TRADE SECRETS

For Gypsy, Amelia, Lotte, Jack and Ava,
my players.

TRADE SECRETS

Australian actors and their craft

Terence Crawford

Currency Press, Sydney

First published in 2005 by
Currency Press Pty Ltd
PO Box 2287
Strawberry Hills NSW 2012 Australia
www.currency.com.au
enquiries@currency.com.au

National Library of Australia Cataloguing-in-Publication Data:
Crawford, Terence.
Trade secrets : Australian actors and their craft.
ISBN 0 86819 763 7.
1. Acting. 2. Actors – Australia – Interviews. I. Title.
792.028

Front cover shows Geoffrey Rush as Subtle from the Company B Belvoir 1996 production of *The Alchemist*. (Photo: Hugh Hartshorne). Back cover shows Terence Crawford as Dr Waxling in the 2001 New Theatre production of *Search and Destroy*.
Cover design by Kate Florance, Currency Press
Printed by Hyde Park Press, Richmond, SA

FOREWORD

John Doyle

I'm still uncertain as to whether acting is art or craft, or both, or whether such a definition matters at all. Having participated in and watched theatre for decades, having seen ordinary performances in State companies and great performances in regional companies and unbelievable performances in amateur companies and spectacular performances in all; having read with interest the biographies of Burton and Olivier and the personal insights from Simon Callow's *On Becoming An Actor* to Michael Green's *Art Of Coarse Acting*, I can only arrive at one conclusion—all roads lead to Rome in the matter. And the roads can be torturous. Coward urged us to not bump into the furniture. And when ordered by his director in a rehearsal exercise to come onto the stage and 'Scare me', Sir John Gielgud is reported to have strolled out and stated simply 'We open in two weeks'. What is clear is that actors can be both craftspeople and artists.

All roads... I remember George Ogilvie directing us to 'walk in circles' as a means, I suppose, of building a group dynamic or ensemble. It worked tremendously well. We walked daily for weeks for ten, fifteen minutes with the group dynamic determining the speed and the duration. Whereas almost all of us stuck it out with open minds, Max Cullen walked with us for half a lap on day one before disappearing through the exit, never to walk again. In the end Max was terrific and our ensemble probably struggled a little in translating our bonding work onto the celluloid. Sometimes there is no justice. The point is, I think, that like all art or craft, some are blessed and many are destined to remain plodders.

In my experience, some actors mimic others, whilst others get inside the 'skin' of character, which can sometimes awkwardly spill over into private life. Some find a character wholly within themselves. Some stay themselves. Some work from the outside in, others from the inside out. Some find the character immediately; some never find it at all. But what is certain is that when you witness a great performance—there is nothing like it.

My first experience with professional theatre was with Aarne Neeme as director and how lucky we were to have a director who knows the theatre from the ground up. Part of his extremely sound advice to us all was to 'get behind the lines'. That phrase says it all really. It sounds so simple and, truth be known, it probably is that simple. But there's more. There is an audience. And when the connection between actor and audience is made, the wave of the play can be ridden together. And you get theatre. This happens when actors are behind their lines. But the journey in getting behind them is intrinsically challenging, simply because some lines require psychological examination, some require physicality and just about all require both.

I can think of few others in a better position to get to the bottom of the mystery as to how our theatre practitioners ply their trade than Terry Crawford. Before he studied at NIDA, Terry was part of the same Newcastle ensemble welded together by Aarne that I was part of. So Terry, too, has seen and known the theatre from the ground up. His precocious and energetic talent was accelerated through his regional theatre experiences where as a teenager he was doing some pretty heavy lifting on stage. It was an amazing time. I remember clearly his dedication to the world of technique and his natural lust for laughs. He refers in his Introduction to *Essington Lewis: I Am Work* and remembers fondly, as I do, that most underestimated theatre practitioner Vic Rooney, some of whose best years as an actor sadly were spent in front of blackboards and amazed students in Newcastle.

And I remember vividly Terry's work in *Essington Lewis* where he played many characters. The play was an organic work in progress by Newcastle playwright John O'Donoghue. In one incarnation Terry was electrician Horst Schmidt, a fleeting character that sadly missed the cut in later productions. Not because of Terry. He did his level best to save the bloke. Horst had the line 'the wiring for the entire steelworks is in my head'. For a whole season Terry was driven by the desire to make that line get a laugh. It was hit or miss. But at the time we wondered how Bille Brown or John Gaden might have approached it.

Now we know.

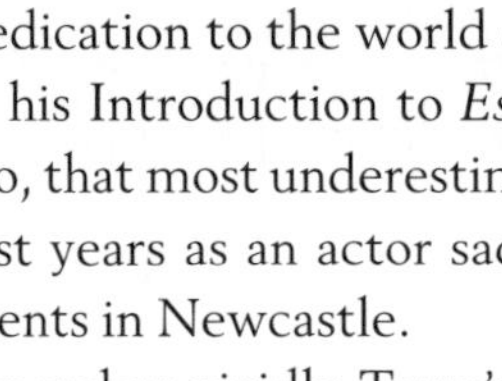

CONTENTS

Foreword JOHN DOYLE *v*

Introduction *1*

Going to the place in the forest BILLE BROWN *11*

If you are just running and not knowing JOEL EDGERTON *27*

The glory of the colours PAMELA RABE *43*

This secret life SEAN O'SHEA *55*

What else do you want me to do? WENDY HUGHES *69*

To see each other's eyes CHARLES 'BUD' TINGWELL *83*

All about the moments HEATHER MITCHELL *95*

It is engendered JOHN GADEN *109*

He's bloody good, this guy ROBERT GRUBB *125*

The unseen character HELEN BUDAY *141*

You give me this and I'll give you that JUDI FARR *155*

Just like falling off a log PAUL GODDARD *167*

Get up and jam PAULA ARUNDELL *189*

He's the holy fool GEOFFREY RUSH *199*

Conclusion *225*

Acknowledgments *229*

'Harry moved forward into the middle of the classroom, into the space that Moody had cleared of desks. Moody raised his wand, pointed it at Harry, and said, "Imperio."

It was the most wonderful feeling. Harry felt a floating sensation as every thought and worry in his head was wiped gently away, leaving nothing but a vague, untraceable happiness. He stood there feeling immensely relaxed, only dimly aware of everyone watching him.'

Harry Potter and The Goblet of Fire
JK Rowling

INTRODUCTION

This book is a response to a nagging feeling I've had for many years that Australian actors are making it up as they go along: that their work processes grow more from their life experience and the way they look at the world than from the pages of any book or the teachings of any guru. The book aims to examine to what extent that hunch is true, how nurture and nature are entangled in the working lives of those pursuing the elusive craft of acting.

Like most actors, I've read Stanislavski, his disciples and his detractors. I've absorbed the theories and the arguments for acting processes that range from the unhelpful minimalism of the 'Just Do It' school to the convoluted, the reductionist, the expansionist, and the just plain whacky. I've entered Primitive Improvisational circles, I've donned the Neutral Mask, I've created my own Clown (a singularly unfunny specimen), I've dwelled on the Given Circumstances, analysed Actions, tightened cues, hit marks, 'dropped in' thoughts, wrestled with Obstacles, ridden laughs, found the light, counted the iambs, mixed the Leichner, and unearthed my inner woman (a sexually acquisitive Newcastle beach chick who, having been discovered, was wisely left on the grainy shore of my young imagination). I've waited for the Truth until it felt like I was sitting on a deserted platform in 40-degree heat, in a ghost town, waiting for the last train to oblivion. I've faked it, I've mugged, I've been transported by sensory memories, effortlessly ridden waves of impulses, I've found myself gloriously drunk 'in the moment', and ingloriously drunk in the greenroom. I've been under the weather and, God knows, I've been over the top. We all have.

Some of these things are part of an actor's rite of passage, others are techniques I've employed again and again as an actor and acting teacher. But rarely in 25 years of acting and teaching—and watching and working with other actors—have I been able to make a clear or consistent link between what is described in any one book, and what I witness people doing.

This, in itself, is not inconsistent with Stanislavski's thinking, or that of many fine teachers and writers over the years. Yet plenty of teachers still enter rooms with acting students and tell them—or allow them to infer—that there is a path of righteousness, and it is found by taking this step, then that one, and so on, with foolproof systematic sameness. A recipe for acting! This is nonsense. Again, the elements may be worthy, but they are pieces of a puzzle that can't be put together by or for all of us in the same way. We must each shape and reshape the pieces to fit a puzzle that makes sense to us, in this gig, at this time. Then we must pull the pieces apart and put them together again for the next role. Generally, I think the piecing together gets quicker with experience, and I think certain pieces are always present—even dominant—for each of us, most of the time.

These are some of the prejudices I held going into this project. To 'out' them as prejudices is important, I think, because they are the things that inevitably describe—or at least inform—the terrain of the conversations that make up the bulk of the book. Here are some others:

- Acting, like breathing, is both a complex and a simple thing. You can choose to—and sometimes must—invest in its complexity, and you can choose to or must at other times invest in its simplicity;
- Acting is sometimes very easy, and sometimes very hard;
- Some actors feel guilty—or are made to feel guilty—when the acting comes easily;
- Actors do—or should do—whatever works;
- No actor is a chameleon;
- Actors never 'become' anyone else, they are always themselves. This is of course just common sense, but I am among those who believe that even pretending to become someone else—though sometimes very helpful—is often a waste of time, that the illusion of 'character' is an audience's privilege, and of limited purpose for most actors, most of the time;
- The distinctions between acting on stage and on screen are often exaggerated;
- The Method (capital T, capital M) is at best a misnomer, at worst a reductionist fantasy;
- The so-called Stanislavskian 'System' and Strasberg's Method are so

> grossly misunderstood, and the gap between them so confused and underestimated, that the mention of either in an acting class or rehearsal room is a negative contribution to the work.

I probably should expand just a little on that last point. I'm not suggesting that these teachers and theorists should not be studied. Obviously, it is the responsibility of those of us who can decipher it all to do so for our students. I'm calling the situation as I commonly see it. I'm sizing the challenge. When I meet a group of students for the first time, they have always heard of Stanislavski, and they have always heard of The Method, and I always wish they hadn't, such is the soggy suet of their comprehension. Personally, I find myself more in awe of Stanislavski's intelligence and doggedness the older I get, and less and less interested in Strasberg's Method as anything other than an obstacle to be overcome. I find greater inspiration in the work of Grotowski, Lecoq, Littlewood, Meisner, Michael Chekhov and others, than the famous American psychologism.

I should say here that the actors in this book by no means endorse all the above dot-points, but severally offer or imply rebuttals to them.

The central question then is this: If actors aren't following the rules of any prescribed, notated, codified, published Process—and there are many great and inspiring books about acting—then what *are* they doing?

What are these actors doing?

I'd like to explain some more about why this book exists, then about the parameters I set for my discussions with the actors.

Australian acting students and Australian actors (and, indeed, Australian theatre and film-goers) have always been able to walk into a good bookshop and buy a book that will give them Olympia Dukakis' views on acting, those of Simon Callow, Uta Hagen, Laurence Olivier, Antony Sher, and maybe even John Wayne or Lassie, but not a word from Helen Buday or Joel Edgerton or Geoffrey Rush. That seemed perverse to me, and improper. Often I've been in class making a point, looking at hungry, sceptical or nervous faces, perhaps relating something I learned from working with someone like John Gaden. And I've thought, If only I could get Gaden to walk in now and say something. Well, at least now I can refer students to a book that contains some of his thoughts. I don't want to be parochial, or disrespectful of the views of esteemed international actors, but surely there's some 'added-value' in reading the opinions that have grown out of an Australian industrial, artistic, political and social context, expressed in our own accents. If you are an acting student, or a young Australian actor, these are the people you may one day work with. You can 'communicate' or argue with the actors in this book, then go straight to a theatre and watch one of them work. These are *your* story-tellers. They are at your service.

So, basically, it's an inversion of the old Everest thing, Why write this book? Because it *isn't* there.

Bille Brown said he thought I was courageous to write the book, given the Australian antipathy towards artists taking themselves too seriously. I wouldn't say courageous, but you do get to a point where negativity makes you either buckle and walk away, or put up a fight. So it is a reaction to those (especially those actors) who think nothing of Steve Waugh writing a whole book about a single cricket innings, yet might accuse the heroes of this book of being self-indulgent for talking about themselves as artists.

There are other pressing reasons why actors need to take themselves seriously, and demand serious respect from society and its authorities.

Over the last five years or so, actor-training institutions in this country have been under siege. Now, there are plenty of people who think there are too many acting schools, and that the natural attrition of the 'market'—that so brutally culls individuals from the ranks of actors—might as well cull institutions as well. But Darwinism is about survival of the fittest. The only principle informing the university sector at the moment with regard to this matter is survival of the cheapest. The fact is that the places under attack are not tin-pot operations. They are among the most prestigious schools and courses in the country.

Perhaps more significant than the undermining of the actor-training sector is the destruction of the theatre network itself throughout Australia. In a country that has only ever flirted with the idea of subsidised art, the last decade has seen support withdrawn from regional theatre companies—a network of companies crucial to the idea of a national theatre industry. The people of major regional centres such as my home town of Newcastle are no longer deemed worthy of having theatre grown for—and out of—their communities. Professional theatre comes to them, not from them: actors as 'carnies', forever foreign. The idea of theatre being an indelible part of the Australian culture, an Australian habit, seems to have been dumped. The establishment of 'flagship' companies (increasingly commercial 'state' theatre companies, and secondary urban 'art-houses') seems to have sunk the rest of the fleet. And this seems to have happened with little dissent, as if our theatrical leaders have been hiding under the bed, hoping the boogie-bean-counter-man doesn't come and get *them*!

What's all this to do with a book about acting? Well, it's all about taking theatre seriously. If we don't take our art and our business seriously, how can we expect the lawyers who run the country to do so?

Conversation is required.

Industry forums, conferences and lecture series do exist, and are perhaps starting to make a difference. We need discourse: inter-industrial and intra-institutional discourse. Stoic silence hasn't worked. Is it possible that our 'no-bullshit' approach is, in fact, bullshit?

The idea of conversation is crucial to the reading of this book. This is not a series of lectures. The actors' responses are subjective, humble, often uncertain, often unconscious of theoretical foundations, honest, sometimes unreasoned, sometimes unsatisfactory, sometimes contradictory, frequently inspiring.

Among the gems and pearls in this book, actors say things that I could never embrace as an actor or teacher—their fallibility is tangible. Infallibility is a privilege that poor teaching affords. It is death to acting. This brings us to a major premise, or 'rule of engagement'.

There will be people here whose work as actors you value more highly than others. There will be people whose acting you don't like at all, or perhaps don't even know. But they are all people whose career achievements cannot be denied. You are asked to put your personal tastes aside, to an extent, or accept them as subjective, in order to fully engage in the reading. Because if you don't, if you allow yourself to discard the views of someone on the basis that you don't think his or her acting is much chop anyway, then you are in danger of missing the point. The processes these actors share with us are processes that *work for them*!

I wanted actors with breadth of experience: people who have worked in different media. In this, I guess I favoured theatre experience because—another prejudice—I believe the theatre is the actor's home-base, and the forum that offers the greatest invitations.

I wanted actors from diverse professional backgrounds. We hear from Bud Tingwell, who learnt his craft on Sydney radio, and in the 'pre-boom' Australian film industry; Judi Farr, who did a mountain of sketch comedy in her formative professional years; Geoffrey Rush, who trained at the famous Lecoq school in Paris; and Pamela Rabe, who studied in her native Canada. There is the inevitable mob from NIDA, but the NIDA that Wendy Hughes attended in 1969 was a very different place to that which Robert Grubb graduated from in 1978, and it was different again for Paul Goddard in the early 1980s, and for Paula Arundell in the early 1990s.

What we learn from the interviews is that the various histories impress themselves upon these artists, creating for each of them a culture, true to itself. They are—as are we all—impressed with the marks of family, lovers, failures and successes, insecurities and pride. And this individual culture that each actor builds is fundamental to the way he or she engages with the work, acting being—more than any other pursuit—the art of one's character, of one's deepest self, one's gruel. This then is a celebration of individuality, of multi-culture (in the broadest sense).

Sadly, the book is not multi-cultural in the narrower, ethnic sense. I reiterate that this is a determinedly *mainstream* reflection. As such, it portrays an industry that does not yet fully embrace or celebrate its ethnic diversity. That said, there would have been a broader ethnicity to the book had all of those invited to take part agreed to do so.

The book also embraces transience. Artists change, their processes evolve (hence some of the confusions about people like Stanislavski and Brecht, who created whole worlds of thought only to shun them and move on). This was a hit-and-run operation. I didn't prep people before the interviews, and I didn't do much patching up afterwards. One shot. What's in their heads about acting, on this day? A more 'sculptured' approach may have brought some benefits, but these were never in my scope. I wanted the rough and ready wisdom of the greenroom rather than the more circumspect reflections of the study. Perhaps, as a consequence, a number of the actors begin cautiously, and only really find their voice in the middle of the interview.

There is a wide age-range of subjects, from late–20s to early–80s. That was one of my solid determinations. I'll never forget the thrilling realisation—when I first started working in theatre professionally and plonked my little shoebox of grease-sticks down next to Vic Rooney's in the dressing room—that this is, in some ways at least, a non-ageist business. (Vic—one of Australia's greatly undervalued leading men—would thunder down on me if I didn't point out that he was only about 45 at the time). It is still one of the things that most excites me about being a theatre-worker. Bud Tingwell and Judi Farr have many more runs on the board than Sean O'Shea, but when the lights come up, they all start from scratch.

I deliberately didn't interview people who spent a great deal of their careers teaching. I didn't want the practised views of folks—like me—who make a substantial part of their living out of talking about acting. Indeed, a number of people in the book are talking in depth here about acting for the first time in their lives, or the first time in decades. Most thanked me for the opportunity to do so, for giving them the chance to explain themselves to themselves, as one put it.

I started by making a list of all the actors whose views I thought would be interesting. That became a list of 113 names. A blowtorch was required. I set up a spreadsheet, mapped out some criteria, and started the wicked, secret fun of giving people 'scores'. The criterion I came to trust most—and I'm extremely grateful to my publishers for encouraging me in this—was my own level of personal excitement at the prospect of chewing the fat with each actor. This then is not a list of the fourteen best actors in the country (though it might be!). Nor is it a list of the most experienced, most intelligent, most famous or most sexy. It is just *my* list. These are some of the people I most wanted to talk to. As I suggested earlier, some others couldn't or wouldn't take part.

With that subjectivity in mind, the introductions to each actor, each chapter, are personalised and subjective too. I try to give a sense of my attraction to the actor, and my experience as an audience member of their work. I've also 'outed' the actors (five out of fourteen) with whom I've worked. I hope you will forgive the extent to which this becomes self-reflective. My intention is to acknowledge all-pervasive subjectivity, and establish an informal tone for the conversations that follow.

I began each interview by asking people to speak about the things they most rely on as actors, the foundation stones of their work, the things they most believe in and trust. I then tried to lead them to put that belief structure into the context of their career, how the 'faith' was formed, and then into the context of existing theories about acting. However, these loosely formulaic aims are often defeated as the conversations go where they will.

I was interested in representing the kinds of issues that I know trouble young actors and actors-in-training. I hoped (hope!) this might put into a manageable context some of those things that seem—when we are 20—to weigh a ton. I asked everyone, for example, to talk about the differences, for them, between acting on stage and on film.

Strong emotional engagement is one of the most difficult challenges an actor faces. There are two broad schools of thought relating to what is actually going on—or what should be going on—when high emotion is called for on stage or screen. It would be counter to the aims of the book for me to go too far into this, or to play my own hand, but in the interests of bringing you into the frame of the discussion (and particularly for those readers who are not actors), let me roughly sketch the terrain.

One school of thought (Stanislavskian) maintains that actors try to find their way to genuine emotional connections during each and every performance (there's huge discussion about how they do this, which we'll leave aside for now). The other belief is that once the requisite emotion is experienced in rehearsal, or is otherwise intellectually and physically 'grasped' by an actor, its physical expression is observed and harnessed (learned and rehearsed), and given to the audience each night. What 'reads' as genuine emotion is in fact a physical display or portrayal of that emotion's 'look' and 'sound'. These are the broad positions. In reality, they are not polar, they overlap and converge in the thinking, writing and acting of many fine practitioners. Not even Stanislavski denies that there is always a degree of monitoring going on: a dual consciousness. Nonetheless, I asked each of the actors to talk about how they approach strong emotional material, and on which side of the controversial divide they stand.

Each interview lasted between one and three hours. What is published here is, on average, about half of what was said. People spoke intelligently and insightfully about the broader industry, and their experiences in it, but I've kept my eyes firmly on the issues of craft, except where the *industrial* insight or revelation was too good to leave out. Actors speak more or less anecdotally. Some adeptly pause to 'unpack' a specific point, others drive us through their experiences, with lessons, secrets, morals 'embedded' in their tales. Some people needed very little prompting throughout, and with others there is more to-ing and fro-ing (that is to say, more from me).

I've wrestled with the enjoyable challenge that faces anyone editing the spoken word. I wanted the chapters to read like conversations, not essays. The dialogue is left in the often-confused cadences and sentence structures of ordinary speech, except where to do so would rob the sentence of its logic or central thought, or be unnecessarily distracting. I've trimmed most ums and ahs, and not bothered with marking pauses or laughter (of which there was much), coffee breaks and so on. Nor have I marked the edit points in the transcripts. Ellipses (...) are used to indicate a trailing or unfinished thought, or when one thought is abandoned for the next. Always, I've sought to balance two things: fidelity to the conversational tone, and ease for the reader.

Another rule of engagement—well, a suggestion: read the book slowly. Give your focus to a different voice, make a different 'friend' each time you open the book. Take a different actor to bed with you, maybe once a week. Let the individual voices in. This approach should allow the repetition in the 'narrative' to be a positive rather than a negative element. As a teacher, repetition doesn't worry me. I know that someone can hear the same point a dozen times, but—maybe because of a particular image or phrase, maybe because of the alignment of the stars, I don't know—only once will a penny drop and the point actually hit home. Also, repetition serves to underline the recurring and dominant concerns. Interestingly, these tend to be the very things that acting theory books most regularly ignore. That's another big can of worms.

I'm aware that the title 'Trade Secrets' makes it all seem foolproof. It is anything but. We learn from these terrific people that it is in fact all about grasping, pecking in the dirt, hacking through the bushes, juggling, chasing rainbows, searching for light, a million sparkles.

'Sparkle, Shirley!', as Mrs Temple used to yell at her little girl. That's the secret.

Going to the place in the forest

BILLE BROWN

Bille Brown describes his career as a 19th-century phenomenon that just happens to be occurring in the 21st century. More simply, he is arguably Australia's most renowned international theatre actor.

Bille grew up in rural Queensland and began working professionally with the Queensland Theatre Company in the early 1970s. In 1976 he joined the Royal Shakespeare Company, where he worked with the great English stage stars of the day. He moved to the US in 1983 where he had success on and off Broadway.

Throughout the late 1980s and early 1990s, Bille continued to work in the States, England and elsewhere in Europe until again making Australia his base in 1996.

Throughout his career, Bille has forged a great and constant bond with QTC. His 30-year contribution to that company was marked by the naming of The Bille Brown Studio. How many actors in their early 50s have a theatre named after them?

South of the border, Bille has thrilled audiences and critics with towering performances at Belvoir St in Ubu *and as Oscar Wilde in* The Judas Kiss, *in Bell Shakespeare productions of* Troilus and Cressida *and* Hamlet, *and in the Sydney Theatre Company's* Howard Katz.

I met Bille on a beautiful, late-summer afternoon at his one-room apartment in an old-fashioned little cranny of Kings Cross, a street lined with two-storey private hotels. I commented that it could be London. Bille agreed, and said that it was also like the little patch of New York that he lived in for four years. It seemed an appropriately 'universal' place to find this self-confessed wandering player.

Bille Brown is a big man: over six feet tall, and solid. He has the wonderful, resonant voice that we associate with a 'classical' actor, and the sophistication and erudition to go with it. But he also has that duality you sometimes spy in country folk who've gone out and met the great world. It's a very endearing quality (Nick Enright had it), a combination of the practical man and the dreamer: part country station master, part exotic genie.

It's been a long apprenticeship, and now—in middle age—I really am looking back at a career that began when I was 17.

Having never been to a drama school, I actually learned while I was in jobs. So the talent—what it is—seemed to be prompted by an innate desire or sense of what to do. The instinct, or the intuition, was constantly being fed and practised by watching other people doing it, by acting with other people. My knowledge is based on the personal experience of being a working professional actor.

If you were to ask me, 'What is acting?', I don't think of it as an artistic enterprise but as a craft, though there is an artistic element to it. A very human and humane art; and it is the art of memory. All acting is memory. The memory of lines, the memory of moves, the memory of what you do, remembering the spontaneous combustion of having been in a rehearsal. The memory of an experience, the memory of an emotion, the memory of a gesture. Associative memories of, say, colours or textures. The way in which your imagination begins to fill up and become fecund, full of all these impressions.

Recently I opened for the first time a very good translation of what Stanislavski actually wrote. And I suddenly realised it was not about particular psychological gestures, it was about the actor connecting to his own physical experience, which is of course memory. Stanislavski was trying to find a way of using the resource of the actual physical being, the actor. Working on yourself, being conscious of your own self, your reality, your being, what you were doing. As one actor once said to me, as we were lying dead at the Royal Shakespeare Company, he said, in a loud whisper, 'You know what I fucking love about this? It's the last fucking existential job available to a man where you don't have to get killed or kill anyone.'

Over the years, whenever anyone has asked me about acting, I've said, Forget about the suspension of disbelief. Let's look at a positive—the obverse of that—the *conspiracy* of *belief*. It begins the minute you engage with the script. You have to conspire together: 'con', together, 'spiro', I breathe. Breath is the partner, the ally of memory, and breath is the secret all actors hold.

Ian McKellen said the live theatre is irreplaceable as an experience, because there comes a point where you—with your human body, with your whole being—are all breathing in the same space, at the same time. And it's breath that carries the vibrations of the imagination out through your body, through the air, into the ears and eyes of the audience.

So in a way that's my understanding of the very pure, atavistic, animal, human contact—*contract* even—with the audience. It's a conspiracy of belief. And I don't think of it as mystical or romantic, I think of it as a very practical thing. Can you hear me? Can you see me? Do you believe what I believe I am?

It's about making up. Not the stuff you put on your face—but making believe. Not only making *yourself* believe, but also making the *audience* believe that I am who I am pretending, aspiring to be.

When I did Oscar Wilde, I read the script thinking of the Stanislavskian mechanism. I began by saying, Wilde says, He says, He moves here, He does that, He thinks that at this moment. I wonder what He feels at this moment? Within a few weeks I found myself dropping the impersonal pronoun and beginning to say: *I* say this, *I* say that. And that, I discovered, was a very telling point.

Does it matter whether you construct that as you becoming Wilde, or as Wilde becoming you? Or is that an unimportant distinction?

It's unimportant. I go back to the innate, the intuition, the instinct. They are the elements, and they happen to you. As John Cleese one day said to me, Every now and then God gives you a joke. Be aware of that.

You're so involved in such a childlike way with rehearsing or reading something, you're seeing it in your head, you're acting it out.

You're talking about a trust in sensitivity, aren't you? A kind of hyper-sensitivity to the space and the people around you?

Absolutely.

That's what you entered the room with when you were 17, a trust in your instincts, and a trust in your capacity to be impressed. And that remains what you enter the room with?

And while you have to be tremendously open to every experience, you realise as you get older that you're cutting back constantly. You're trying less hard. I think now, in my late 40s and early 50s, I'm about to become a better actor. I'm doing less. I'm trusting more. I'm not trying to elaborate. I've become suspicious of the great gift of my theatricality. I'm learning more to trust in the simplicity of things and the humanity of things.

Some people say to me, You seem able to easily contact your emotional centre, and I say, I always could, but it was beaten out of me. The whole culture of, Get control of your emotions. I feel it's only now that I've begun to trust the purer instincts, intelligently and discerningly, and in relationship with other good actors, and with directors of genius. And there *are* directors of genius. I rate Neil Armfield as one.

It is such an intense personal act of trust for you to go into the area of play, the area of imagination, the area of engagement with what you have to do as an actor, and have someone there who is both objective and compassionate. The objectivity is very important.

We talk about concentration—and this is something I learned in the RSC from watching very good 'classical actors'—there always had to be an *objective* concentration. You couldn't just *subjectively* concentrate on being in the role, saying the lines. You needed real commitment, but you also needed an *objective* concentration. There is that minute censor that is both listening to the audience, hearing the play in its most pure form, yet at the same time allowing you to be brave and courageous enough to go where the moment of performance takes you.

I think a problem with a lot of actors is that they go onto the stage in front of an audience and just rehearse the play. You can't do that. That's when theatre becomes deadly, predictable and quite dull. You really have to approach it like a good footy match. Sometimes you win, sometimes you lose. Sometimes you fumble the ball. A penalty is given against you. You know, the great theatre of my childhood was not so much the St Patrick's concerts, but the big rugby matches. Operatic activities with all the excitement and passion of, How's it going to turn out?

Can you talk a little bit more about that distinction you made between what you do in the rehearsal room and what you do on stage? Where does the idea of exploration fit into that? Does exploration happen on both sides of that equation?

It does, and it can be very exciting when it happens in a performance and you think, This actor has now gone to a new place. That is spontaneous. God has given him a joke, you know?

There is that inspirational element. The theatre has always been that, when you think about the origins of the Western theatre, the Dionysian cult where our theatre began. Going to the place in the forest, removing the external clothes, singing, dancing, hoping God will enter you, preparing yourself—the rehearsal, as it were. And then in the performance you get *extasis*, the ecstasy, which is the indwelling of the God. It's programmed into our species, this particular activity. It's the purest element of us, no matter how sophisticated or austere the play may be, it is, to some degree, those elements that truly make it a human activity.

And also, it seems to me, it is these elements that make it artful. If you are seeking to be 'touched by God'–in the broadest secular sense–when you are going onstage–

It's the gamble you take as an audience and an actor. It may or may not work that night.

Nina in Chekhov's *Seagull* talks about the appalling feeling of knowing that one is acting badly.

And one does it all the time. Bad acting is an occupational hazard. What one must do is make all the right moves, to try and cast all the right spells in the hope that there is that alchemical contact. And when it happens, it's unforgettable.

So you're saying that if you stay on track, as it were–even if you acknowledge that your work, at this moment, is not 'graced'–if you stay on track the spirit may re-enter?

The spirit may re-enter.

I love the idea of the medium. The actor as a medium. That idea works all the way through. You make sounds, you transmit the play, and at the same time there is a state where, with true artistic humility—and good actors have artistic humility—there is that extraordinarily precious place where you, the audience and the play cohere. The sense of, Oh my goodness, where did that come from? The inspiration. The trade secret: inspiration. Remember the line that Stoppard wrote for Geoffrey's character in *Shakespeare in Love*: 'It's a mystery'.

Participation in the mysteries, that takes us back to the Greeks—our very atavistic heritage in the Western theatre, pagan, absolutely in-the-guts. That heartbeat, that pulse. The irredeemable heartbeat. Breathing together, hearts pumping together. Breathtaking, spellbinding, all those words that critics reach for. That human element. It's the one that I connect with constantly.

If you want to know a trade secret: Going to the place where it will happen, despite all the preparation that one has made in rehearsal, it's on the night, in the moment. All those things that drama teachers are constantly trying to say. They may sound baffling, but they're very practical, very simple.

You spoke about having access to your emotional life. You portrayed it as just a part of your life, that you managed to keep alive the sensitivity of childhood, to an extent. What about when a role carries large expectations of what we might call 'big emotional bits'? How do you deal with that kind of expectation?

I go back to my overriding thing that it is the art of memory. And emotion is the quickest contact between the actor's imagination and the actor's physical memory—his experience of his own life, his observation of other lives, of the human condition. It's the quickest contact.

How does it work with those big roles? Well, often the big roles have so many technical and physical demands that it all balances out. When I've played the big Shakespearean roles, and big roles like *The Judas Kiss* or the Count in *The Marriage of Figaro* or, recently, *Howard Katz*, I don't approach them emotionally. I approach them thoughtfully, cautiously, and quite practically. I eat the words. One has to use every means.

On three occasions I've played a woman. Once for a whole year. You know, I'm a big, strapping fella, so I thought, What sort of woman am I? And I thought, Well, I'm Mae West. So I had a memory of Mae West's voice and her body. Still, I couldn't arrive at being this woman. But it eventually happened when I imagined her walking in shoes. It took the director two weeks to convince me to get into the shoes. When I did it happened instantly, and I thought, Oh, it's like this. It was only in the third week that I put on the rehearsal skirt. So in a way, one balances out the physical demands of the role.

Playing Henry the Fifth, for example, is probably more physically demanding than playing Hamlet. He's a trumpet. He constantly sings and bellows in battle until virtually the end of the play. Then he has 20 minutes where he puts the trumpet away, and has to woo Katherine. To do that eight times a week for months is physically exhausting, and you have to get the body ready to run that marathon. You have to get used to tackling it. A very unemotional man. Only two emotional moments: 'I was not angry since I came to France'; and the other is in the darkness of the night: 'Upon the king'. Both of them are quite shallow emotions, so I had to use

Bille Brown as Oscar Wilde in the 1999 Company B Belvoir production of *The Judas Kiss*. (Photo: Julian Watt)

the obligation, the contract with the writer, which is *those words*. And sometimes it's easiest to just *start* with them, and trust that you get them right.

An actor should have an ear. Both an ear for listening to what everyone else is saying, and also what effect, what impact, what impression—in the true sense of the word—he is having on the other actors, so that he is constantly being fed back with the energy and information, with the informed breath he needs, so that when he hears those things, he doesn't have to *think*. It is spontaneously *evoked*.

That practical exercise is what some in this country would call very technical acting. But I mean, come on! If you want a brain surgeon or a plumber surely you want some technical skill.

And the harnessing of that capacity to catch the inspiration is itself a technical skill.

Yes. We have a sentimental love for the golden amateurism of our sportsmen, but those athletes are elite, technically skilled, hugely motivated, profoundly focussed, self-interested beings. And that's what I think the actor has to be as well, particularly with big classical works. His obligation is to reignite an idea and to give it life for the moment of the performance, and to infect or affect the memory of the audience. And that requires a generosity of spirit. It doesn't need you to be generous as a person, it needs generosity of spirit. Artistic modesty, humility. You don't have to be modest to be an actor. In fact modesty is often second-rate, but humility is something quite remarkable.

The actor is involved with the elements. 'What is this quintessence of dust?' You know? The angel and the dust in *us*. Why go to drama school when you can read *Hamlet*? It is a treatise on acting.

When you were talking about Henry 5–

That was an unusual situation for me. It was thrilling because what I wanted coincided exactly with what Henry was about. Henry wanted to prove himself a king. I wanted to prove myself a big, butch man who could speak, climb ladders, do sword fights, sustain that amount of energy. I was 33 with the reputation of being an eccentric, light comedian. I had huge doubts about myself, so I didn't have to act doubt. Initially, the role seemed impossible for me. But what I was feeling as a man and an actor engaged to play that part was precisely analogous to what Henry was going through. No acting required.

Ironically, after that, the next part I had was Falstaff. I went from, you know, running up and down those battlements and leading men to war, to Falstaff, the complete opposite. Before I put on the fat-suit, I *thought* fat. I actually dreamt myself into that fat-suit.

We've been talking about the internal, mystical, psychological, alchemical aspects, but acting is also very practical. It's about doors, shoes, walking, turning. Being heard, being fat, being skinny, being naked. There is a whole series of very practical aspects that I really think is the great beauty of the craft, and shouldn't be poo-pooed. There's an enormous amount of fraudulent time-wasting in challenging young people psychologically, when they should be given very practical tasks. After all, that is what you are given if, like me, you've had a long apprenticeship.

In my first year at the RSC, I understudied 27 parts, I died twice nightly, I was third rat on the coach. But I was watching, every night. Peggy Ashcroft, Ian McKellen, Allan Howard, and all those wonderful young actors. I also saw older actors, much older actors. And I started to see my place. To understand what world I belonged to.

To me, the world of acting was that marvellous moment at the School of Arts at Biloela, where, up against a horrendously tasteless backdrop which included, you know, a couple of blackfellas standing and looking at a starry sky, Alexander Hay and the Young Elizabethan Players came onto the stage and did 'What country, friend, is this?' What country indeed! I wanted them to take me away. The whole air, the whole place melted and became something else. It was transformed by the fact that they were there. I thought, Oh my God, they are my tribe. I belong to that!

And the theatre is dangerous. It's filled with sexuality. It's filled, too, with glamour. Not cheap glamour, but the deep, deep glamour of humanity. I remember—I must have still been a virgin—but I remember when I first saw Rex Cramphorn. I thought, There is an angel pointing in that direction. And in a way, people like Rex, they were the watchers, the messenger-angels.

I feel I'm only coming good now that I'm in my 50s. My gift, where the soul is closest to the skin, is blooming at this stage of my life. And that is a trade secret, knowing not only *what* you are but *where* you are.

Can we go back to your focus on memory? Memory is such a loaded and troubled thing in actor parlance because of the whole Strasbergian experiments in Affective Memory–

Crap! The classic moment for me was when I was playing Oscar Wilde, when Constance says to him, Give up Alfred Douglas and I will let you see your children. She uses the children. And that was really all he had left.

Now, I don't have children, so I had to find an emotional connection to that sense of loss. And I remembered when I left home. My father, elderly and dying. My mother, worrying about this long trip I was about to make. I wouldn't be back for many years. I remembered the look on their faces, the fact that maybe that was the last time they'd see me. I remembered the timbre of my mother's voice, the timbre of my father's voice—a very unemotional Australian bloke—as he thought, This is a child I will never see again. I mean, I was a grown man, but I was suddenly rendered almost a child. I remembered *that*. *That* was my memory! Of course, I couldn't think of that when I was onstage, but in the privacy of rehearsal, in the space that had been allowed me, I was able to take a moment to say, Oh, yeah. My children. Then you have to recreate it, in a way, in performance, and trust that it will be there. You don't plan it. You don't say, Oh-oh, here comes the big moment. It just happens because you've rehearsed it and then you come to perform it.

That's probably closer to Meisner. I've never been to a Meisner class in my life. But when I was in America I worked with a lot of actors, and I listened. I rehearsed with a couple of older people who had been taught by him and I listened. I found the wonderful thing about them was generosity, a sense of humour and a profound lack of pretension. That was wonderful.

You're talking about the accessing of memory consciously in rehearsal, then incidentally in performance, without torturing yourself?

Oh yes, torturing yourself, that's bullshit. Joy. What did Brecht say? Gaiety is the essence of the theatre. If there is no gaiety in the theatre, then it is not a play. Joy. Gaiety. Even in the darkest, most horrendous, horrible theatrical experience for the character, there must be a joy, that gaiety. And I don't mean it in the cheap sense at all. Although, by the same token, the wonder of the theatre is that it is both high and low. The theatre has to be filled with the most wondrous cries of joy and pain, but it should be full of farts too. I love that. Which is why most actors will tell you, in a business where it's very hard to judge whether you're being good or bad, Shakespeare is still the measure. In playing Shakespeare, we can still have that objective measure, because everything is embraced within that extraordinary challenge.

Once you're able to distinguish the discrete component items within that greater challenge, do you then also compartmentalise the practical things that need to be done to achieve them? Does that mean that one day in the rehearsal room may at times be devoted to the cracking of a particular thing? That there may be a particular focus?

Oh, yeah. You find something in particular and think, *That* is the key. That is the central thing. Once you've got that, you know you can expand out from it, then the rest is ocean and swimming. And good directors know it. Neil Armfield has a real nose for that. He will actually go back and re-rehearse something once we've arrived at the point where he knows, That's it.

I've been praised and criticised for having a sense of style, and I say this: When a professional pianist sits down they can sight-read, they can find out what the writer needs. They can hear it, imagine it, and somehow recognise what is needed in the playing. The writer's voice is in what is written down. The same with a play. What is style? It's not affecting attitude or gesture. In fact, it's avoiding that, really. You can do it if you *need* it. I mean, we are rag and bone men. You've got to use every single resource to arrive at the heart of the matter. Knowing what works, and sometimes trusting that fact even though you can't explain it in words.

So you may enter a journey with a sense that there is a very particular element to be cracked: If I can crack this element, everything else will flow. I'll gain a kind of liberation.

Yes. And then you stand in a different relationship to the rest of the play, because you realise how things must be done. And that was one of the things about Sam Mendes. He was tremendously brave. He would abandon a whole scheme or process, to go back.

Because he'd recognised some magic?

Yes. Let's start again, but let's not lose that. Let's be able to find our way in the dark back to that particular feeling.

Now we get to the converse of the Nina thing. What is the physical sensation of knowing that you are acting well?

If you stop for a moment—and this is Olivier, not me—if you stop for a moment and think, Oh, that was good, you're fucked. You're absolutely fucked.

Is that to say you know it's been good when you get offstage?

Yes, or wonder how it could have happened. How the fuck did I do that?

I wanted to ask you about that international perspective, because you've had many international colleagues. And obviously I'm asking you to generalise, but is it different walking into a rehearsal room in Australia as opposed to walking into an American or English room?

Yes. All three are different. I think Australians are too servile towards directors. I find that I want a true sense of companionship and comradeship with a director. But with some directors, you walk into the room and think, Right, I'm going to have to spend most of my energy trying to interpret what this director wants.

Does that mean you don't think we are overly blessed with inspiring or skilfully cooperative directors in Australia?

They don't have enough chance to practise.

I found in my early days of working in the RSC as an actor, you didn't expect to be shown what to do and how to do it, you were expected to come with your instrument tuned.

I worked with some superb directors in America. Particularly émigré Americans from Eastern Europe, and also a generation of directors who had grown up inheritors of Tyrone Guthrie, Elia Kazan, Uta Hagen, Stella

Adler—more than Lee Strasberg, I thought Stella Adler. And directors who had grown up in the aesthetic bounds of people like Sandy Meisner. Directors who understood what their role was in relation to the actor, both in a personal relationship, and in terms of a professional bond.

A director creates the *atmosphere* of a rehearsal room, an actor the *demands* of a rehearsal room. And he sets those demands not through any personal quirk but simply by being there, ready, tuned, anticipating. I think an actor should walk into that room with his animal instincts, and he must know what to do.

One has to be completely open, or if you are closed it's because you want the director to come in and open things in a different way. You must be sending very clear signals to the director, and the director must be responding with very clear signals. Which brings me back to people like Neil and Sam and Trevor Nunn, Terry Hands. They listen and they watch. They listen for and watch what is being given. Give them something! Own that room! Some actors look like they don't belong on the stage, they don't belong in the part.

This thing of tuning–

Yes. Ready. Tuned. Aware.

There's almost a folkloric view of Australian actors. One often hears how Australians are unprepared to do classes, to tune the instrument between jobs and that sort of stuff. We're sold the image of our American counterparts obsessively doing the opposite. Is that your experience, and is that relevant to what you're talking about in relation to the different cultures?

Sometimes those 'workshops of the week' are so time-wasting, ill-founded, money-wasting and indulgent because they are not focussed on the task at hand.

Now sometimes you have a brilliant director, a good relationship where you can devise games, exercises, things so skilfully aligned to what is required for the play that the transition from workshop to the actual thing is marvellous and thrilling, and the imagination is freed. But mostly it is, Do that at home.

Sometimes a vocal warm-up is wonderful.

But for me the whole preparation begins around four o'clock. When I shower, when I sleep, when I think about the trip to the theatre. This is all integral. The real life. I have begun a trajectory to land at that place and

I am giving my life over to that particular exercise, not in a grand, artistic way, but in a very practical way.

I've watched actors do elaborate warm-ups—vocal, physical—then go into their dressing room because they haven't eaten, and it smells of McDonald's or yesterday's Chinese heated up, and you think, What is the relationship between your preparation and that?

That's not to say that there aren't some exercises that are absolutely wonderful. Singing together. That can bring a group of actors together to focus on what is required.

How do you spend the half-hour?

I like hearing the half, going onto the stage and into the theatre without the audience. I like going into the auditorium and looking back at the stage. I like hearing and watching the preparation of the stage management. Hearing the calls. I love when the temperature changes, when you hear, Going to blue, and they let the house in. Those rituals of preparation, almost like incantations. They are recognised, they're familiar, they're very practical. They resonate inside one. They call on the memory, and I find I'm beginning to leave myself with the same ease that I do when I'm undressing and putting on clothes. I make mental notes to myself. I go through the script. I always keep the script with me, in my dressing room. I go through it. I make mental notes. I think about other notes. I hear the calls, and you can hear, via the tannoy, the audience. To listen to them, to go to that place—

There's that wonderful expression: The house is live.

The house is live! All the various integral elements of the trade, the processes of the trade, become part of your preparation. Sometimes you can be distracted and have a laugh with another actor, but other times you don't want to speak.

If I'm playing in an intense, passionate relationship with a woman or with another man in the company, I'll just touch base with them. There's nothing holy about it. You try not to make it pretentious. And all the time there is that other world coming, coming closer.

Some actors like to look at the audience, like to know who's out there. I don't particularly. I like them to be anonymous until that moment they define themselves in that performance. In *The Judas Kiss*, I would listen: Oh, he got that laugh. What did they think of that? Oh, they've disapproved of the nudity already. Oh, that was good. Oh, he's done that different.

And sometimes you simply sit in silence.

Someone saw Chekhov. He was sitting, doing nothing. I think he was smoking a cigarette. And they said, What's he doing? The reply was, He's writing. In a way it's exactly the same for me when I perform these fairly mundane activities. What am I doing? I'm acting.

Nourishment of the imagination is the greatest gift that the actor can give himself, and it's certainly what he does for his audience. He actually *nourishes* the 'third being', as I think they call it in the world of the mystics, the being that is taking impressions of the experience of life.

That is a real trade secret, knowing what to do in order to *allow* yourself to do it. And sometimes it requires no preparation at all.

In a long run, you know, it all begins so fresh, so exciting, and then after a while... We used to say in long runs at the RSC, Don't rehearse in the wings. Don't do it in the wings, do it on the stage! You know? Bring it all onto the stage.

Someone once said—one of the great Russian actors who came to talk to us—someone said to him, It's so thrilling and exciting when you come onto the stage, even in such a small part. And he said, Yes, I'm always thinking of more important things I must do to get me off. What do you mean? Well, yes, my character drops in to do this, but I have a whole other play that is about *me*! And off I go. It's happening in the wings. I can stay with you for a moment, I can tell you this because it is very important, but *my* play is happening. You have only seen this much. I have a whole other world that I belong to!

We are all the leading role in our own–

In our own lives, yes. And we're just getting a glimpse of it. We see a moment perhaps passing by, but your character has a whole other life.

It's about being buoyed by your imagination, isn't it?

Absolutely.

And there's no limit to how much you can buoy yourself.

We're getting into the Buddhist and Zen thing here. We make our own life. We are thinking it into existence. We are dreaming, singing the world into existence. If we didn't sing it into existence, it wouldn't be there. And in a way it is that, the bravery, the outrageousness that buoys you.

Germaine Greer writes about the Aboriginal artist, Emily Kngwarreye, who was pressed to give titles to her paintings. She didn't give them titles. But she understood what was being asked, and she said they were all called Awelye. And everyone thought this was marvellous. But what she was saying was, All of you. What is in the painting? All of you. Awelye. Awelye. And that's a very good description of both ourselves as a nation, and oneself as an artist. Particularly as an Australian artist and an actor. It's not just about all of *us*, it's about Awelye. All of *you*. And in a way, Awelye is what I mean by the memory. There must be effort, and a degree of suffering, but not the intentional inflicting of pain, more a sense of... Awelye. All of you.

What you're doing is very courageous, in a way. It's considered very bad form in this country to talk seriously about one's art, to take oneself very seriously as a professional artist in 21st-century Australia.

When I was given the Hayes Gordon Award recently, that was what I was most proud of. I said, I accept this award because it has taken me 30 years to say what I am. I am both a man of the theatre, an Australian, and a professional artist. It is my living. My *living*, in the true sense of the word. I make.

If you are just running and not knowing

JOEL EDGERTON

Joel graduated from Theatre Nepean in 1994. Since then he has appeared in many stage productions with Sydney Theatre Company and—perhaps most notably—with Bell Shakespeare, growing Prince Hal into King Henry the Fifth in two of that company's most celebrated productions.

Joel's film career continues to blossom in the dual orbits of Australian and international production. From the former category there is Erskineville Kings, Praise, Ned Kelly, *among others, and from the latter,* Star Wars: Episode Two: Attack of the Clones *and* King Arthur. *He is perhaps most widely known, loved and admired in Australia as Will in the hugely successful TV series,* The Secret Life of Us.

I first saw Joel act in a disused science lab in western Sydney in 1993, while he was a second-year acting student. He was playing Angelo from Shakespeare's Measure for Measure *in a famous scene where the character has the outrageous gall to attempt to seduce a young nun, Isabella, who has come to him to seek leniency for her brother, whom Angelo has sentenced to die. I've seen the scene played many times, with Angelo's lust usually somewhat stunted by his awareness of his own sexual perversity. Not so with Joel. He went after his Isabella like a hungry lion ripping into hapless prey. I was there as a guest director, looking to cast* Love's Labour's Lost, *and Joel's power and magnetism made him a shoe-in for the leading role of Berowne, whose genius is to know—while surrounded by pretension and stupidity—that life is for living.*

It was Joel's first Shakespearean role, and his hunger for the work, his preparedness to go all out, was inspiring and refreshing. The production fell into place around his professionalism and athletic leadership. The greatest shock for me came on the closing night. I'd assumed—having been so knocked out by the intelligence and humility of his process—that he must have been a very mature 23 or 24. He told me he was about to turn 18!

A couple of years later I had the privilege of acting with him in a production of Caryl Churchill's visceral adaptation of Seneca's Thyestes. *Joel had to torture me onstage, and he did. I mean, he really did!*

Interestingly, Joel reflects in this interview on that kind of take-no-prisoners power that he threw at everything in the early years of his acting.

We met at his Darlinghurst apartment. He proudly showed me the trailer from the soon-to-be-released King Arthur. *He spoke about that experience—its ups and downs—and how it had led him to do more writing. On the day, at 30-ish, Joel seemed confident, humble, and also a little uncertain about exactly what it is he's hungering for in the future. But the hunger is so palpable that it leaves no doubt that it will be sated.*

One is left with the impression—both from close quarters and from the back row of a cinema or theatre—that Joel really does share the essence of Shakespeare's Berowne: he knows that life is for living.

I think acting is something you never come close to understanding completely. It's only been in the last couple of years that I've understood that I'm comfortable with it at all. And that understanding has really come from just relaxing.

I kind of describe it as being under-prepared yet—and this might sound confusing—being well-prepared at the same time. In other words, prepared in terms of understanding the material you are working with, understanding the terrain your character floats in, but forgetting everything else.

Perhaps the best way to describe it is instinct and intuition. For me, the first instinct always seems right. Then, by being relaxed enough to be intuitive, and allowing answers to *reveal* themselves, I don't need to try and make a plan or a map of the way things should look.

Set yourself boundaries, but don't make them too strict.

This might sound pretty obvious, but don't allow yourself to premeditate the way a piece of dialogue should move or where it should end up. Or how you should sound or where the inflections should lie. To me these are all scientific things that should be used only in a technical, analytical way.

So when you divide things into what should be prepared and what should be unprepared, the performative decisions are things you put in the unprepared basket?

Yeah. I'm talking about when you walk onto a film or television set in particular. It's hard to do the same thing with theatre, because you really can't expect the other actors to deal with under-preparedness in theatre. I mean, to not know your lines when you're getting close to the opening night of a play is very selfish.

Okay, but you're suggesting that not knowing your lines *is* one of these 'un-preparation' strategies in relation to working on a film set?

Yeah. I may not even have looked at them the night before.

So what's the specific advantage of that process? And I'm wondering how common it is.

I've come across a few people on film sets that do similar things. The thing is, you risk being judged. People don't know whether or not you're just being lazy. I'm talking about a long-running TV series, for instance. Some people turn up every day and they're word-perfect, some people don't. And it's often the people who aren't word-perfect that are the most fascinating to work with or to watch.

In that circumstance, the unprepared category of things is allowed for by what is prepared, isn't it?

Yeah.

This way of working implies a trust in your instincts and a trust that it's going to be okay. So what is the trust built on?

You're relying on your own sense that you don't want to look stupid and fail. You're trusting the *thoughts behind* the words before you actually learn the words. It's like a tradesman who understands the way building or plumbing or masonry work, but when he arrives at the job he won't yet know the gauge of the pipes or the angles to cut the masonry.

And so the specific challenges of the day's work are to be embraced and trusted by the wealth of trade knowledge you have behind you?

Yeah. If you've ever been to a beach headland and run across the rocks, it's an exciting thing to do. If you are just running and not knowing, all you can do is look at the next rock that you're going to land on. You don't know if it's going to tilt, or if you're going to have to jump twice as far because there's a rock pool. The only decision you make is to just step out, not knowing the predicted route. To just decide along the way.

The problem with preplanning is that, unless you've put in a lot of preplanning, thought of every option, walked into every room of possibility, you may be shutting out other possibilities by not allowing yourself to freefall. And that's when your imagination will come to your rescue. That's when—especially on film—your whole cognitive response to things appears, just as it does in life.

What I aim for is to make the atmosphere for acting as similar as possible to real life—I don't know what you're going to say, and I don't know what I'm going to say after you've said what you're going to say, because I don't know what you're going to say yet.

But you do trust that whatever you're going to say is going to be organic in some way. In the artificial life of acting, how do you build a similar faith? The running over the rocks thing is... You're trusting your agility. You're just backing yourself, really.

Yeah. You're backing yourself.

Because of that trade knowledge we talked about, that the electrician or the plumber has?

But that trade knowledge is not so much acting training. It's just life, and being comfortable in your own skin. That's separate from acting training.

Hopefully, as an actor, you get to the platform where you forget about the nerves, the eagerness to get the job, your ambition, being nervous because this director is someone you know, or the actor that's already cast in the film is important, or the theatre company is one you've never worked with before.

Of course, no one can teach you how to get over nerves. Maybe someone can. It's funny, but working the way I do can create more nerves because you go, I'm not prepared. I'm not really prepared. I could actually mess my lines up. Who gives a shit? But in a way, this approach allows you to forget about all the other nerves, because you've got to concentrate so hard.

The thing of preparing alone in a room, I've done that loads of times. You rehearse by yourself for a scene that has two people. You decide that when you get to the part where your character says, 'How dare you do that to me', after Rita has said, 'Get out of my house', you know you're going to give your line nine out of ten on the Richter Scale. Then you walk onto the set and your Rita says, 'Get out of my house' in a pleading, crumbling kind of way. Now you've rehearsed your nine on the Richter Scale, you can tell you should reduce it to a three, but because you've rehearsed it as a nine, you've *got* to do it as a nine! And you know that's going to win you your mini-Oscar for the day. So I've worked hard at getting rid of that.

Part of what led me to working the way I do now came from the belief I had earlier in my career that in order to have an effect over the audience, or the other person I was acting with, I often needed to feel like I was in some kind of pain, or I had to be exhausted.

That it had to be difficult?

Yeah. A strain. And then I thought, Well, in life, nothing is strained. You might feel pain, you might feel upset, you might feel angry, but if you're going to express yourself, you just express yourself at the drop of a hat, you don't wind yourself up like a generator. So why do actors need to wind themselves up? Why do some actors need to do push-ups backstage? Or run around and beat their chests to simulate a frantic state, when it's really about breath and honesty and understanding and intelligence? These are things that you're ready for in life.

In life, yelling doesn't strain your voice—unless you've been doing it for minutes. But I'd often find myself halfway through the run of a play, and if I could bring my throat outside of my body, it would look hideous. It would feel damaged because I'd been yelling, and I was feeling that I had to yell because I'd yelled in rehearsal and it worked.

And so an aesthetic expectation had grown around that moment? This is a loud moment.

Yeah, whereas why couldn't it be *not* a loud moment? Or why couldn't it be a loud moment one night and not a loud moment the next night, as long as the two actors are ready to take the plunge?

What allows a readiness between two actors for that to be okay?

The shortest and best answer to that is pure listening. There are times when you meet up with some other actors to do some work and you think, Yeah, that person and I are meant to dance, or work together in that way. Dancing actually is probably a pretty good explanation for it. Whereas you meet another actor and there's no click. It's really about listening. And you can see it when actors are listening. You can really see it.

When it comes to drawing comparisons between theatre, film and television, there are so many similarities and a lot of differences too.

One of the important differences in theatre is the size of the auditorium. To play in a theatre with 1,000 seats is very different to playing in a theatre with 80 or 100 seats. A small theatre draws the requirements of playing on stage closer to a performance that you could pull off in front of a camera. But then, even with a camera, the shot size becomes integral. In a larger shot, you might play a scene like you would in the theatre, but in a shot that's from your chin to the top of your forehead you can get away with the most minute whisper, the most minute expression. But the truth behind things should always be the same whether on stage or on film.

So, that moment that is going to be played in all sorts of different-sized theatres, and is also going to be shot on film with extreme close-ups, has an essential kind of truth to it. The implication being that there are knobs and dials that you're quite happy to slide up and down.

Adjust. Yeah.

Obviously, the awareness of your body is going to be extreme in a big theatre. Does that mean you just cut your head off and not worry about your body in an extreme close-up?

No. The rest of your body is involved, it just won't be caught on film. A good example of that is, say, the end of *Devil's Advocate*. Al Pacino has this huge speech as the Devil. You could take that and put it right on stage. Put a lot of Nicholas Cage's performance in *Moonstruck* on stage. He does enormous things on film.

There are no rules. To decide that you should do a particular thing, or not do a particular thing, is just cutting off opportunities.

In film, someone else is looking after so much of your performance. And in theatre too. The director is looking after spatial relationships between two characters, and how much dynamism that creates, and how much malevolence or how much love that creates. In film, whatever is keeping two people apart or bringing them together, that part is handled by the positioning of the camera, by the editor and the director. You might have to play a love scene from quite a distance because that's the way it looks best. So you've got to put a lot of faith in other people.

The way it is on the stage is the way the audience will perceive it. The audience doesn't have a camera. In an intimate scene they can't see your eyes. But in film you can see an intimate scene from every which way. Every angle. It's a luxury. Whereas in the theatre you have a responsibility to find other ways of expressing things. Some people really know how their body fits in space, and those people tend to be adept at working in the theatre. They know how to express with every part of their body. Geoffrey Rush is really good at that. His fingers have electricity or something.

What's the extent of your feeling of possession of the spatiality of a stage?

With my under-preparedness, one thing I *am* prepared for is having some imaginative idea of the boundaries in which that character fits in the world of the play.

Well, what you're talking about there is what *is* prepared. See, the word you said earlier, before you said under-prepared, was relaxation. In a way this is a kind of sophisticated preparedness of its own, isn't it? You are preparing to be relaxed?

Yeah.

You're determined that you're going to walk into the room with a level of relaxation and receptivity. What else is supporting you, allowing you to do that?

I did a really interesting workshop about why actors get nervous. And why they don't share the fact that they get nervous. And why actors sabotage themselves on the first day of rehearsal. All sorts of things.

Get all actors in a room and say, Let's all admit that we think we're all hopeless. On the first day of rehearsal. People are going to find out that we're phoneys. And that's an extension of a great idea in life. Everybody on the planet—people on the top floors of buildings who run corporations, everybody anywhere—part of them thinks, People are going to find out I'm a phoney. And you can relate it to acting. People think you've got to put your best foot forward in rehearsal, as you've got to put your best foot forward in life. You've got to be great, you know?

Part of what allows me to not let nerves or sabotaging thoughts come into my head is to know the imaginative world that I'm in, and to make it tangible. It's almost like the dialogue and the lines are secondary.

So in a scene where a character is well established in a society, and is questioning the arrival of a newcomer, being prepared might mean being sure that your feet are just planted right on the ground. Complete stillness and confidence.

You mean that not just in a metaphorical sense, you mean as a physical decision?

A physical decision. If I'm playing a character arriving in a room to meet somebody about getting a job, almost more important to me than the lines is, What does the room look like? Is my character arriving to meet the right person? That kind of process allows me to think whether I'll get the job or not get the job. And if I feel physically uncomfortable to the point where I don't look confident, how do I feign feeling comfortable? Those thoughts are more important to me than just getting to my first line.

And those things become both intellectual and physical. If somebody said, Okay, before you start the scene, what does this room look like?, you'd actually have an answer. Or, What is this person doing? It shouldn't be about making a decision like, I'm going to surprise this person, or, I'm going to emote, or, I'm going to cry. Take all that pressure *off* yourself. What am I looking at? Where am I? How do I feel? What is happening? Almost like being a kid and playing.

In a way, that's what it becomes. Being a kid, creeping through the forest. There could be monsters around. How does that feel? It's amazing how freeing that can be. Fantastically freeing.

It can be broken down in a methodical way but, hopefully, all those steps can happen at once. To the point where, if you are given a piece of paper that has a few things on it, a few scraps of dialogue, you make very fast decisions. You know where the world is. You know where the person you are playing sits in that world. You know what the person thinks of themselves. You know so much that it then becomes just an imaginary exercise where you either instantly connect or you don't.

I'm interested in how you've progressed toward this kind of world view, as it sits at this point in time. Were there major fuck-ups along the way that made you see things in this way? Or were there major enlightenments and epiphanies, where you stumbled on wonderful things, and they made you think, Gee, I'm going to buy some of this and carry some of this with me?

The bits that taught me more along the way were probably moments when I was disappointed in myself because I knew that I'd contrived a moment, or contrived stuff on stage, and was praised for it. It felt corrupt to me, because I was receiving an accolade or a thankyou or praise for doing something that I knew was sneaky.

To live life as a contrivance in acting would be... I wouldn't do it. As much as I think there'd be some joy in pulling the wool over people's eyes—and that's what a lot of acting is. You know, you're not *really* upset but you make everybody *believe* that, in the context of the story, you *are* this person who's really upset. And then they get upset along with you.

I mean, that's really kind of fun. Even a tragedy should be fun. You might have woken up feeling fantastic. Then you go off to work, you make everyone believe that your life is a mess, and they buy into it. That's exciting. But if you're just contriving it, then the only excitement is the effect you're having over the audience.

But I think there's something else to it that's fun, and that's transforming *yourself*.

I'd like to ask you again to go back to when you were starting out. I'm keen to talk with you about that because you're still a young actor. What do you recall being the things you were obsessed about, the things that concerned you—both positive and negative—when you were 17, 19, 21, at acting school and in the early years beyond acting school? What were you putting your money on then?

It was almost like I was trying to act backwards. I think I misinterpreted drama school in a lot of ways. I became obsessed with my voice. I'd just left high school and I had quite a high voice. I think the natural process of getting a bit older helped, also concentrating on voice exercises helped. But I think vocal exercises can be a waste of time for a lot of people. Because if an actor decides that they have to sound a particular way, then they're monitoring themselves. And that's one of the last things, one of the things you should bury.

Sure, you might want to get someone's voice centred. But I don't know if any amount of 'budda-gudda-budda-gudda' is going to do that. I think it's deeper than that, deeper than 'red-lorry-yellow-lorry'. I see the value in that, and I see the value in articulation—

What is the value?

God. Good question. I don't know. The value in those classes, I think, was gaining a certain amount of confidence with other actors and with yourself. And agility of voice, especially when it came to, say, classical acting in theatre. And to understand the resonance inside your own body. But, for a kid like me, growing up in Dural, I just thought, What am I doing?

And then someone told me, someone pointed out that I had a lisp, and that was the fuckin' worst thing. I mean, in a way, the best thing, but the worst thing at that time. The best thing because it taught me to go, Who gives a fuck?

I went off to a speech place where I remember a waiting room with someone in a wheelchair who was learning to talk again. And here I was, an able-bodied young guy who could actually communicate in any circumstance as long as there was English being spoken, but who had a very slight lisp. And it had become like a hot air balloon inside my body, something that had to be expelled like a tumour. And the thought attached to this was, If you don't get rid of this problem, you won't work in film or television. And you think, Fuck!

So I go off to do a lesson and I've got this notebook and I'm up for $80 a session for who knows how many sessions. And then I thought, I can't buy into this. I have my voice. I'm a human being. Who gives a fuck?!

I've learned a lot about acting from reality TV shows. Why do we all get hooked on them? You get anybody, real people, put them on TV, watch them talk and move, and they're fascinating.

So to say that an actor isn't ready to be a good performer until they look right or sound right… Isn't it just about finding your expression? Finding *your* way of doing things, without being constricted, you know? Not being onstage going, Oh, God, I'm thinking about where my hands are.

Look, there's a huge problem, I think, when you get a bunch of young people together who want to be actors. They want to be famous, they want to be stars, or they're desperate for something. And human desperation can be quite ugly. I'm being pretty harsh here, but desperation can be ugly when somebody *needs* something. Now, neediness is going to create blockages, because if you need something, then the other side of it is, What if I don't get it? And the what-if-I-don't-get-it side sabotages an actor. How do you get rid of that?

The other side of that equation is the fact that sometimes you get good actors out of people who don't want to be actors, but then those kind of people can run into other problems like not being able to fully express themselves.

Somewhere in between lies the person who's relaxed and at ease with who they are, is willing to express it, is willing to be ugly or in pain, willing to show every facet of their real self. And this person is not so over-eager that they sabotage themselves along the way, or contrive what they think the end product should look like. Somewhere in that zone, I reckon, is an ease of acting that just flows like water. But it's hard to find.

But again you're talking about what makes one conducive to it. Desperation is not conducive to finding what you might call this artistic realm in which you're going to relate, and you're going to find the

spatiality. Desperation is just one of those things that fucks you up. Stops you from getting the job done.

Yeah.

What does it feel like when you're contriving, or feeling that you're acting badly?

I'll draw another analogy. I like going for a run, but I much prefer it if every time I go for a run it's in a new spot. I get to look at something new. When I'm running towards a bend, I don't know what's around the bend. I'm not treading in the same footsteps every time.

I think that's why I got a little bit disappointed with the theatre. I'd go out there every night and get angry or upset with myself because I didn't think there was anything new in that night's performance, as opposed to the night before. But that's not your job in the theatre, necessarily. That's when it becomes about entertaining *yourself*. It should be about entertaining the audience and telling a story. And the audience on Tuesday isn't going to know what it was like on Monday—they're not comparing it. But you as an actor are.

You feel like you are literally going through the motions?

Yeah. I've just worked out all my footprints. So it's about actually being a part of the discovery as well.

Presumably you think that your sense of discovering stuff is going to translate as something of more value to the audience too.

Yeah.

So talk about that in the context of a big Shakespearean lead.

I recently had the experience—and I wouldn't recommend it—of watching tapes of sections of *Henry 4* and *Henry 5*, the productions I was involved in. I thought there was much more of an organic process going on for me with *Henry 4*, and that I brought more technical expertise or understanding to *Henry 5*. And I think the result is that *Henry 5*, to me, was a better performance for the stage. I rose to meet the language more than I did in *Henry 4*. I felt like in *Henry 4* I was thinking the right thoughts, but the words themselves were dropping a lot. I wasn't flying with the language. But I felt wonderful on stage. It felt really organic. But after listening to the tapes in a clinical way, *Henry 5* seemed much more watchable, and probably would have been to an audience as well. But that's with hindsight, you know.

Isn't it also true that that might be a way of describing the two different roles? *Henry 4* is about a young guy–

Exactly. And certainly that was behind a lot of the thinking and discussion that went into it. Actually taking the mantle of the king in *Henry 5* was a parallel to taking the mantle of the next level of a Shakespearean character.

And a character who's turning himself from a sensualist into an orator. What about the physical sensation of when you know you're acting really well?

There is no physical sensation, I reckon. It's almost like you wouldn't even be able to remember the sensation. I mean, you could describe it as a lightness and an ease, as opposed to the stuff I was talking about before—you know, feeling like you're winding a generator or running a marathon or screwing yourself into a ball just to feel like you're feeling great human emotion.

I think the great sensation of communicating well is just… It's a lightness and a responsiveness that is almost indestructible. I don't know, that makes it sound like a religious experience but it *is* almost. It's a confidence. It's an ease, I guess.

What happens when it's a cathartic scene or a very aggressive scene or a life-changing, gut-wrenching moment for a character?

Oh, far out. I reckon you've got to approach it step by step. Climbing a mountain is a lot more achievable if you're going from base camp to the first-stop hut, then to the next, then re-checking your gear and going on to the next one.

The trouble with emotion is that it becomes like this big flag on the horizon. It's like you go, Okay, I'm going along here taking each step as it comes, but I can almost see in my peripheral vision that I've got to yell or abuse somebody or break down and cry. And you can't just cross your fingers and hope for the best. And you can't necessarily go, Well, if I don't feel it I'm not going to do it. The audience have paid $45 a ticket. They're not going to stand for that.

You've got to do something in that moment that's pretty extraordinary, so immediately, you're freakin' out on your way to that spot. You're not concentrating on the 20 lines of dialogue that come before, and you're not listening well to all the other actors. You're singing that song 'What About Me?' in your head. You're going, What am I going to do in that moment?

John Gaden as Falstaff and Joel Edgerton as Prince Hal in the 1998 Bell Shakespeare production of *Henry 4*. (Photo: Branco Gaica)

And the hardest thing is: How do you actually just relax and treat that scene like you would a scene about getting the milk from the shops? Because if you can—the theory being that your preparedness, listening and responding in the moment, will make you better prepared to do your breakdown scene. If you stop in at all the points along the way, if you're honest and true and you listen—the way you do in any other scene—you should be better prepared for that moment.

I guess it goes back to that whole running along the rocks thing. You have to stay true all along the way. It's like one of those scientific theories about the way particles of matter create things in the universe or something, like, I know the theory is there but show it to me in practice!

Stanislavski. How clear or concise or fulsome is your understanding of what that's all about, and does it mean anything to you in the way you go about what you do?

Some of the things I think about and apply in my head do relate to it, but in all honesty, I never relate to it terms of *him* or thinking about his *process*. In terms of what we used to call the VOTE sheet, at drama school: Victory, Objective, Tactics, Expectations. After a certain amount of practice, I think they just become automatic. You read a piece of material, those things fall into place. After a while you hope you don't have to write them down ever again.

So you don't make a lot of notes?

No.

You would never write a character biography?

No, no.

Would you ever analyse actions, and attach verbs, and flip through a thesaurus and things like that?

No, I would never do that stuff. But I write loose notes. In my version I think about a character as being like a wheel that has a centre and spokes. If you want your wheel to work properly, you need to have a lot of dimension to the spokes so that they'll hold it up and make it roll properly, make it real. One of the spokes might be understanding your character's victories. Another might be that stuff we talked about before—their status within the situation, you know, or their familiarity with the room. One of them might be how worldly or educated that person is. You just look at them in all different imaginary ways.

And all that stuff you learn at drama school, like, What animal is most like this person? If, when you approach a character, those things don't immediately occur to you, it could be a good thing to look at it in terms of the wheel. Think about those animal things. Think about their physical energy. Think about drastically different situations than those of the context of the play—how they make a cup of coffee. Whatever it is that you think about in that 'outside-in' way, it'll give you a fuller idea of that person as a real person.

So you think all that stuff that's done in acting school, things you might spend a class on, or you might spend a week on, or you might spend a whole term on, in your case, is all stuff that becomes organic?

Yeah.

But you do believe that in this organic and unstudied way, you still cover a lot of that terrain?

Yeah. Yeah. But as sort of grabbing thoughts. It just becomes part of your way of proceeding when you start thinking about that story or about that character.

I think Method acting is a term that has this kind of magic attached to it. This idea that someone is a Method actor and that they really *become* the person they're playing. I think it's more about a tenacity of imagination, and a lack of censorship within people that allows them to go, In between shooting scenes I'm going to stay in this imaginative world, rather than go and have chit-chats over a cup of tea or coffee. I'm just going to allow myself to stay in the right terrain.

I think you have to be careful saying these people *become* somebody else. Their contrivance and their imagination—the rhythms of their speech, maybe, and their mannerisms—allow them to sound, to move, to *be* this other person. But they *aren't* that other person. If they were, then we'd be worried about them and we'd put them away.

The reason I like being an actor is because of the feeling of being able to express myself beyond the things I'm comfortable doing in life. In life I'm not very assertive. I don't enjoy tension. I don't enjoy aggression, but I love it if I get the licence to express it. I don't enjoy being timid or stifling my own expression and interaction in society, but if I get the licence to do it as a character, I get joy out of it—to be *all* the sides of me. I have a body of knowledge from what I've seen and heard and experienced.

You can use yourself as a kind of equaliser. Like you were talking about before, turning things up and down, certain sides of yourself. You're always being nine tenths of yourself, more or less, but you're hiding certain parts of yourself. It might be your sympathy or your tenderness. In acting you get to do things other than be yourself.

What about the use of your own emotional life, and your own emotional experiences in a role?

To use and draw on your own experiences and emotional experiences or situations in your life is always a handy kind of tool, because you've been there, you've experienced it.

Particularly those big moments we were talking about before, perhaps? Some people would say that one of the things that helps you get there is thinking about any experience that's analogous. I'm wondering if you've done that, and if so, how it works.

I find it quite hard, that stuff. Like saying, I'm going to relate the scene between you and I to another moment in my life. Because then, I think, for me it's like there are three people in the scene. It's like you're dragging a large prop into the scene. It means I have to stop communicating *directly* with you, and go via another port of call, before I can get back to you and it becomes about you and me again. It feels like, you know, reaching over to the table behind you to get the salt, or something. That's how I'd describe it.

Whereas, don't I try and use my imagination just to make it more about you and me than remembering when my dog died, or how I felt about visiting my grandmother in hospital, in order to try and conjure up an emotional state? It makes me feel as if I'm leaving you and becoming all about *myself* for a moment, and then once I've prepared and I've had that memory, then I can get back to communicating with *you*. That's not about really *listening* and *communicating* with you, so I don't like that stuff. I've tried it.

Some people might have a quicker response to a fleeting thought and then come back. I don't know how other people's brains work. They might be able to disappear into that memory and come back. Or make that memory complicit with the moment of communicating with another person. I guess that's a question of the agility of other people's thoughts and imagination.

For me... I want to stay at the table. Stay there.

The glory of the colours

PAMELA RABE

Pamela Rabe was born in Canada and studied acting at the Playhouse Acting School in Vancouver. She began working professionally at the Vancouver Playhouse, before making Australia her home in the early 1980s. She quickly established herself as a leading player on the Melbourne stage, and has since grown to national eminence as an actor of enormous skill, with an engaging mix of heartiness and finesse.

Pamela is equally at home in the 'high-fiction' of roles like the Wicked Witch of the West in The Wizard of Oz, *in classical leading roles like Beatrice in* Much Ado About Nothing, *and in the aching realism of* The Beauty Queen of Leenane.

Pamela has won two Sydney Critics' Circle Awards, and no fewer than five of Melbourne's prestigious Green Room Awards. Her best-known film role has been in Samantha Lang's The Well, *for which she won numerous awards both in Australia and overseas.*

Of all the times I've enjoyed Pamela's work onstage, the one that really sticks with me is her performance as the tragic Beauty Queen of Leenane. I felt her hopeless isolation. I dreamed her dreams with her. She's a whip-you-away-to-another-world kind of actor, a presence of rare power.

I met her 'on the road', in her apartment at the bottom of George Street, just a stone's throw from the Sydney Opera House, where she was playing in Coward's Blithe Spirit. *It seemed ironic to me that this actor should be so concerned about her sense of purpose and worth when surrounded by the mountainous office blocks of the CBD, and the often unhappy pen-pushing lives that fill them. I reckon she's doing alright.*

The drama school I went to in Canada was founded on passion, commitment and reason for being, really.

Not bad things to found an art school on.

Absolutely. The people who taught me had a great impact on me, yet the things they held most dear might not necessarily agree with what I most dearly believe in now. I suspect that whatever resonated with me, I conveniently turned around into thinking that's what they meant, and therefore that's what I'm going to run with.

That's possibly inevitable.

Yeah, that's what being taught is all about. You respond to ideas that somebody's feeding you, but it's about how those ideas *land*.

Nonetheless I recognised, right from the start, that in the act of exploring performance I was losing the self-consciousness that had plagued my childhood.

It had that sense of vocation. Anybody, not just a performer, but anybody who does anything, that point at which they no longer question their—not exactly their right to do it, but it's like that—that moment carries this sense of vocation.

And somehow—and these moments might still be few—I can get on a roll with what I'm doing, and nothing gets in the way. Nothing. I'm not aware of listening to myself, judging myself, watching myself. Obviously you are on some level because it's a highly artificial exercise, but I don't question myself or my—not *right* to expression—but I don't question my ability to express. Some things, we are hormonally programmed to enjoy.

It goes hand in hand with a constant feeling of guilt, because it feels highly self-indulgent, you know, because it's you up there doing it, and it's about you tapping into your imaginative responses to ideas. And yes, it's in order to entertain people, but you're not solving the problems of famine and war. Even though you may be affecting people. In some circumstances people have said their lives have been changed by an experience of watching something. But because it's linked with an essentially self-indulgent activity, everything is always tinged, for me, with a kind of guilt or mistrust and a wariness of pretension and wankery.

The passion and commitment of the drama school I attended influenced my belief that I must be absolutely 150 per cent committed to working as hard as I can, be as true to the whole, and engage every part of my being to do the job I've been asked to do. If I can't I should quit.

Oh, yes, and the other part of it is to make it look as easy as possible. The audience should not be aware of anything. They should be able to share the same lack of self-consciousness as you. If they're aware of you being a technically good actor—*Oh, isn't she wonderful!*—that's actually distancing them from the story that's being told or the ideas that are being expressed.

That's kind of my one commitment, to the idea that we should all lose ourselves in the experience in order to go somewhere together. Sometimes that can be for a totally frivolous reason. It can be just to feel good and forget who you are for a couple of hours. Sometimes it's about receiving great ideas, or about being shaken up and made to think differently.

I'm aware that even the phrase 'self-consciousness' doesn't satisfy what it is I'm talking about. But I suppose it's the loss of criticism, of self-criticism. I always think of a metaphor that somebody used: If you look at a stained-glass window from one side, all you see is the soldering and the muck and the mess and how the thing's been put together. But if you go around to the other side, all you see is the glory of the colours. You actually lose the mechanics. And it's that kind of quality with the self-conscious thing that I'm trying to get at.

That's a rich, over-arching point of personal/professional philosophy. But where do you actually start your work? What are your first steps, in a practical sense?

The first thing I do when somebody offers me something is read it, and in that reading something has to click. I have to get excited by something. Something touches me. Sometimes I feel excited by the energy of the writing, but often it's because the character I've been asked to play has a moment which tugs something.

What would you then be looking to achieve, in the early stages of rehearsal?

I would say trust. That's the thing I'm quite addicted to.

I'm not a very social person. I'm quite uncomfortable in a social context, but the times when I feel unselfconscious as a human being are when I'm in a room with people putting a piece of theatre together. So first of all I'll be trying to work out where I fit in the balance of energies and personalities in the room. That's not a clear-cut thing. You're just—on a non-intellectual level—just sort of feeling where you fit in. You think, *Well, this is the group we are, and we've been presented with the design, and a context, and we've got a director, and we're all kind of sensing what the world of* whatever we're in for is. We're all throwing our own private responses to the work into the centre of the room. We're starting to form a kind of shape. But more than anything, at the end of the first week I'd be looking for trust. In order to do the job as well as we can, we have to not be frightened. And it's a love affair too. You actually want to be seduced by everybody. You want it to be brilliant.

I think every actor—whether consciously or not—makes an assessment, quickly, about whether and how much they're going to allow themselves to be used or abused or humiliated, made to look foolish or bad. And everybody makes a kind of decision somewhere along the line about whether and how much they're going to engage their survival techniques. And everybody's got them, even if they say they haven't, they've got them.

I think that another thing I took from my formal acting training was the knowledge that nobody owes you. Nobody has a responsibility to make you look good. If you can't do it, the director doesn't do your job for you. If somebody's technique doesn't jibe with yours, it's your responsibility to make it work.

Sometimes you can have really horrendous experiences. You find yourself with a director and you don't like the way they work. I've worked with a few pretty insane directors, and it's really unsettling. I hate that. You want them to be the least neurotic person in the room, not the most! Some directors don't deal with the whole power thing very happily or well. That can create a very unpleasant environment to work in.

And there are often times when you know the piece actually might work, but the path to getting there is going to be a bit unpleasant. You're going to have to knuckle down and think, Right, how do I serve this the best way I can? That sometimes can get to the point of, How do I come away from this without looking as bad as everything else? Which, to me, is the least desirable circumstance. But there have been a couple where I've thought, This whole thing stinks so badly, and it's so awful, and so many people have been disengaged from what they're doing, from their own talent, their own belief in themselves. Everybody has just crumbled, and this piece is crap and we shouldn't actually be asking money from people to watch it. But we're on the road of no return. Those are the ones where the power of the social group gets you through. Sometimes the closest friendships are formed in difficult projects because you've all gone though a very odd hell.

I've said that on a fundamental level I'm striving for a loss of self-consciousness for everybody, for *everybody*—but the primary responsibility is to an audience. The germ of it begins with a personal response to something, but I don't believe it lives there. It's not all about how *I* feel about something. It's not inward looking. I firmly believe it's about a group of people telling a story together. And yes, there's a kind of loop that involves me and my very personal responses, and yes, it would be completely different if one link in that chain were different, but essentially it is a *group* responsibility. We create it together.

And that ripples out into a whole area of belief in terms of how you work spatially with other actors, and how you converse with other actors on a professional level.

I get into trouble sometimes because I talk a lot in the rehearsal room. But I've come to a point where I believe in talking to other actors about what you need in the hope that they will share those same things with you. And there are some actors who don't like that. To them, it sounds too much like 'notes'. There's an old-fashioned acting belief that we shouldn't give each other notes. So you have to be very careful about how you articulate stuff like that. Even something as simple as, It would really help this moment—in story-telling terms—if it doesn't get in the way of what you're doing, could you possibly be there, do this, in order to help that? And that is a borderline imposition on another actor who may be, you know, guarding their turf.

You basically work out the people that you can work with in that way, the people that you can trust, and the people that you can't.

For example, Greg Stone and I, we've worked on things a number of times, and it's great because we've got to a point where we trust each other on that level. We take great delight in the forensic process of trying to get a moment to work really well. But there are some people you just know would not take that on, so you don't bother. And that's fine. *Everybody's* different.

Apart from that quite substantial agenda of sensitivities, do you start rehearsing plays with other things weighing on your mind in relation to the particular play? For example, *The Wizard of Oz*, a piece that carries a very particular aesthetic expectation?

When you say aesthetic, do you mean style?

I guess that's the word I'm avoiding, yeah.

Because I think that's a really important thing. That's also one of the things you're assessing really strongly in that first week. Because there are a million

Pamela Rabe as Paige and Stephen Curry as Mike in the 2004 Melbourne Theatre Company production of *Dinner*. (Photo: Jeff Busby)

different ways to do Noel Coward, music theatre, Irish pot-boiling melodrama. Sometimes it's very much imposed. You get a very strong sense of what it is because there's a house-style involved.

Neil Armfield cast me in a production of *The Ham Funeral* with Brian Thomson doing the set, and Kerry Walker and Max Cullen in the cast. I'd seen a number of Neil's productions prior to that experience, so that you kind of walk into the room and right away some style options are already narrowed down. Right away you're thinking, Ah, I think I have an idea of the world that this is going to exist in, and a little of what's expected of me. You're still shooting off like a catherine-wheel in terms of your choices and how to do the job the best you can, but you've got a much stronger idea of the kind of niche in which this is going to exist. Much more so than when you walk into a room with a director and a group of actors whom you've never worked with or seen before. Then you're not quite sure what's expected of you.

That kind of experience, like your *Ham Funeral* experience, could be read as a really strong and helpful guide, or it could be read as an inhibition.

No, I think it's fantastic. It just saves time. You can get down to the nitty-gritty.

I also get off on all that stuff—and I may be completely wrong, and people may think, Well, that's what I hate about her work—but I love all the different styles of performance.

When things have ended up manifesting in highly fictional ways–

When you say fictional you mean grotesque? The big stuff.

Yeah, the big stuff. How and when does that come in?

I suppose it often just hinges on a couple of moments when you think, Oh, okay, I think I understand what that's about. And then you start responding to things that are thrown at you. You start responding to what they dress you in. But also it's about thinking, What do I represent in this whole story here? What part of the story am I serving? What is my character here for? Can I push that? How far can I push it? Then you have to trust the director and your fellow actors to let you know when you've pushed it too far.

Are there not points where you know you have to make a big leap? I think of the Wicked Witch, for example. Was there a thing pressing on you, a voice saying, Well, one of these days I'm going to have to start getting pretty witchy?

That's a tricky one. Different work environments have different demands and requirements.

A lot of people come to a musical—a commercial musical especially—with everything learnt, everything ready, and a performance pretty much in the can, which is kind of anathema to me in terms of how I would normally like to work, but I also kind of get off on the demand that that makes.

Right, they're going to get frightened very quickly—I might get fired—if I don't come up with something pretty quickly. I'm paid to be braver.

And that can be liberating as well. It just takes one little tick in the room, whether it's the fact you make the chorus people laugh or—

I often say to people that acting is a confidence game, and one has to be acquiring confidence–

Absolutely, and you're looking around. I mean, commercial theatre productions, they're big, big structures. And with *The Wizard of* Oz I had a few pointers, indicators that this is where my character was *expected* to fit in to the whole.

I adored her. There's nothing nicer and more fun than being purely nasty, and a bit stupid at the same time. And she's the one character who has a connection to the audience, who is allowed to have a kind of a wink with the audience, and that's a great treat. I enjoy all that.

I actually think the wink is there, even in the most straightforwardly fourth-wall presentations. It's a fundamental belief. I do believe very strongly in the... I can only call it the wink, but that sounds too open and crass. It ties in with that thing of the audience understanding that you are really fully present, and with them in the room, and sharing something, and giving them something very special on an individual, intimate level.

So it's the acknowledgment that, even if the play is ostensibly set long ago and far away, the more important reality, the most important 'given circumstance', is the room you are all in, and this moment that you're all sharing? Like, Where is this play set? Well, in one sense, it's set in 19th-century Russia, but more significantly, it's set in Melbourne, tonight.

Yeah. Which is actually, I suppose, the fundamental antidote to the guilt thing, the self-indulgent element. Deep down I believe in the pleasure that we all derive, and that I derive as an audience member, from being in a space with people. From being present, sharing something with somebody else.

One must never degrade the experience or cheapen it. You shouldn't fuck around with it either. You have a responsibility to be consistently of a high quality. Perhaps it makes me a more boring actor.

That's an interesting and perhaps sobering point, associating consistency and quality with being boring.

Look, there's a group of actors who are just temperamentally predisposed to believe that their greatest work comes totally by surprising themselves, being different every night. And they will go to great lengths to kind of shake it up all the time, because they feel that's the way they produce their best work. But they may actually be producing inferior work six or seven times out of ten. And then there are those who feel that primarily it's about a kind of consistency of quality, which means they may never get to the high highs of excitement, for either themselves or the audience. But to me it's trying to get a balance of the two. I suspect, however, that I tip over into the slightly staid, boring category, striving to have a consistent level of quality.

I'd love you to talk more about that difficult gap between what is set and what is given freedom. Between the leash and to what extent one can let oneself off the leash.

Well, that, I suppose, is about the work that you do beforehand, and how your brain works in terms of how you structure a performance.

I remember being quite hurt when Ruth Cracknell described me in an interview as someone who had everything worked out to the finest detail. Everything set. To me it implied that my work had no life or freshness. I know that's not what she meant, but that's kind of what it sounded like. I thought, Oh God, is that what it looks like? Because I don't feel that that's what it is, but maybe that *is* what it is. But I'd like to think of it as adhering to a more kind of Grotowski 'technique sets you free' kind of thing. The idea that if you create enough, like… what's the word? Enough, like in a race, enough flags, enough posts to hang onto along the way, you can soar. And you can. Again, it's about safety and trust in order to throw yourself deeply into stuff. If I can create a kind of framework that is quite strong.

Like orienteering flags, or pegs along a path? And it's possible to put too many of them in, so that there's no room between, and it's possible to have them too far apart?

But it's how you reach for the pegs, too. Sometimes the pegs can save you.

Take the example of a long run of something like a musical show. It's such a highly artificial environment. You're miked. You're getting no acoustic sound from your fellow actors. You're dealing with a lot of different kinds of acting. Just the nature of the experience of playing to a 2,500 – 3,000-seat theatre can create… Everybody's in their own sort of vacuum. It's highly choreographed, highly artificial. Dancing and singing to that same beat for months and months. It can sometimes just push you towards autopilot.

The pegs can be useful there, but you have to resist the urge to just reach for them. It's *how* you reach for the pegs that's important. Yes, if the pegs get too close together they… No, I don't mind that. Those pegs can be like sardines as long as you go for them freshly. It's about trusting that they're there, but not thinking about them.

The people who are plunging in and flailing and being very different and very exciting—quite electric on stage—are people who have the pegs quite far apart, and they really enjoy the adrenaline rush and the thrill of what happens if they crash and don't make it to the next peg. The more anal people, like me, have the pegs fairly close together, because I know that should inspiration fail me, should the fresh discovery not be there between this peg and that peg, I know that I will get to the end, and the overall experience for the audience will be not so different to when I'm actually firing on all cylinders.

You mentioned Grotowski. Of course, his legacy reminds us that this sort of process, or this way of looking at performance, is not *anti* emotional engagement. It's not something one does *instead* of being emotionally engaged.

No, it's to help it, actually.

You talk about doing *The Wizard of Oz*, and taking on the form of something, and almost prematurely saying, Well, here's the form. And, as you said, there is also a kind of *industrial* reality that comes into play: you have commercial expectations on you. You can't say, Look, I've decided that she's actually all these different things.

Yes. Before we began it was made clear to me that this production was a faithful recreation on stage of the MGM film. And within that framework my character had a little bit of licence to have some fun with the notion of it being a live performance.

I went for the size of it, the big stuff, and it filled up pretty quickly. I just turned up the volume on Margaret Hamilton, which then, through me, produced some other things, and you'd get approval and disapproval, and you go with the stuff that you get approval for.

Sometimes young actors seem to resist the notion that there are knobs and dials, and you can turn things up and down, because they're concerned about things feeling right *before* they're explored. What does it do to your gizzards when you accept the reality of technique? What's the link between your guts—and you've used this gesture of germination in your gut—what's the link between that and going for the big stuff?

Well, that is interesting. I remember Simon Phillips said that was something he could count on, that if he wanted size, but still an emotional connection to what was going on in the core of the character, he could count on me. And I take that as a great compliment. A little double-edged, because you have to be able to turn the knobs down when you need to. But for me, I get off on the style of things. And I'm not talking just about externals, but that different stories require different kinds of artifice, different levels of the wink. There's an awareness of the performance.

I love the use of the word 'artifice'. It's one of the words in teaching that I love to 'out', because people otherwise are inclined to pretend that it is–

Completely exclusive of emotional truth. You can be highly artificial, and absolutely truthful at the same time.

And, indeed, is it not so that embracing the artifice can be a conduit to the truth?

Absolutely. In fact, some of the most moving experiences I have had as an audience member have been watching the most artificial things.

I think of something like Shakespeare. The level of artifice in Shakespeare is huge, and one can see bad productions that are all artifice and one can see as bad–possibly worse–productions that are all what Keith Bain once called toenail-picking truth, ignoring the artifice. But I think one of the reasons, and part of the fun of why Shakespeare survives, is that it can be both. It can embrace all 20th-century, post-psychologising–

Yeah, and I love just running the gamut of all those. Things that are almost borderline dance to something that's so filmic and naturalistic. I get off on that. I might push things a little bit far because I'm having fun, but I am commenting on my response to what I see as an already pre-established style. I don't see any kind of betrayal of my responsibility to emotional truth in having fun with that. Which is a bit unusual. When I went overseas to work in Canada a few years ago, that was commented on.

Unusual that you were embracing the artificiality?

Yes. They seemed to think that if you're that big you can't be truthful. But I was taught by English people, not Canadians, for the most part. It was an environment where there was a big dividing line between highly artificial disciplines—including the work of a lot of comedians—and *drama*. And the drama was—particularly1970s, early 80s—was real kitchen sink, Actors Studio, truth stuff.

Yes, well, we're kind of the same age, and were at acting school at the same time, and I remember certainly that 'technique' was a dirty word. We didn't want to be technical, we wanted to be truthful.

And I think we were responding to new-wave cinema.

I guess so. Responding to *Raging Bull* and all the rest of it, and not seeing the technique in it.

It's as much a style as anything else.

Yes, and as prone to bullshit as any other style, be it cod-Pacino or cod-Molière. *Truth* can be the most annoying of affectations.

Yeah. And the whole point is story-telling. So a process of selection is in place even if it is the most 'naturalistic' of stories.

I think the tensions between the sort of highly artificial performance styles and those that are much more sort of low-key and grounded in naturalistic detail, the tension between those two has created a kind of hybrid style which is particularly Australian. I don't really know why or how it is, but I think that's true. And now I'm so much a part of it that it's harder to see. But I remember feeling it quite strongly in the first decade that I was here.

There's often a kind of mistrust of naked emotional commitment to things, other than when it's at its most naturalistic and filmic. There's a great love for the high camp, of big style, especially if it's really clear to the audience that you're sending yourself up. I just find it a really fascinating kind of style that pervades a lot of stuff I see.

It's perhaps informed by something so simple as the fact that a lot of the rehearsal spaces we work in are very noisy. In Sydney, in every place I've ever rehearsed in… The Wharf, for example, the most beautiful of locations, to the point of being quite distracting, but it's… You can't hear! If it's a sunny day there's the noise of helicopters and the harbour all around you, and if it's raining you're drowned out. The cacophony of rain on the tin roof is deafening. And the places that I've rehearsed with for Belvoir are the same. It's like there's so much noise everywhere that, by necessity, it's created an interesting style, and had an imperceptible—well slightly perceptible—impact on the evolution of what's considered to be truth, and truthfulness.

This secret life

SEAN O'SHEA

Working constantly with student actors, one becomes aware of the young professionals in the industry who are exciting the students. Certain names keep cropping up as students rave about and rip into the productions they've seen.

When I was a student in the early 80s, Heather Mitchell was one such role model. Over the last five years, I've been aware that Sean O'Shea's work has been touching a chord with that highly critical section of the audience that is made up of student actors. Sean's been making a pretty big impact on everybody else too with the combination of intelligence and ease with which he works.

I first saw Sean as a rather peculiar, near-Chekhovian Puck for Penrith's Railway St Theatre, a company for which he has worked a number of times. Its production of Favourite Names for Boys *was an example of what I call pure theatre, in which the time, the place, the people and the material all seem essential to the mix. It was a piece to which Sean was passionately connected, and it showed in his fine work.*

Sean has also worked extensively with Bell Shakespeare, including playing Antipholus of Ephesus in the wonderfully warm, funny and generous John Bell production of A Comedy of Errors.

Sean was chuffed to be invited into the pages of this book, and humbly suggested he be placed in a section for the 'not quite distinguished'. Not a bit of it! Read on.

Ultimately, my inspiration or passion for a piece of work must come from the writing. In an ideal world that would be the starting and finishing point. Many times that's not the case.

Because the quality of the writing differs so greatly? From TV commercials to Chekhov?

Exactly. If you were just going for what you need to keep you sustained, you'd never do television commercials. I don't think anyone does them for any other reason but survival and paying the rent. Unfortunately it's one of the realities.

You underwent formal training in Western Australia. Can you talk a bit about what you were taught to do, and can you relate that to what you actually do?

I had a wonderful three years at WAAPA, as opposed to a lot of the people I talk to who look back at their training and speak of the many nervous breakdowns and of still bearing the scars and all that kind of stuff. For me it was an enormous part of growing as a person, not just whether or not I became a better actor. I was too terrified to act when I went to acting school. I mean, I think I was good enough to act, but I was a very frightened, shy, timid person.

And you felt the course allowed you to be that, yet was conducive to you growing as a person?

Absolutely. I don't think I could possibly have ended up being an actor if I hadn't gone through some kind of experience like that at acting school, which was much more important than what they taught me about how to act and how to approach a play.

How did that nurturing aspect manifest? Was it just a general tone and attitude of the place?

Yes. I just felt very supported there. I felt like they actually believed I was good enough to be doing this. So I never really had to justify my presence there. I also had an extremely good run. There was a very good mix of people teaching quite different stuff, some approaching things from traditional angles and others coming from much more left of field.

That investment in you as a person at a young age, and that development of yourself as a human being, does that have a place in the way you approach the work now?

In terms of how you value yourself as a human being? God, I would hope so. I think if you lose track of that you might as well forget it. I mean, that's in the good jobs. The ones when you actually feel like you're doing something and you're a part of something that's saying something you believe in.

For me the exciting time is when you are inspired or impassioned by a piece of writing and you feel that the play is actually informed by who *you* are as well as the writer, and the good group of people who you are working with.

The play is informed by who *you* are? Presumably, that's a connection to being trained in a way that gave you a sense of who you were?

Yeah, and I don't think actors should have to apologise for that. We should be opinionated. Any kind of person in the arts should be an opinionated person. And you should ultimately be trying to bring that to the work, I think.

What's in your head and in your body at the point you start rehearsal? What are you aiming for?

It's not all that methodical for me. I was taught some methodical ways and I have to say that they're not all that helpful for me.

The thing that I'm looking for first is a kind of intuitive, intimate connection to the work, to the writing. And that doesn't just mean I want to read the play and like it, or I want to read the play and think what my character thinks.

The plays where I've felt I've done my best work, I've sort of approached a little bit left of field. It's an intuitive leap. For *Julius Caesar* I got extremely obsessed with Russian politics and approached it from that. So I think people can approach a play like that: How does this play inform me? What does this play say to me? What does it make me think of? Even if it's not what the writer first intended. I mean, obviously Shakespeare wasn't writing a play about Russian politics, but it was a way that got me to feel like I was absolutely part of it rather than just sort of interpreting.

So the Russian politics thing was a private connection, not a collective production connection?

Absolutely. Before I walked into the rehearsal room. And I've done that with a number of plays. I often look for side jumps like that. And I could keep that to myself, but all the time I'm trying to relate it back to the play. It opens up the play for me rather than that big Stanislavskian, What if I was in this situation?

Sean O'Shea as Jaques in the 2003 Bell Shakespeare production of *As You Like It*. (Photo: Heidrun Löhr)

Is that something you'd always do? Look for this parallel?

It's not something you can make happen, but it normally happens with me in plays that really excite me. The complex plays that you can work on for a long time and still wonder what they're about.

What's it arming you with? You've got this other extra imaginative support, I guess, or lateral fuel. How does it actually arm you when you walk into the room?

Fuel is good. It does, it fuels you with a passion for the work.

I've been in productions, extremely successful productions like *A Comedy of Errors*, and I sort of hold my breath and gulp a bit when I think about it. I'm not great at stuff like that. But it was a terribly successful production, and it's a great consolation that night after night you're performing for people who are having a wonderful time—and I'm not putting that down—but I get bored in those kind of plays. It's because I haven't got the imaginative support to get me through. Whereas plays like *As You Like It* and *Julius Caesar* and *Twelfth Night*, you can be in those plays for years and still find new levels.

So you're finding a kind of multi-levelled respect for the play?

And also, we're not afraid to say, Well, this is *my* take on this. This is what happened when *I* read this play, you know? Rather than just say, You've got to serve the play. Well, the play can serve *me* as well. This is me plus this play in this time.

You're engaged in a deeply imaginative way, and also in a worldly way, a political and contextual way?

Yeah. Yes.

You see a purpose to the play beyond Elizabethan England or Ancient Rome?

Beyond, yeah, and beyond the story we're telling. The story that we're telling is marvellous, but for me, there's almost this secret life to it, as well. I don't care if other people don't get it. It was never my plan: I'm going to play Jaques and I want people to go, Oh, look, he's drawing parallels to Native Americans. I mean, far from it. I hate those productions where we go, Okay, now we're on Mars or whatever. That's childish. What can we do to this play to *update* it, or make it relevant? I can't bear that. If it's not relevant, if you have to make it relevant, then let's not do it.

Yes, what's implied by that approach is, We don't actually think this is a very good play.

Completely, and with Shakespeare we're stuck with that all the time. We have such difficulties doing those plays, though, because people have such preconceptions about them because they've been put on the pedestal as a kind of *high culture*. And I think a lot of people going to see the classics have this idea that culture is somehow a bit like medicine or something. It's very distasteful but good for you, so we'll sit there and be bored for three hours once every six months and it will make us better human beings.

In terms of your process, we've got you into the room. We've got you to the first rehearsal.

These are the ideal ones, where I go in and I'm really thrilled. I've prepared the background.

Yeah, you've made this investment in the play and you feel that it's taking root in you.

The sidelines do give me investment. They connect me to the writing in a big way, and make me really thrilled to be doing something extremely worthwhile.

So what's next? What do you look for once you're in the room, with this enthusiasm and with this connection?

Then you hold your breath while they go through the design presentation, while the director does an introductory spiel. It sounds very flippant but I do think there's an element of truth in that, holding your breath. I think we've been a little bit hijacked by conceptual designers and directors and stuff like that, so I do hold my breath through that.

Then I'm looking for things that ring true for me. And I kind of grasp at them. One moment in one scene, somewhere, when you first start, and you're going through that appallingly awkward phase when you get up from the table and you're standing on the floor.

Can you really focus on what happens in that moment? You're clunking around feeling pretty shitty and a few things happen. What's the sensory experience of discovering those little–?

I think the sensory experience is that you feel at ease. That suddenly all of the awful self-consciousness and, Oh, God, what am I doing? How did I get this job?, all this falls away and you think, Yes, that's right. I'll hang onto that. There's a way into this character through that.

How do you make it kind of seep out into all the other moments?

You just find the next moment, and find the next one and find the next one, and you start to join up the dots. Hopefully the distance between those comfort zones gets smaller and smaller as you keep going. Doesn't always happen.

But it's a *feeling* thing for me, as opposed to clothes and walks and voices and stuff like that. Those other things come very late for me, if at all.

I'm not one of those disguise actors. I quite like watching actors who are, but I'm not one of those different-in-every-role-type people. Even though in my head I might have gone off in very different directions, it always somehow ends up with *me*, which can be rather disappointing for some people when they go to the theatre. There are people who just want to watch some kind of essence of something, I suppose, but there are also people who are into the disguise element of theatre, the chameleon aspect. And sometimes that can be exciting to watch, but it's certainly not my strong point.

What do you do between rehearsals?

Just get into it more and more. Identify the bits that are working. If that's working for me, why? It's kind of an empathy thing. The more I go, Yeah, I understand that moment; and the more moments I understand, the more I understand the man.

I think we always judge our work from a feeling thing: Well, that felt all right so it must have been okay. But how do you know that always follows? Sometimes you can watch stuff, and think while you're watching it that the actor is feeling very good in this role but, um, it's not working for me. Still, that's certainly how I judge it for myself.

Well, you don't really have a choice, do you? Your only choice is to be constantly paranoid.

I am pretty tough on myself. I don't always get to the stage of thinking, Well, I feel comfortable with this so it must be good.

When you say you're tough on yourself, what kind of criticisms are you making, and when are you making them?

I think everything I'm in is a dog. I'm one of those actors. Nothing I'm in is ever good enough. I don't spend a lot of time going, I'm hopeless, I'm hopeless. I don't find that a very interesting quality in some people I work with, but I do get quite obsessed with how can we make the ideas in this more—

I'm not a director, but I do think directorially a lot. When I'm in a scene, I'm not just thinking, How am I identifying with the person I'm playing?, but, How is the story being perceived? And how are the ideas being perceived? And do we have that right? And do we even think we know what this play is about—particularly the big complex pieces? I get very troubled by being in a six-month run, and halfway through the run you think, I'm not sure we as a group have even decided what this play's about. And I suppose they're directorial questions—

Well, there's no reason why actors shouldn't have a stake in them.

They should. And too often I think direction has become about this conceptual stuff. You know, What is this production of *Romeo and Juliet* about? Well, it's set in Mussolini's Italy. That's not what the play's *about*. We've got so used to, That's how we do theatre now—you know, we're going to set it in a stack of cards, a card-house, or in space-age costumes—but that's not even beginning to come to terms with the question of what is the play *about*. So I'm tough on myself with regard to that, and tough on the whole process because I don't often feel that I'm part of a group where you agree on that. When you do, they're the joyous moments. But I'd say they're a very small minority, when somehow this group of people have come to terms with what this piece is about.

It sounds like an intellectual process, but it's also a sensory process, of sensing that you're all in the same play, or all in the same story. Not just a kind of actorly connectedness that might be described in a Meisner-type way, but an intellectual or conceptual connectedness.

Yeah. God, yeah. And intellect has become a really dirty word, I think, when people talk about acting or acting-training. You know, Don't be intellectual, get out of your head. If you have intellectual ideas, I don't think they have to cancel out the sensory part. They can co-exist. I think the really good productions have both of those things.

I think that when people talk about intellectualising as a danger, they are talking about—in the moment—there being too much monitoring of what one is doing.

Yeah, and that thing where people use it as a defence mechanism. Well, I'll just sit here and talk, because the longer I talk, I'm putting off the inevitable of having to get up and try to immerse myself in this role. That's using an intellectual approach to avoid what you have to do.

Immersion is a good word, having to immerse yourself in a role, and finding these connections that bring ease. So you're linking these things together and you're finding this pattern that hopefully leads to as much prolonged ease as possible?

That's the plan, yes. It's never that conscious, you just kind of do it. But you are aware of moments where it goes click, click, click, and it slots into place and you think, Well, yes, I'll take that as a sign, that that particular moment is where I'm on the right track. And so, more of that, I'll pursue that.

What happens when the feelings of self-consciousness remain, for a scene or a beat or a moment or an Act? Are there times when you think, Well, the intuition hasn't found it for me.

There are many times. Then, for me, it's like, Okay, what are we doing? That is the methodical part of my training, of which there was quite a bit.

I don't go through a whole script and write down an action for every moment any more than I think any other actor does, but I do find it's a useful strategy when you're stuck. And I do come back to it a fair bit. I will say to a director, Well, I don't know what you're talking about. What's the action? And thankfully most of them know what you're talking about, which I think they should.

Because if it has eluded you—and you think, Okay, I'm stuck—the chances are you're doing something wrong. You're not actually playing what is written. Or there are two actors in the scene and they're playing different things. Or you don't think the scene is about the same thing the director thinks it's about. So then I think you need something to initiate the conversation like, What are you doing? What do you want? How are you going to get it? What action are you playing? Things like this are a good way to start that. And thankfully, for most of us now, it's pretty much a common language.

But then when you get on your feet again, are you trusting that that conversation will have had some kind of effect and you can go back on and intuit some more? Or are there times when you lead with something other than your intuition?

There absolutely are. There might be times when you go, Look, it could be this, this or this. Here's six things, so we'll just get up and try each one and see which one is best for all of us. And that's not an intuitive thing, that's being quite methodical.

Moments of intuition and inspiration are probably much less than the methodical slog, really. What's the story? That's a question I will ask a director. What's the story we're telling? So we can say, Okay, A walks in, finds B, they have this argument and they separate. We all go, Okay, let's tell *that* story, because actually that's not what I was telling at all. *That's* not about intuition.

It's dramaturgy, really.

Yes, and trial and error. Because maybe you have to try a number of stories before you go, Oh, okay. And in complex plays there's often more than one story that you can tell. You can play some scenes a hundred different ways, so we all need to agree which of those hundred ways we're going to play it. And that can be just sheer methodical slog.

When you talk about not being interested in disguise, does that mean that finding ease is, like, *it*? The end of your job? Because presumably people who really like disguise go from that and then look for ways in which it might inform what moustache to wear.

Well, do they? Or do they find the moustache and go the other way? And that's fine. There are some brilliant actors who do that. And sometimes scripts demand you look different.

Where do you sit in relation to the portrayal of high emotion on stage? Are you of the 'display it' school or the 'feel it' school? Are they, indeed, two different schools?

I'm somewhere in between. In an ideal world, I would rather go for the real emotion. But I think it's a pretty extraordinary actor who can do that eight times a week for six months.

I think I can tell if I'm sitting out there in the audience that you're really just indicating. I don't think that works at all. Some actors would say, Look, I was just indicating. I wasn't really going for it. But I don't think they're always the best judge of that.

It's a different sensation from when you find it the first time and how it would be absolutely in life. You know, if you've got to play something deeply hard, like your life falling apart or something. I just think there's middle ground.

Talk about what that is. Talk about how it's not a polarity.

I think you can teach yourself, over time, to enter the moment without indicating and just bullshitting, but without it actually killing you as well. We've all worked with people who *do* have to experience it night after night and it's just not good for their sanity. Similarly, some actors come to mind who seem obsessed with this idea of just walking through stuff and indicating. A discerning audience can spot that. If you invest nothing in it, I think a discerning audience can tell.

The thing that surprises me about that approach is that if you are being accurate, gesturally and tonally, I don't know how you can avoid being moved. You are literally *moving yourself.*

That's what I mean. When people say, I wasn't really going through it, I was just... um...

But something does happen once you recreate something like that. And it can feel terribly real in the moment, but then you can walk into the wings and it just completely falls away. And you're fine. And that's what it needs to be, otherwise you're on that dangerous sort of sanity-dodgy ground. Whereas the first time you ever find the emotion, or if you've really experienced it in your life, then obviously you can't just walk off and forget about it. And they are different. And the fact that you can just walk into the wings and be fine doesn't mean that you bullshitted your way through it. I mean, bullshitting your way through it is kind of cheating your audience by not actually *trying* to go there.

It's not something that really bothers me too much. I never feel like I'm bullshitting my way through stuff. I think it's just one of the easier things in acting, you know, it's not a huge problem for me.

I think that it's one of the things that's widely misunderstood. And you've described it very well, that bi-play of literally going through the motions and at the same time making a real connection. So you are both in control *and* emotionally connected.

And surely that's what the craft is all about. You're going out and you're repeating something, you are *re*-hearsing something, doing something over and over again. It's a different process from going through it in life, but that doesn't mean that you're just walking through it. You *can* walk through it, but that's just ripping off the audience.

You've done a lot of Shakespearean work. What are the specific demands, for you personally, approaching that work?

Shakespeare asks a whole bunch of different things, makes different demands on you in terms of technique. The more you do, the better equipped you are to deal with the language. But in terms of the actual heart and essence of what is acting, there's no kind of *Shakespearean* acting as opposed to other acting.

The thing that first surprised me after working on plays like Shakespeare, where you're dealing with very heightened text, is that it opens up much more for me when I go back to naturalistic text. You might think, Is this just going to make me better at doing Shakespeare and Restoration and very wordy kind of stuff? But I don't find it does at all. It opens up all sorts of scripts, and it makes you look at writing with more—

Expertise, perhaps?

Well, it would be nice to think more expertise, but you don't take it for granted. You really try and pull the text apart and see what's there. You're still ultimately trying to own it, no matter who wrote it. You've still got to own it. And, God, that can sometimes be the hard thing about Shakespeare, you know, not just getting your mouth around the words and the actual nuts-and-bolts technique of the verse, but making it sound like they are absolutely the words you *have* to say. Now! Nothing else will do! Because it's so heightened that it requires a slightly heightened—not heightened playing, but a heightened sense of being.

What does it do to your body? That 'height'? Does it feel different in your body?

Yeah, it does. I always try to get the Shakespeare lines down a bit quicker because I think you can feel that thing of you're doing it but it's not in your body. And that's useful for any theatre, but it's quite palpable when you do Shakespeare. You think, I've just got these words down, they're rolling around in my head but they haven't quite… they're not sitting in me yet. And because the language is more complex that tends to take a little more time for me than it does if I'm dealing with more naturalistic language.

This thing of words sinking down into yourself. Is that something that might happen in these connection moments? Is that a part of that feeling?

Yes, yes. Absolutely.

Words become embodied?

Words become embodied. You find the need to say them rather than struggle with the technique of, How do I say this? And, Where do I breathe? How do I get through this sentence which is actually five lines of quite complex imagery? You stop thinking about all that when you actually find the need to say them. They may be just brief moments but, yeah, you hang onto those.

Look, the best way to find out what the scene is about is to get up and do it. Those times when you find yourself spending weeks sitting around tables with people, I want to beat my head against the wall.

There are so many acting techniques and practitioners now, the whole Stanislavskian thing is thought to be a bit passé. That's the feeling I get. But like it or not, he's the most influential practitioner of the 20th century and the launching pad for a lot of the other guys. It just seems to me that we need a common language, and that seems to be it.

And you can't reduce acting to a formula. It's not like, if you explain what actions and objectives are, then *anyone* could act. I mean, that's crazy. It's just a way of describing—one of many ways of describing—what it is that actors seem to be able to do. And sometimes they need to be able to talk about it.

And sometimes they don't.

Yeah, sometimes they don't. But when we *do* need to talk about it, that seems as good a start as anything else. It's also a little less ethereal than a lot of the other approaches. I mean, it's not that hard to understand. But I don't think it needs to be our master either. Like, I can't walk on stage unless I've written down, in the margin of my text, what my action is, and stuff like that—those things we were told to do. I don't think there's an actor in the world who does that.

Given whatever pride and frustrations you have about where you're at on this road—do you have a sense of where you'd like to get to, artistically, as an actor?

I obsess about that all the time, and give myself a hard time about it, like lots of us do. It's not about, I was supposed to have achieved this and this by the time I was 40, but about how can I continue to find this fulfilling? That obsesses me because, you know, it's given me great, great joys. I wouldn't want anyone to read this and think, He's just whingeing. I've been extremely lucky and it's given me great joys, but also there is a sense of, What do you strive for? Who are the people you want to work for? Who are the theatre companies that you want to—? And you don't see a lot of that in this country to keep you going. All the companies in this country are capable of doing good work, and they do every now and then, but—

I always look back at the stuff that has been the most fulfilling for me, and it's been when I have felt that I have had a real investment in the work, that I have had some kind of creative—not control—but creative *input*, rather than just being used for the skills I have—you know, Oh, he's a good interpreter of stories, or of this role, so we'll kind of use him—but I've actually felt more an intrinsic part of the creative process. God, one of them was a co-op, another was a piece I wrote myself.

Ultimately we should all be really tough on the work we're doing. Are we, as a community of artists, doing work that we can be proud of and that we think is worth doing? I don't know, Terry, it sounds wanky and it's hard to explain. We should take responsibility for our own work, work together, and in some kind of way grow as the people *in* it along with the people *watching* it. That it serves some kind of purpose. And we all know that it can. We've all seen theatre like that, that blows us away. And if that becomes increasingly difficult to achieve, then it becomes harder to imagine yourself hanging in there, you know? Particularly when you don't have a career like

Geoffrey Rush or Cate Blanchett. The good bits have got to be really, really, *really* good to sustain you in the bits that are crap. And most of it's crap. I mean, most of it *is*, you know? Like, we all kind of… I did a guesty on one of our Australian dramas the other day and, you know, we're all bending over backwards to get into stuff like that, and when you do, you think, Why? You get no money for it and you think, This is nonsense.

So you really do just have to find the occasional jobs that sustain you through all the rest of it. And that's got a lot to do with working with people you want to work with, and saying stuff that you feel is important to say, and all those things. I suppose people might think I'm being naïve and unrealistic but, you know, what's the point of going into it if you don't hang onto that?

What else do you want me to do?

WENDY HUGHES

Wendy Hughes graduated from NIDA in 1970. In retrospect, it seems the industry had been longing for her. And why not? She seems to embody a stack of fascinating paradoxes. She is simultaneously academic and sensual, statuesque and fragile, careful and wilful, approachable and exotic.

I first saw her on stage when—as an 18-year-old—I caught the train down from Newcastle to see Cat on a Hot Tin Roof *at the Sydney Opera House. She was a perfect cat, playing alongside two of Australia's great actors, Ron Haddrick and the amazing, late John Hargreaves, with whom she enjoyed a beautiful professional partnership in theatre and film.*

By that point, Wendy had already appeared in seminal Australian movies like Newsfront *and* My Brilliant Career, *and was on the verge of a trilogy of films that was to cement her place as one of the finest film actors of her generation, anywhere! Paul Cox's* Lonely Hearts *and* My First Wife, *and Carl Schultz's production of Sumner Locke Elliot's* Careful, He Might Hear You *are all exquisite films. I should think that any Australian actor could die happy having been in any one of them. Wendy was at the centre of all three.*

Wendy has played Chekhov, Coward, Williams, Buzo and Williamson for our major theatre companies. She has appeared in over 20 films and has worked extensively on television drama both in Australia and the US. She has appeared in The Heist, Donor, A Woman Named Jackie, Homicide: A Year on the Street *and* Star Trek *in the US, and on Australian television in* Return to Eden, The Man from Snowy River *and in the leading role of* State Coroner.

I met Wendy at Currency House on Cleveland Street in Sydney. She was talking about acting for the first time—in any detail—for at least 20 years. She was generous but reserved, halting, polite, humble, and sometimes wickedly funny. She was both earthy and ethereal. My paradoxical impressions continue…

Meanwhile, do yourself the greatest of movie-watching favours: If you haven't seen them, hunt down copies of those two Cox *films, and of* Careful, He Might Hear You, *and see what greatness the Australian film industry flirted with back then, and what class Wendy Hughes brings to the whole shebang.*

Mostly, I've got used to relying on my instinct. Human instinct. What will work and what won't, via me. I mean, part of it is coming from Wendy Hughes' personality, and I'll change it to, you know, someone else, but, ultimately, the deep core is coming from me.

It helps if you have a really good script. That means, Phew, I can do something with this. If it's something slighter, you have to embellish it and put something more of your own into it, I think.

You're talking about experience. Years of experience and being able to trust your instincts?

Yes.

Can you remember what you took from that early experience of going to acting school, and what you applied?

Everything I could. I was straight out of high school and I couldn't believe I got into drama school. For me it was like this new world opening up. I just listened to everything we were given, went in there with full gusto.

We did the classics. I particularly took notice of the voice stuff and weighed into that. I just went at everything they threw at me, saying, Oh, yes, I'll try that. I'll try that. And sometimes it was terrible. As you say, it's experience. Sometimes you'd hear yourself and say, Oh, that's not working. That's terrible. But as you go on you get it to work more often.

But sometimes I still can't get it to work, or sound right. It just doesn't feel real. It jars. You think it's too much like yourself, and that's instinct. It's this huge clanger, like a bell that goes off. Especially with film acting. I can do five, six takes and it will work, and there'll be one that just does not work, and I'll say, No, that's not right. It's an instinct thing, I think. It just stands out like a beacon that it's not real. And the director will say it's fine, and I'll say, No it wasn't. And sometimes I'm wrong.

Well, on film I guess the director has what she or he believes is the take in the can that they like. On stage it's different, isn't it? Because in theatre if your ideas and the director's are at odds, that's another kind of artistic and industrial issue, isn't it?

Normally you come to a compromise. Mostly, I want to please the director. You do, because they have the overall vision. I mean, I'll try everything a director wants, but if it's not working they eventually agree. I mean, they see it's not working.

You say you tried everything at drama school. What things worked? What were the things you took from the training and felt you could invest in?

Well, you're fearless at that age. You just try everything, and sometimes you don't know if you're making a fool of yourself or not. But learning to use my voice—which I didn't know how to use before—was wonderful, and gave me a sense of achievement and power because I knew I could reach people at the back of the theatre.

Did it change the way that you spoke? Your accent, for example?

Yes. But I wanted that. I didn't like the way I spoke. I didn't like that Australian… I was brought up in that working-class thing.

Is there an element of the work that you always look to crack? Something that you always feel will bring a level of comfort, a level of liberation?

Accent is something to do with that. And the voice level. But again, I'll just tread through it, and instinctively know if I'm getting there. That gets harder with film. In theatre it's much easier because you have a lot of rehearsal.

What are the signs that you're getting there?

I'm not freaking out.

Are you more relaxed?

Yeah, more relaxed. I'm not as manic—not that I get manic—but I'm not as nervous. I'm not going over and over the lines. Yeah, comfort has a lot to do with it. I think rehearsal too has a lot to do with it, and somehow you find it.

You can't always do that in film. And that's why in film you are often cast to type. Because they've seen you before and they think, Oh, she can do that. So you don't get to stretch a lot, although in *Careful, He Might Hear You*, that was nothing to do with me, my background or anything. With that, though, we had a couple of weeks' rehearsal with a wonderful director called Carl Schultz, and I worked very hard on that with the accent and just imagining what that woman's life was like. We had the book as well, of course, which helped. But sometimes I wouldn't know until I'd seen a couple of rushes, and I'd go, Okay, yeah, yeah, it's not me, and I'd see someone else. I've sort of got it, but it was still sort of—it was a couple of weeks before I felt secure. The costumes helped a lot too. They were extraordinary costumes.

Well, that's an interesting thing too. The external stimuli. Is that often a comfort?

Yeah, it can be, especially in period clothes. That takes you somewhere else. But ultimately it's getting inside someone's skin and head. Sometimes you understand it intellectually, and you'll go there emotionally, but when you come out of it you think, But I could never think like that. It's hard to imagine, but that's what you have to do. You have to imagine.

You talked about doing imaginative preparation. What might that entail?

I would make a whole history. Where she came from, who her siblings were, what she might think about things, what kind of men she's been with, and I'll just wander around with that in my head, often talk out aloud, you know, and write things down.

Even for *State Coroner* I wrote down a whole history because the material is so foreign to me, someone coming from that whole legal and medical… I just don't… I'm not there. So I went to the coroner, spoke to a couple of coroners. I went to autopsies. I did all of that. So even though she's a modern character, she's so far removed from where I come from, that I wrote a whole sort of history on her.

And then you have to throw it away. Once you've done all that, and you're into the character and you're doing it, then hopefully, instinctively you're going, No, hang on, she wouldn't do it like that, or, She wouldn't say that because she's come from here or there or whatever.

If you haven't done the research, and you go into a scene where you are perhaps making even oblique references to the professional stuff, then you're going to feel–?

I couldn't do it. I'd have to at least write something. You know, how long did she go to university? And how long did she study? And who she met. All that kind of stuff. What her mother and father were like.

Because it just makes you feel at ease?

With who she is, and who I'm supposed to be representing. Who I am. And then when you're doing it for a while, you're able to say, Oh, she'd never say it like that, or, She'd never say this. You get a whole feel for her, because then she's *become* you, really, or she's *part* of you, and you can actually say to the writers, Look, I don't want her to do that because I don't think she would. Because you told me in episode whatever that she was this, so now I'm contradicting myself. And they go, Oh, yes.

And the more you have stored in your database about the kind of life off-screen or off-stage then the more authority you have to make that call.

Yeah. You just feel like you've done a little bit of work. You just can't walk on cold. Well, I suppose you can if it's a character you've played a lot, but with something new, I just can't do that. I'd feel a bit blasé. Maybe it doesn't make any difference. I don't know. It makes a difference to me, though, because I can speak with authority because I've done the history and research. That makes me feel more comfortable.

Those types of things, things like writing fictional biographical notes about a character–

I think it's quite common with actors.

They're the kind of exercises, presumably, that you learned at acting school that you thought were of value, and have continued to–

Yeah, yeah, I think at some point that would have come up. Definitely.

What does Stanislavski mean to you? Is it significant to you?

I think it was. It's so long since I read any of that stuff. Same thing with The Method. It makes sense to a certain extent. I just can't take it to where you're meant to be able to take it. I use some of it, but I don't want to get too immersed, because then I'd lose control, and I don't think—

You're talking about recovering emotional stuff?

Emotional stuff. Yeah. That's the only thing that I came away with.

Right. So to you, that's what it was?

Yes. And you use that to a certain extent, you know, to get upset. But that's *you* getting upset, it's not the *character*. You're using yourself and your emotions and your flashbacks or whatever—I do use that to some extent. But that's all I've taken from Stanislavski.

What do you do when you have a role that obviously calls for big, tough emotional stuff?

It's scary. It's the most recent thing I did. *Who is Sylvia*, by Edward Albee. It's the most wonderful role. With a huge scene at the end. I'd just dread it every night. Dread it and love it at the same time. It was written in such a way that he just took you there. I'd miss fusing the emotional thing I wanted to get to a couple of times, but not very often. Only a couple of times I never quite got there.

What was along the path of getting there? What did you set yourself along that path?

Well, it was complete anger, and overwhelming disappointment, and on the verge of... Just horrific. But what helps is, I go around smashing items on the set, and it all builds. So you would just let it build. And with the smashing of furniture, it all just became this one long rage, with this immense explosion at the end. Sometimes it gets so intense that I've just got to pull it back, because I know I'll lose it. I don't like that.

Maybe The Method is to just go with it. I still believe you have to retain some kind of control or you become *you* and not the *character*. There've been several nights when I've thought, God, if I really let this go I don't think the audience would want to look at it, because it would be too real, too heavy. I think it's a problem if things are too real. It would have been *Wendy* losing it, which is not the thing. It's a really fine line.

I did it once on film, in a Paul Cox film. I was crying and it felt so real. I mean, *really* sort of feeling it and all of that. Then I did a take where I didn't feel it the same and didn't cry as much. And we saw the two of them, and the one where to me it felt really real and crying, wasn't the best take. The other one where I was in control was better. Because the one where I'd really let it all go was so—I'd hidden myself. I hadn't actually done anything. I thought I had, but because it was Wendy hiding herself, instinctively feeling somehow embarrassed, you couldn't see anything. You couldn't see my eyes or anything. So it's weird. If it gets too subjective it's not right.

So you're balancing the human reality with a kind of aesthetic, artistic, technical reality?

Technical. Yes. To me, it can't not be technical. And if you *do* lose it—I don't know, maybe it can be great. It just frightens me to lose it totally, because I think the audience would freak.

And yet, you talked a few times about the idea of wanting it to get buried in yourself, get rooted in yourself before you find the ease and the comfort and the security. So at the point where the furniture is being smashed up and these stimuli are being experienced, they're being *really* experienced, by Wendy, at that point, aren't they?

Oh, yeah.

And they need to be in order to get there?

In order to get there. Exactly. Yeah. You don't really change into that other person. It's acting. That's the thing. But sometimes Wendy can get so carried away that you could go right off and—I don't think I'd let myself go there. I never could. I could never really lose it. Because also you've still got to talk, so it's never totally naturalistic. Maybe in film it can be more realistic and naturalistic.

Although there are limits there too, aren't there? Because there are still as many technical demands on you in film.

Totally.

And you're surrounded by people hassling you all the time, doing final checks and all that kind of stuff.

Exactly, and that's the thing. To be able to stay and concentrate and still be able to deliver with all that going on, it's very difficult.

A flow-on in theatre can be a lot easier than film. It's very hard in film, to forget everything's there and deliver. That's a real craft. An art, I think, and some people are better at it than others.

Is the distance between the disciplines of acting on stage and acting on film—?

It's all based in realism. Being real. On stage, even though it's out of the ordinary, and it's theatrical, even within your bigness and theatricality, it has to sound real. And that's the same in film. In film, though, because your head is so big on that screen, you don't have to project. You can be realer. It's very seductive, film, because you can be real, and the scripts are realer, and all that.

If you can act in theatre, you can act on film. Sometimes film actors can't act on stage, though. Because they haven't learnt a technique. You need a certain voice production and technique, and you have to look like you're able to move, too, on a stage, not just shuffling along. So it's probably harder for film actors who have never been on stage to go and do a theatre production than vice-versa.

My first few times on film and television, though, weren't very good. But then you learn the technique. Then it becomes a challenge to work in with the camera and still be able to deliver. It's always a challenge. I like that.

Truth. Emotional truth. It's all about trying to look like you belong there.

As long as you have the essential truth, and you know what you're getting at, and you know what the character is getting at, the director can say, Can you do it like this? Can you do it like that? And you can. It's easy. Yeah, sure. Some people say, Oh, I don't know if I can do it like that. I say, Yeah, sure. What else do you want me to do? Yeah, sure. As long as I know what I'm doing.

And sometimes someone might say, Try something. And I'll say, Yeah, I'll try it. But I'm not sure about it. Then I'll say, No, it's not right. It's just not right. And they'll back off then. Often. Because I've given it to them a few different ways and they'll see that it doesn't work, and they'll go, Oh, no, forget it.

How do you spend the half-hour before going onstage?

I always have to get in at least one-and-a-half hours before. I can't stand being in only an hour before. I'll talk to the other actors, make a cup of coffee, have a cigarette, slowly put on a bit of make-up. I do a bit of voice warm-up, not much, and I'm normally ready by the half. Then I'll just wander around, read. I've got to be ready at least 20 minutes before.

In order to relax or in order to hype yourself up?

In order to hype myself up. No, not relax. In order to *hype it up*! And always before I go on I think, What am I doing? This is just the stupidest way to earn a living. I've got to go on there, find out my husband's been fucking a goat, go off my face, throw things. It's just cry, sob, scream, rant, rave. Oh, well, here we go. It just seems so ridiculous. It didn't used to as much. It's just as I get older it seems so weird.

Does it seem less significant?

No, no, because it's a ritual that's thousands and thousands and thousands of years old. But sometimes it just feels like an odd way to be behaving.

When you approach a piece and there are expectations of things, like accent, and belief systems of the society of the play, and things like that, do you tackle it wholly all the time, or do you sometimes compartmentalise those things? Today I'm going to focus on getting this sound right, for instance, and I don't care if other things fall by the wayside.

No. I think I do it pretty much as a whole, because the compartments end up being the whole. Do I just concentrate on the accent? I might go in there thinking I'll do that, but then before I know it the whole emotional thing invades all that and it's discarded. I suppose with theatre, because you have a decent rehearsal period, I'll just take it day by day. Because you discuss it so much beforehand, you get freaked out. You go, I don't know how I'm going to do this. But then, as the process goes on, you hopefully get a bit more comfortable. No, I don't think I put things in different compartments.

So your approach seems fairly methodical in as much as you are leading with your instincts, all the time.

Yep.

You've talked a lot about hearing something being right or hearing something being wrong. You also trust your self-monitoring systems a lot.

Yes. Yes I do.

And you also have a firm faith in imaginative homework?

Yeah. A couple of years ago I did *Sweet Bird of Youth*, by Tennessee Williams. And because I'd done Tennessee Williams before, and because we've all read so much about Williams and where he's come from and his whole history, with something like that you don't have to do quite as much.

So it's a bit like you've been on this planet before?

Yes, because you've been in his world before.

Another of the things that young actors sometimes stress about and wonder about the efficacy of is the business of actions and the playing of actions. Are you familiar with that?

No. I probably was once.

I do sometimes go through the whole thing of, you know, What does this person want? Now, what is my—? No, I won't just say the line. What is the attitude? Is it angry? Is it manipulative? Often you don't have to do that, though, because it's just so plain obvious. So what you see is what you get. Normally that's a part of just understanding the script, and—no, I don't believe in that stuff.

I try to be physically still on stage—maybe not so much in film. I don't like mess, too much hand movement. I like to keep it simple. Which is not me. Unless it really calls for something flamboyant. But I don't like too many messy moves. Sometimes, I think, What do you do with your hands? Well, you've just got to keep them still. Oh, I'm clasping my hands again, mmm… Oh, I'm crossing my arms now. Now, let's just see if you can actually stand there with them by your side. So I'll go through all of that. It sort of comes automatically. I just go, No, I don't want to be that busy, it's really boring. There's something so much more powerful about someone who's still on stage.

But if you're working and you're having that conversation with yourself, do you welcome that conversation, or is it a thing of, Oh, my God, what am I doing going on with all that?

No, I don't mind it at all because I'm so used to it. It's just a part of the process. I'll still be delivering the lines the way they should be, while the other part of the brain is just going, No, you're not going to move again. I don't want all those messy things happening that don't mean anything.

So again that's a really strong self-monitoring thing that you have, which a lot of people think of in a negative way, but you use as a part of your comfort, part of your security?

Yeah, because I'm in control. Part of me is outside it. It's just part of the way I work. Sometimes you miss a bit. You go, Oh, gee, I didn't want it to come out like that. But then you do another bit really well.

How do you know you've done it well?

Well, the audience. You can hear a pin drop. That's why it's tougher on film. There it's just instinct. Oh, yeah that bit, mmm, maybe that bit—they might cut that bit. Whatever. But often in theatre you can tell by the audience. Especially through long speeches. And you go, Oh, no, I'll speed this bit up because I can feel, I can sense that person's going to cough in a

Wendy Hughes as Alexandra Del Lago in the 2002 Melbourne Theatre Company production of *Sweet Bird of Youth*. (Photo: Jeff Busby)

minute, and I can sense someone over there getting the lollies out. I mean, you sense all of that. Totally conscious of the audience. And sometimes I just demand that they listen.

How do you do that?

I don't know, I just think, You're gonna fuckin' listen! And sometimes I feel I've just lost them, so I'll pick up the pace or do something so it changes.

It's extraordinary, isn't it, the detail, the fineness of one's appreciation of the most minute... I mean, I always think it's amazing that people can sit in the audience and eat lollies and think that the actors don't know. And in fact you know exactly what everyone is doing, and you know the difference between the sound of a Mintie and the sound of a Crunchie bar.

Yeah. I know. And they just think you can't hear. Or often the matinees, where they all just sit talking to one another because they think they're watching telly. That's just shocking.

You've worked quite a bit with American actors. Have you found American actors—and I'm asking you to generalise—have you found them more or less methodical than Australian actors? More or less tied to a prescribed way of doing things, or have you found them equally individualistic in their approach?

Equally. Just as insecure as everyone else.

You spoke really well about the emotional heights of the play you were just doing, and I'm really interested in the physical activity that helped you to get literally wound up. Is the approach to doing a scene like that different in a film?

Yeah, it would be. Maybe you could do it in one take if you had about three different cameras, but then it gets hard because you get other people in the way and all of that. No, probably it would be chopped into pieces. That's hard because you can't—you've got to keep it all boiling under the surface. And you've got to turn it on and off. That's where concentration and just keeping everything going on… That's the tough part. The hanging around and keeping everything still there, and then being able to bring it out. That's really hard. It requires real staying in the moment and concentration.

Sometimes you think, Oh, please don't talk to me now, I'm trying to get it together here, and they're going to say Action soon and I'm going to have to have it all together. There might be 50 or 100 people around and they want to chat. And you go, No, just leave me alone, I'm trying to get into this. And people will. They'll just leave you alone. Because it's that thing that sometimes you don't get the chance to work into it. You've just got to deliver. Sometimes you do and sometimes you don't. Sometimes you'll get another go at it and maybe by the second or third take you've worked yourself back into it again.

You've talked about wanting it to be you. The security comes when—

I don't want it to be *me*. No, it's got to be the *character*, but it has to come *through* you, so obviously there's always a little bit of you in there, or your take on things. Unless it's really, really so different from you, and you can totally go into a—But often it's not, especially with modern stuff. I can't quite explain it. You want it to be as it's been written but obviously some of you always gets in there.

But that connection that you suggested early on in our talk, this tying-of-your-guts kind of gesture–

Mmm—

When a character is most–in terms of thoughts and manner and belief systems–most unlike you, most distant from you, that gut-tying thing is not diminished, is it? Or is it?

Well, it depends if it's an emotional scene or not, I think. You've got to try and connect on a sort of gut level. Yeah, definitely. Especially if it's emotional.

You've got to intellectually empathise with them?

Yeah, and emotionally. Yeah, because otherwise you couldn't get to those emotional areas. Especially with, like, *Sweet Bird of Youth*. She was so off-the-planet, but fabulous. I mean, parts of her are probably like me but she was so extravagant and tragic. I suppose you just go with it. So then Wendy goes with it and you have to get into the emotional things and make them hers, even though you know it's really Wendy pretending to be her. It all just meshes into this other personality.

Is it another personality or is it a realm of behaviour?

Yeah, that's it. I think that's what it is. I'm giving all these things to Wendy. Ultimately, it's *acting*! It can be really good acting where you go, Gee, you forgot it was Wendy or you forgot it was whoever. Yeah, that's where you want to get to.

Sometimes you do disappear, and you think, This character can take over. It's great when that happens. You're allowing Wendy to take on all these other things. Sometimes you've gone through some stuff and that's what you can draw on, but other times you've never been there so then you're imagining it.

Is it easier when it's stuff that's part of your personal experience?

Probably, probably. The thing is, though, I can do imagination. You know, you really can.

So when there's no clear autobiographical link to something, it's not an inhibiting thing.

No, no. It's a leap of faith. You invent something.

You invent a link?

Yeah.

And it's just as strong and real for you as if it were really connected to your actual experience?

It can be.

Depending on how strongly you've created it?

I suppose, yeah. Whether you've pulled it off or not. Exactly. There are lots of things we actors haven't done in our lives, and you've got to—

Believe that you could?

Yeah.

Great.

That all make sense?

I'm glad we chewed that over a bit more.

Yeah, I'm glad you did that too.

To see each other's eyes

CHARLES 'BUD' TINGWELL

I have a copy of Eric Reade's tome, History and Heartburn: The saga of Australian film, 1896 to 1978. *In the extensive index, only two names have more references attached to them than Bud Tingwell's. They are the names of our pioneering directors, Raymond Longford and Ken G. Hall. No other actor comes within cooee of Bud.*

Bud Tingwell began his film career as a schoolboy in Coming Up Smiling *in 1939. After spending the war in a fighter cockpit, he had to wait until 1945 to deliver his first lines, in one of the best 'American' films made in Australia in that decade,* Smithy.

After some time in Hollywood (delightfully recalled in his recently published autobiography), Bud spent from 1956 to 1973 in England, playing in a number of hit plays and films, and starring in the medical drama, Emergency Ward 10.

*He returned to Australia and did a mountain of television work for Crawfords, including three years as Inspector Reg Lawson in the best long-running cop show Australia has ever made—still!—*Homicide.

In the last decade, Bud has appeared in The Castle, Tulip, The Craic, The Wog Boy, Innocence, Ned Kelly, *and every one of them he's graced. When he appears on the screen I have an immediate reaction, This director is no fool; Bud Tingwell's in it! As a matter of fact, a few of the other actors in this book drew the same happy conclusion about me when I told them Bud was involved. John Gaden talked about a moment in the courtroom scene of* The Castle *when he felt that Bud's connection to the moment was so real that it shocked him.*

Bud was a leading man throughout the highs and lows of the Australian film industry in the 1940s and 1950s, an industry that kangaroo-jumped more often than it cruised. Arguably, the same might be said of the Australian film industry today, and Bud's still playing his part, sincerely, and straight-down-the-line.

When I met Bud at his Melbourne home, I was excited about meeting such a distinguished 'old' actor. Though in his 80s, the actor I met was full of boyish enthusiasm for his work, and thinking deeply about the nuances of his current role in The Carer, *as he approached his 200th performance of the play. There are plenty of staid old actors about, I guess, but Bud's not one of them.*

I've always felt—perhaps not everyone would agree with me—that performance is very much part of our species. I worked with the Ooldea Aboriginal people in 1949 over quite a few months on the film *Bitter Springs*—and we had no language in common—and most of their communication seemed to be performance. They picked up the skills of being film actors extremely fast, and seemed to understand the philosophy of it. To such an extent that when our sound recordist wanted to get an extra track of a crowd scene, with them running up over a hill—the visual shooting had been done earlier in the shoot. He'd had trouble with the soundtrack and wanted them to reproduce that scene. Now, for skilled film actors that can be hard with many weeks of work on other things in between. But I watched them preparing themselves, and they duplicated exactly what they'd done weeks before, even to allocating… I imagine they were saying, You came over here, You shouted, You did this, You threw a spear, or whatever. It was fascinating to watch.

And when my son and daughter were—I don't know—six and four or something, in the back garden of our house in London when I was working over there, I used to watch them being totally absorbed, very quickly, in whatever game they were playing. Not just them but their mates from school. If they were being spacemen or explorers or whatever they were being, they very quickly got into the story they were inventing. I remember saying to my wife, If you look at it, that's really perfect performance, because they're nowhere else. They're really right in that story.

Some of the best work by actors I've seen was in something called Talking Stick. We actors would get together with a coordinator, not a director, and we would read—in front of small audiences at a small art gallery in Fitzroy—well-known works by some of the great writers, and some new plays. There was never an allowance for directing, so the first time you did it was the first time you tried it with your fellow actor. I did a two-hander by John Mortimer with Bruce Kerr. It was one of the most exhilarating experiences I've had. Sure, we were reading, and we had about 20 or 30 people watching, but I had no idea what Bruce was going to do. It was not influenced at all by formal production or direction.

So it all adds up to me thinking that within us, as a species, we learn to act. You learn to be polite to the boss, even though you don't like him. You know, all those sort of things. And I think if we muck about with that too much and formalise it too much then maybe we're taking away some of the innate freshness of the performance.

I'm arriving—after all these years—at a few things that certainly are helping me. Stanislavski—well documented in *An Actor Prepares* and *My Life in Art*—and the New York people, were trying, I think, to distil that very thing we've got inside us.

I've arrived at an oversimplified version of the task, but it's stood me in very good stead, especially when I had the lead in a play in London for two years. I gave 800 performances of a lovely comedy called *There's a Girl in My Soup*. In every performance I tried to think as closely as possible the real thoughts that I imagined were going on inside the character. I found that to be a fantastic exercise. I do it with *The Carer*—I'm about to do my 200th performance of that—and I'm finding it fresh all the time.

I went to see a drama teacher/actor mate of mine taking part in a big sort of stand-up comedy show in one of the hotels here in Melbourne. It was very interesting to see a whole lot of chaps who weren't professional comedians having a go. One of them is a radio announcer in one of the community radio stations, and he came up and spoke to me afterwards. He'd interviewed me once—and I had vaguely remembered him, but not the circumstances—and he said I talked a lot in the interview about the thought processes being the most powerful thing an actor's got. And he said that in all the reading he'd done, I was the only one who'd ever tried to put that down as such an important thing. I said, Well, it's not me, it was really Spencer Tracy way back in 1948 or something. I read an article by him. He said, 'Think. Really think. Listen. Really listen.' And he just repeated those words all the way down the column. Now if you look at the simplicity of his work, which was wonderful, he's never *not* thinking, it seems, and never *not* listening, if it's appropriate for the scene.

John Saul—great actor/director in Sydney in the post-war years, and a great friend of Peter Finch—they did a lot of experimenting together, particular in relation to Stanislavski's work. He is still probably the best

Don Barker, John Stanton, Gary Day and Charles 'Bud' Tingwell as Inspector Reg Lawson in *Homicide*.

director I've ever worked with. Huge influence on Rod Taylor, people like that. He could come up with the simplest notes. Shortest, simplest notes that would illuminate enormously. When Rod went to Hollywood he talked so much about John that they tried to get John to go over to Hollywood, but he wouldn't go. He said, I don't know much about film and telly, I only know radio and theatre.

John used to write me a letter if he saw a performance, whether it was telly, film or sometimes the theatre, and just analyse, in the gentlest, most positive way, what I was doing. I've got them all somewhere in a trunk. I think it's nearly time to get those letters out. There'd be a wealth of information in them.

On one of our final performances on a relatively recent tour of *The Carer*, the actor Alan David Lee came to see me, and he reminded me that I'd directed him in a film years ago which was apparently his first job out of NIDA. He said I gave him a tip or a direction which has been extraordinarily powerful for him ever since—this is 20 years ago. Apparently at some stage he was worried about a scene. I suggested he just *think* it and the camera will photograph it. And he said, I did exactly that and it's been one of the most useful things I've ever been told. And that's about as simple as you can get. I think it's what children do.

Saw Angela Punch-McGregor talking to George Negus on television last night. What startled me about her was that she's never lost her fear of the camera. She said, That black hole thing out there, looking at you. One of the most important things that Stanislavski ever talked about was what he called Solitude in Public. And the Circle of Attention. I find that enormously valuable. If you become reasonably skilled at using those facilities, gee, it's an amazingly important thing. To have 1,000 people out front, and you're alone on stage, is an extraordinarily powerful, marvellous feeling.

As I remember, he… I haven't re-read *An Actor Prepares* for quite some time. I must do it again, but I read it over and over many, many years ago. But in my memory the Circle of Attention was started because one of the young actors said, Oh, I feel so exposed on stage. And so—this is obviously short-cutting it like mad—I think I remember they turned the lights out, got the actor to sit in a chair, put one very sharp spotlight on him, and said, Now, how do you feel? He said, Oh, much better. Can't see anything. And I think he moved around and the spotlight followed him, and all the exercises around about then were to achieve that feeling of being alone—in that case—without the need to have just a spotlight. But when I first started in films, because of the lighting requirements of the film lenses and things in those days, you often, in front of a camera, felt as if you were in that spotlight, because of the way they had to light the scene, with far more light than they need now. You were never aware of all the other people around on the movie set.

The first time I'd got terribly conscious of that in an important scene was in a film called *Kangaroo*, that Maureen O'Hara came out to do, way back in 1950. It was directed by the great Lewis Milestone, who directed *All Quiet on the Western Front*. He was one of the great European-American directors. I was having to play this fairly emotional scene with Maureen O'Hara, Chips Rafferty, whom I knew but not all that well in those days. This huge and important film crew from America were filming the first film in Australia with one of the great directors of the world. And, oh, it was an awful experience. Because we were on location in South Australia, a location interior—which was a beautifully built house that they could pull walls down and put the camera anywhere they wanted—was brightly lit all the time because of that amazing South Australian light. And I lost that wonderful comfort of not being able to see the crew, that you would get in an ordinary, good old-fashioned studio. It was awful.

But when I read Stanislavski that really had a tremendous significance for me. Johnny Saul would talk about it. We tried to achieve it even in a radio studio, that Circle of Attention, just around the microphone.

I've seen lots of examples of people trying to *demonstrate* what they were supposed to be in a scene. When I was doing a lot of directing—particularly for Crawfords—they had three actors, excellent actors, brilliantly cast as three mates in the Australian army early in World War II, and Hector Crawford contacted me and he said, It's just not working. Go to a rehearsal room and work with them for a while and see what's happening. Well, I got them to run a scene. They were busy *being* those characters, but not working with each other. So I said, Forget all the character things, just concentrate on each other. You're supposed to be three close mates. Well, the next time they ran it, it was magical. Now, I'm not suggesting I'm terribly clever to have picked it, it wasn't me. It was Johnny Saul, Stanislavski. You'll see evidence of it in nearly everything Spencer Tracy did, and I keep thinking about that, 'Listen. Really listen. Think. Really think.' And frankly, that's about all I've got in the way of information.

It's like accepting that the complexity of situations can conspire to challenge that spontaneity, and the devices that you employ are things to diffuse those challenges, and try and keep it simple.

Yeah. Yeah. Another time... It was a marvellous experience working with Rachel Griffiths on a little film she wrote called *Tulip*. We did it as an experiment in thought processes. I don't remember discussing anything other than what the fella I was playing was *thinking* at any time. If she had a suggestion, it was a suggestion of what he might be thinking. Then maybe I'd put a layer of something else on or take a layer away. Golly, it was stimulating. I don't think I've ever felt so comfortable in front of a camera. The film had a lot of sort of gentle success everywhere with festivals. The rumour was she was being offered an Academy Award nomination—which I'm told we were offered for *Innocence*, but it's a very expensive thing if you're an independent film-maker.

You mean the lobbying?

Well, you've got to buy a lot of cassettes for all the members. Paul Cox told me we were offered an Academy Award for *Innocence*. And he said, If you don't mind I can't accept it. Because they worked out it was going to cost him $100,000 to buy that many cassettes for the Academy members—5,000 members!

That's extraordinary that it can inhibit–

Oh, yeah. I mentioned it at a Producers' Guild meeting recently, and our current president had two examples of smallish documentaries which were highly regarded. In each case it was going to cost about $40,000 or $50,000 to accept the nomination. To get the number of cassettes! But for Paul, 100,000 American bucks is an awful lot of money out of his next project. Fine if you've got MGM or Fox behind you. I was surprised to hear that that was the situation, but it sort of makes sense. Someone's got to pay for the bloody cassettes at $20 a go.

It seems sort of archaic.

Doesn't it? Yes. Delightfully ordinary or something.

Yeah, that's right. One of the really interesting things that you've been talking about is... There might be a tendency for people to think that before the acting schools started, that before NIDA and the Ensemble, somehow people didn't talk about acting, or people didn't think about it. But what's really interesting is that you're talking about a period that is pre-50s, and you depict professional actors engaging with the world of thought about acting very conscientiously on the job, possibly more so than they do now.

Probably, yeah. And I think it takes one... Well, Johnny Saul, to me, was the one who attracted thoughtful people around him. And I'm sure he was sent-up rotten by people who thought, Oh, it's a lot of rubbish.

We developed—there was Rod Taylor, me, sometimes Ken Wayne who was another Aussie actor who was not as well known as he should be—and we'd go down to John's house at Newport on a Saturday night, and we'd start talking when we got there, and we'd share a bottle of wine, but often we would talk until dawn. Looking back, there was nothing we hadn't discussed. That was an extraordinary period.

And then you had the experience of going to England and having a leading role in a quite long-running television series. What kind of lessons did that instil in you?

The ambitions for that show were tiny. It was designed to run for three or four weeks to fill a gap in the production schedules which changed because of the ending of a thing called The Toddlers' Truce. The Toddlers' Truce meant that every television set used to go blank and silent for one hour at night between six and seven so Mum could get the kids to bed.

So it was a non-program?

Absolutely nothing. No test-card. Nothing. So when that stopped—

What a good idea.

It sounds brilliant now. Anyhow, the show was purely designed to fill that gap. And they thought maybe in three or four weeks other programs would be up and running properly.

What new acting challenges did that present?

Oh, concentration. It was like the theatre. It was live to air. No recording process of any kind.

I was asked to do episodes 1, 2 and 4, and that was it, we'd go home. We went to air live on 19 February 1957, on a Tuesday night. The next day we were nearly as big as sliced bread. It was an extraordinary reaction, so they were busy re-writing all the background stories, such as they were. A lot of them hadn't been revealed. Mine hadn't been revealed, but they thought I probably had a sick wife somewhere which probably made me a bit bad-tempered—the bad-tempered Aussie. By the Friday episode, she was a sick fiancée, by the following Friday, she was a sick sister in the Isle of Wight, but nobody ever met her. I was just supposed to be sort of worried about her, and that made me go crook at the young nurse if she dropped the tray of instruments, you know?

Anthony Keary was a marvellous director, wonderful producer. Scottish chap with a good acting-in-rep background. Had a habit of saying, That's wonderful, darlings. Just a little more *real*. And walk away. And if you tried to say, Sorry…? He'd go, No, you know what I mean. And that's one of the most valuable directing tools I've ever used. And I believe almost any actor, especially with a bit of experience, has got a little meter that says, Oh, yeah, you were as phoney as a two-bob watch.

It's interesting, isn't it, that sometimes a simple and frank thing like that works remarkably well, don't you think?

Yeah. People like Albert Finney came in to work with us. Teddy Woodward came in and, you know, very established actors and beaut blokes. Finney came in only because he loved what we were doing as an ensemble. I got to know him quite well. Woodward too, great to work with. He came in as a nutty patient about to jump off the roof of the hospital. He was so good that a year later they got him back as the chest surgeon. Then I was asked if I would mind becoming the chest surgeon because Teddy had been offered

Mercutio at Stratford, and if I was prepared to become the chest surgeon he could go to Stratford.

I used to get leave to do movies, and all Tony wanted to know was when I wanted to come back. He said, If you can give us three weeks' notice that'd be good and we can get the scripts adjusted. But on one occasion he wrote me out overnight so I could go to Africa on a film. I mean, the goodwill was amazing. And we became huge, we had 27 million viewers per episode. Half the country watched us, the other half watched the BBC.

But the disciplines were fantastic. Because we used to really prepare. Tony used his time better than anybody, I thought. He didn't muck about with too much deep and meaningful stuff. As long as it was real and believable. And that fitted everything that Johnny Saul had been talking about with me. I don't remember Tony and I having any deep and meaningful chats about it, though.

But you had the resources—because of your experiences back in Australia—to deal with someone saying, It needs to be more real, then walking away.

Yes. Oh, sure. Yeah, exactly.

I had one of the best-written drama moments I'd ever had in anything in that show. It was to try to tell a colleague—Peter Howell, lovely actor—that his wife had just died behind the screens. It was so beautifully, simply written. I was out of shot for a while, then I come in, go to see her. Camera didn't follow me in, but she's gone while I was in there behind the screens.

We used to rehearse outside in a rehearsal room first, then come in about ten in the morning and start running and rehearsing the rest of the day with cameras and crew, then do the show live about seven-thirty. And about four in the afternoon I really thought I'd hit the big emotional stuff, and it felt great. All that. Director came out and said, Uh-uh, I can see you doing it. And walked away. And I thought, Oh. That's right! And what I hadn't done when I went behind the screens was, a) determine the moment when she died, and b) what would my thought process really be if this was real? Knowing that the husband was in the vicinity, probably in the next ward.

I remember the thought I took was, How am I going to tell him? Not, *What* I'm going to tell him, just, *How*? I know I'll run into him in a minute. So I walked out—and this is now live on air—and suddenly the ward went funny. It was just an ordinary set but it felt longer. I found it slightly difficult to walk, but I got there.

Peter came in right on cue. I walked around, tried to tell him something, whatever, then he walked behind the screens and I'm now out of the show. That's it. I can go and sit down and wait for the credits to run after the show. Well, I looked around and the whole studio had gone dead quiet. The credits rolled, and right at the very end there was the logo—TV London or something. Then that studio erupted. Wow, what a show!

I was telling Rod Taylor this, as an example of how Johnny Saul's feelings had come into, say, that episode. He said, Yeah, but did the audience get it? I said, Mate, all over the country the phones rang red hot that night. And we thought it was one of the confirming moments of that show. Now, clever me, had hit only the right thought processes. Not great acting. Nothing, you know? And what astonished me was the strange physical feeling of the legs not working all that well. And not really being able to say what I should have been saying according to the script. But it wasn't like a careless actor changing it or anything, it was all terribly appropriate. That was still probably one of the most powerful acting experiences I've ever had. And it started with the director saying, Uh-uh, I can see you doing it.

So you had found a simple, motivating mechanism, which was a thought?

Yes. And it wasn't a great, intelligent thought. It was just, How am I going to tell him? As simple as that.

One of the things I love about doing *The Carer* is I can try whatever I want—not to change anything physical, all the moves are exactly the same—but I've got a lot of freedom within the thought processes.

A lot of people believe that *The Castle* was a lovely, funny comedy, but we treated it as a drama. I don't remember Rob Sitch ever mentioning the words 'funny' or 'comedy' when he was directing. And we rehearsed it like a radio play. We had four four-hour sessions, sitting around in a room. All the cast, the whole cast—small parts, large parts, whatever—and that was really exhilarating. Then we started shooting. I directed *The Glass Menagerie* like that because we couldn't get into the theatre for about a week. I said, Well, let's sit around and read it for a week and see what happens. Oo, and it was magic. Wonderful! Not just to read it, it was performance reading, proper radio-type—

Where you kind of grow from just reading into—

And playing with each other, looking across, as we used to. In good radio production I used to love watching the really good actors looking up from the script to work with the other person, and even, if the mic was in the way, to move it to see each other's eyes.

I guess that's a long way around, but that's what Stanislavski was sort of on about. That kind of involvement with people. And I still believe that if audiences don't really believe, they're not really going to go on the journey with you, they'll hang back a bit.

All about the moments

HEATHER MITCHELL

When I reflect on the many performances I've seen Heather Mitchell give, the word that comes to mind is grace. It should be no surprise that it's the same word that pops into one's head when one is with her offstage too.

Like John Gaden, Bud Tingwell and others, Heather is one of those actors who seems to trade on her natural sense of decency, generosity and integrity. We instinctively believe the work on stage because we sense those essential qualities in the person.

On graduating from NIDA in 1980, Heather seemed to immediately appear on every director's casting wish-list. She has since played leading roles with all of Australia's major theatre companies, including Barbara in Major Barbara, *Yelenei in* Uncle Vanya, *Virgilia in* Coriolanus, *Hermoine in* A Winter's Tale, *Anna in* Burn This *and, just prior to our conversation, Charlotte in* The Real Thing, *with the Sydney Theatre Company.*

Heather has appeared in dozens of Aussie TV series and mini-series, and in films including Malcolm, Proof, Children of the Revolution *and* Thank God He Met Lizzie.

Thank God I met Heather Mitchell to record her self-effacing yet acutely detailed impressions of the sensations of being on stage.

I put my first faith in the writer. If it's a period piece I try and do as much research as I can on the period, so when we have discussions I'll know what I'm talking about, what happened at that time, the environment the character is living in.

Preparing more than that to me seems foolish. The director, no matter how collaborative they want to be, or not, has definite ideas about how they see it. The other actors have their ideas as well, so I don't see any point in doing any more work than that, because I like to think of theatre as a collaborative process.

I don't think I've changed in what I bring into the rehearsal room since the very first time. I'm always very excited to see the other people, and I go wanting to have fun. And I don't feel scared, I don't feel nervous, I don't feel anxious about sitting down and doing the first read. I don't try and do a performance or anything, I don't put any pressure on myself to come up with something in that first read.

So what steps do you take to build from there?

Often people say I look worried, but I'm not. I think I become almost… It's almost a sensory overload thing when I first get up, like I'm wanting everything to respond. It's not worry at all, but it's like this neutral place that people interpret as me being worried. But I'm actually neutral. People think I'm thinking a lot, and I'm not, I'm just—

That's your professional state?

Yeah.

So there's no particular preparation to find that state? You trust that you're going to just turn it on?

Yes.

I like to get up quickly. I don't want to sit around talking. I try to be very aware of the space.

I like to know the direction I'm going in. If there hasn't been a discussion toward some sort of understanding of the parameters of a scene, if the director is being secretive in some way, I become frustrated.

The very first time you get up and play, I don't mind. You just get up and anything can happen. But fairly quickly, you need some framework, even if it's the wrong one. I've found with some directors I've worked with, there wasn't any framework. And you can get, like, into the third week of rehearsal and you're still not sure what's really going on in the scene. It just seems that the focus of the scene is dictated by whoever's performance is the most showy.

I keep going back to the script all the time. I try to find out what the writer is trying to get out of it before I try and find out—

And does that have to be explicit? Does it have to be collectively agreed upon?

I think the intention eventually has to be agreed upon. I mean, I've been in things where it wasn't agreed upon and, during the run of the play, it just goes all over the place. And it becomes more and more obvious that the audience is a bit lost, and *you* start to feel a bit lost.

Basically, the first week of rehearsal—if it's been a great first week, striving, striving, striving, trying to keep your imagination free—is very much a process of osmosis. I don't do a hell of a lot of worrying. I try to keep my head out of it, out of rehearsal.

Talk about your head entering and leaving the process. When is your head useful?

My head's useful when you get to the point in rehearsal when something's not happening and you stand and discuss why.

Do you feel, physiologically, this kind of switch from the part of your brain that you act with and the part of your brain that you analyse with?

Yes, but... It's tricky, isn't it? God. I'd say yes, but when you're rehearsing you're using both parts simultaneously. It's a simultaneous thing. You're never... It's only when you're actually performing—and it happens rarely in performing—that you're totally free from any sort of brain-censorship or any kind of brain activity other than playing that moment from the scene. So no. No, that's not—

Your head is involved all the time. I think it's that thing that all actors, I'm sure, have an ability to observe themselves while in the moment. So you can feel very much in the moment, *doing* something, but you're *observing* yourself at the same time. So I've got that going on all the time. I think that's the thing. Most actors have that ability.

When I'm in rehearsal I'm not thinking in terms of character. I think that's the main thing. I'm just responding as *me*. Definitely. I'm never thinking of character until the last week of rehearsal.

And when you do start thinking about character, what might it lead you to do?

It's usually through revelations. It's usually through, Oh, I get it. *That* happens. Oh, and that happens, and *that* seems to go with *that*. Through something that has happened spontaneously on the floor you are given insight, and something clicks and you go, That's right. And you can see an agreement, the director doesn't have to say anything, but there is an agreement that it has worked.

You're meeting the script, and then three weeks into rehearsal you're recognising that *it* is doing certain things to *you*?

Yes. Exactly. But how does that happen? How does that happen so suddenly? It seems that for two weeks—this is what I don't understand about the process—for two weeks you'll just be working on it, and responding as yourself, your own intuitive responses to things—and hopefully a little more imaginatively than you would when you're just living your life—and then it seems quite sudden that things click. Like, *Oh*, I get it.

Often it will come through something the director has said. Even one word, sometimes. Something either you think of yourself, or something that's said during the day, or something that's happened, and you think, Ah, that's the key. It's almost like getting a little key, and you go, Oh. *That* influences you: how she responds to other people in general, how she feels about herself. It's some little comment, that just kind of triggers. It's not that I depend on it in every rehearsal. If it doesn't happen it doesn't happen. But usually something happens, and all the other things I've done then make sense. Every other thing then takes on a slightly different nuance.

So if you start with this neutrality, and then sometimes—and it's a welcome thing—you have this moment of differentiation in relation to the character, which sheds a whole and distinct light on the work. Does that point then encourage you to push things in a behaviourally more distinct way?

Yeah, it gives you the confidence to push things that bit further. When you get really imaginative responses to things is when you get those little keys into the character. And then you can go, Okay, I'll take it this way. And then you go, Oh, no, no, no. Until I get those little clues I find it hard to just kind of get up and start. I see some actors who just get up and start performing, and I just go, Whoa! Whoa! I just cannot, I just don't do that. I get up and I'm very small. I'm quite small, just plot, plot, plotting it through until one of those little moments happens, and then my imaginative response comes into play.

What happens if it doesn't?

That hasn't happened yet. Which is not to say there haven't been *performances* that haven't worked for me. That's definitely happened. But I guess that's where your technique comes in. That you do know how to analyse a script and you've learned those fundamental things so if you really are stuck, you can go back and work something out.

What are some of the things—things that we might associate with acting school exercises, with being trained—what of those things might you actually apply at this stage of your career?

Well, plotting your character's journey, where you're going, from A to B. What all the other characters say about you, what you say about other people. When it appears that you're being quite consciously honest about things, when you're not.

What else from your training remains essential to your practice today?

I always go to rehearsal with a good free voice. I'd spend a good 20 minutes lying on the floor, breathing deeply. Then getting upside down, getting the soft palette working, making sure the neck is free. Just those very simple, basic, voice exercises, because I really feel that if the voice isn't free and the neck isn't free it's very hard to be imaginative and creative.

Would you do that every day of rehearsal?

Yep. Every day.

In something I did recently, opening night came, and it was one of those terrible feelings like I'd forgotten to go to school when I had to sit for an exam. I couldn't remember having such a feeling. I felt like I'd missed out on doing the rehearsals. I really felt like I was in a nightmare. And I went on stage and the audience—I really didn't know what I was doing—I walked on stage and the audience totally informed me as to how to approach the role.

So presumably that moment-that-informs-all in rehearsal hadn't happened?

No. Well, I thought it had, but then the notes I was getting from the director were contradicting my instincts and understanding, so there was an at-odds. I'm not usually… I have nerves on opening night, but I'm excited. I love anything with a celebratory feel. I love the first day of rehearsal because there's that feeling. I love opening nights because there's that thing of everyone being together, for each other. I love that feeling. But I was terrified. Absolutely terrified. I felt like I didn't know what was going to come out, even though I'd mentioned it to one of the actors, and they said, You'll be fine, you'll be fine, you've been doing it for four weeks. And I thought, I don't feel like I've been there at all.

There were some days in rehearsal when I went in going, I don't know what I'm doing. I'll just get up and do anything. And I would. I'd just go into rehearsal and try and do anything, but I didn't really know what I was doing. And yet, when I initially read the script, I thought, I can do this. I can see myself doing this. I actually thought, This'll be easy.

And I can't say I was great on that first night or anything, but the audience totally informed me how to start working on it. And of course the director said, That's what I wanted all along. And I thought, Yeah, I get it. It's just that somehow we hadn't had the same conversations going on. It was frightening. And it also made me question, Had I not been responding correctly? Had I been deluding myself in rehearsal? Had I not been taking notes properly? It was quite a confronting experience. I've never experienced that before. It was the first time I'd felt that I'd had to save myself.

Out of all of that, what did I learn? Out of all of that, in terms of my process, I learned that it all comes back to the sort of relationship you have with the director. And understanding the moments.

When you're up working on something with the other actor or actors, it's the moments. It's all about the moments. And if the moments are put in a context of what they're—not necessarily about—but what they all add up to, then you can play, you can really muck around, you can do anything. But if you don't think the director understands what those moments are aiming towards, then it's really, really difficult. They're just a whole lot of little bubbles floating around. They need to be put inside a little snowdome or something, you know?

I also get very upset when a director—this happens not so much in theatre, more in film—when a director keeps things from the actor because they think, Well, I know about this, the actor doesn't need to know about this. I suppose they do that because they think they'll just cut around it anyway. But I like to know the parameters I'm working in. I feel much more secure to play.

If there's a problem with a director, that's when you've just got to go straight back to your own self, somehow not let it worry you. You've just got to rise above taking it personally. Because you do, you do take it very personally. You think, They hate me, they hate what I'm doing, they wish they hadn't cast me. You've got to rise totally above that. You have to let go of that, get along with them, and go back to your own instincts. Totally trust your own instincts. And usually it'll get you through. Even if it's not an inspired piece of work, it *will* get you through.

So tell me about when you are relying on your own instincts.

Well, it's a combination of instincts and experience. Experience comes in too because… Let's say it's a comedy. There are certain rules of comedy. How to make a gag work. How to go through to the end of the line. And without an audience it's very difficult to know if that gag is working, so you have to do it technically. If the director doesn't understand comedy, has chosen to do a comedy but just doesn't understand it, you have to trust those techniques you know. They might look stupid in rehearsal—but you have to go, Okay, they don't understand that you have to have an audience to make this look good. And you have to have a certain amount of confidence to know it will work. Even though that's not being the character, that's just technique. It's not instinct, it's technique.

In terms of instincts, it's a tricky one, because you can walk into rehearsal and do a scene in which you're confronted with something—you react with horror to the situation and suddenly have to break down and cry or something. The first time you do it, it feels fantastic. You think, Oh, my God, that's fantastic! That must be the way to do it! And the next time you do it you just can't get it up. You can't do it. And you think, But my instincts said that it was right. And that's when I think you have to go back and say, That felt right in that moment but it doesn't work in the context of what comes next. So you have to throw it away and find something else which works—employ your instincts *again* to find another way of doing it.

See, sometimes you find it and you can't find it again, and there's a reason you can't find it again, and it's about finding what that reason is. I've found that sometimes my immediate response to something—it was a good response, it felt right, it seemed right—but it wasn't right because it wasn't in context. It's hard to let go of it if it felt so good. That's when you have to trust your instincts but not indulge them. You have to be able to let go of stuff that felt right, but is not necessarily right in context, or with what the other actor is doing. Unless the writer specifically asks for it, *then* you have to find a way of keeping it.

I would say NIDA was for me—apart from the technical voice work and stuff—it was three years of observation, becoming more aware internally, emotionally, physically, intuitively, and employing that awareness in acting exercises and production. It's not taught so much as nurtured. It's an exploration. I don't think you have to go to psychotherapy or anything like that. There are things you can click into immediately, and other things you can't. Which is why some people are repeatedly cast in certain types of roles, and other people in others. We all access different things easily. So to become a more diverse actor, I suppose the idea is to find more and

Heather Mitchell as Ruth in the 1992 Sydney Theatre Company production of *The Homecoming*. (Photo: Tracey Schramm)

more things to use from one's life experience rather than from things you've been taught. You can have huge life experiences that you repress and don't want to access. It's about having those experiences and allowing yourself to be in touch with them, and not negating them. Being able to use them.

Other people are brilliant technicians, can do it totally technically. I think someone like John Gaden is such a brilliant… He's so brilliant technically as well as intuitively, imaginatively. He can produce those things technically.

But what is technical?

Oh, I don't know. I don't know. But I don't turn myself inside out if I can't access stuff. I mean I've certainly done performances where I haven't accessed stuff. I've just done it purely technically. That's for sure.

So describe the feeling of doing something technically.

Well, when you do something technically you're very aware. You're standing outside of yourself, observing yourself, helping yourself. It's almost like you're outside as a puppeteer helping yourself get through the moment. You're totally not there. Maybe not totally not there, but you're outside of yourself, you know? You're having trouble. You feel really empty. You think, Oh, God. You've just got so much in your head. You're trying to unclutter yourself. You're trying to just remain in the moment. So technically, to get through it you would—

Fortunately your body will remember. Your muscles will remember because you've done it so many times. Your muscles will just go through the process. That's why human beings are so extraordinary because your muscles will just go through all the things you've done night after night, and emotionally—it's like the emotional memory will sustain you even though you're not there. So I think you just cheat it a bit, try to access something emotionally even if it's not in the right area. You access something emotionally just so it's something true.

Sometimes you've got to realise that emotional scenes can grow way beyond where they started, and even though it feels great… Sometimes by having that experience where it defeats you, getting to it is wonderful because it takes you back to the truth of it, and makes you do it far more simply. And you go, Oh, I think I've gone way too far. I need to bring it back. That's always the trick with any show, I think, where you play a role that does require a large emotional response to things. They grow and grow. It's very hard to get a consistency.

Another technical thing I do is get a list of words—lots of words, active words—and almost every scene, before I go on, I take a different word with me, in my head. It will just give a slightly different colour or shade to the way I enter into the scene. Something appropriate, not totally inappropriate to the scene, just something that gives you something other to think about—before you walk on—other than yourself. You're thinking about the scene, or something you didn't do the night before, or something you want to achieve in the scene. Usually it's an active word, something to help you affect the other person.

What's the best way to feel, when you walk on?

Before I go on? Oh, one of the best things is to feel happy. It's almost like a feeling of love for the audience. I often look—if I can see an audience before a show—I'll just see one person. I don't want to see their face, I just want to see a blur of them. I don't want to know who it is or anything. It's something outside of the play itself, and if I can just feel a love for the audience, it takes me away from thinking about myself or the play.

The best feeling is to go on without anything. Absolutely nothing, just a relaxed and prepared body.

So this relaxation you've got to walk on with, how do you reconcile that with notions of where the character is coming from, and what specific energy you are supposed to be coming on with? Does that challenge that?

No, it enhances that. If you're really relaxed—I don't mean tired—then you can access those things really easily. It's the nights when you're tired or stressed that you have to work up those things. A show I did a while ago, one of the actors spent so much of the night getting himself so worked up into the role—a fairly aggressive role—and he's backstage getting worked up, worked up, worked up, and it was exhausting all of us. By the time he got onstage, he still had the energy, but he didn't have nearly as much. The energy he had backstage was much more interesting than what he took onstage. He'd used it all up.

Relaxation. It's very much about internal energy, I think. It's a state of non-critical... You cannot be critical in that state. And you're not judgemental, you're not even thinking. It's a total, wonderful readiness. A state of readiness. And that's something that George Ogilvie, as a teacher, did a lot of work on. It's to do with focus. It's almost like... It's not a meditative state, but it's a state of being totally prepared for anything.

I think it has a lot of correlations with meditation.

I like to mediate before I do a performance. And I do a number of kinesiology exercises, getting the left and right brain—the left and right hemisphere—connected, which you do by crossing the mid-line of the body. They're very simple exercises. I find if I do a vocal warm-up, I do a bit of a physical warm-up. Not a really strenuous one, more like some yoga, some stretching and a bit of jumping. And I do a bit of meditation, usually a good hour or so before I come into the theatre. Then a couple of minutes of left and right brain stuff. Then I feel really prepared and relaxed and ready for anything. And there's that wonderful feeling which, you know, you long to have all the time, where you're on stage and if anything gets thrown at you, you can deal with it. You feel so in control, but out of control. Aware of the audience, aware of everything. Everything's heightened and wonderful. That comes from repeated preparedness. If you repeat that, if that becomes your program, I think you eventually get that experience much more often.

What does it feel like when it misses, in your body?

It's terrible. You feel totally exposed. You feel every pore, every bit of you is being observed, scrutinised. You become overly self-conscious. I think to ever feel self-conscious on stage, it just breaks everything. It's a slowness of the brain. You just can't seem to focus. Your peripheral vision isn't working. You feel your responses are slow. You feel you're missing. If there are laughs, you're missing them. You're missing all the technical bits. It's just awful. My first response is I just want to run away, and my second response is I want to apologise to everybody. Sometimes you can pull yourself out of it. I don't know how, but you pull yourself out of it. You go on. You get back into the groove.

You've constantly got to remind yourself—as the actor—while you're doing the run of a show, to never hold onto the way it felt the day before. You've just got to let go of that. Just enjoy it.

I was going to ask you about your take on the differences of acting on screen?

I think with a film I would plot the character's through-line, where they're going, what they're doing. You do all those things quite technically, and write them all down, simply because you're working out of context, out of sequence. So you need to have reference points to remind you of the sequence of events, emotionally, what's going on. I'm much more analytical earlier on than I would be in theatre because there you've got a four-week rehearsal process, and it's much more collaborative.

Film work is not as collaborative, usually. Often you'll have a director who's sitting behind the video split. Some directors—amazingly enough—can do that and say only two words to you the whole time, and get really good work, and get fantastic projects happening because they have such a strong idea of what it is they're making. They can see it already. A lot of directors in film and television are not very visual. Some are, and the ones that are, and know what they're after, and have cast exactly what they imagined, they get great work out of you whether you're aware of it or not. And there are others who sit behind the video split because they don't know what they're doing, and they haven't got a great idea of how it's all going to come together, and you're all fumbling around together.

But I think in terms of acting, you're just filling a different kind of emotional space. The information you're giving is different. You're giving a different quantity of information in theatre than you are in film.

Look, for me, my level of confidence in theatre is greater than film, definitely. But my level of confidence in film is getting better all the time. The more I do, the more confident I get. From learning and becoming more aware of the technical things, and therefore feeling more comfortable. You know, you do one of those episodes of those serials, and no matter how confident you are, you feel like the visitor. It's pretty demoralising doing those things because the fundamental thing is that you're not really part of it.

Well, it's a bit of a sliding scale, isn't it? Because sometimes one can be made to feel part of it, and sometimes one can be made to feel like a barnacle.

Absolutely. You come in and do your little bit, then you walk away and they call you up four hours later, do another little bit, then you go home. I think fundamentally most actors want to be part of some sort of creative process. They don't want to just come on and do their bit. What they do want—I think, most actors—is to feel that they're being trusted with some information and knowledge about the piece that they're working on, and to feel part of that. You don't just want to be a hired labourer, you know?

Well, if you link that to the foundation that you're trying to achieve in rehearsal, the neutrality and openness, it becomes problematic, doesn't it? Because if you're in a working environment that seems fundamentally uninterested in you achieving those things, then it completely undermines the essential foundations of your process, doesn't it?

Absolutely. And, look, it's very difficult with that stuff, because you have to walk in with the character all worked out, and basically, when I say the character all worked out, it's pretty much you responding to those things within those given circumstances. You haven't done any detailed work.

You've talked about the more analytical approach in these circumstances, so you've gone through a *virtual* rehearsal process. You're trying to imagine what a rehearsal process might be like?

Might be like, exactly. You have to skip that.

But what you *do* walk into that's different is a set, where it's all decked out—the sort of place where, in theatre you might have after four weeks, on film you walk straight in. You've got the set. You've got the clothes. You're given all these externals so you have to learn how to use the externals to *create*. You come in with your internal stuff and you don't have to take the externals on, because you're *in* them. It does a lot of the work for you. You might be in half-shadow, so that does a lot for you emotionally. You don't have to construct any of that.

I remember the first film role I ever had—it was television actually—was a big job, and I'd done only theatre before that. The producer and the director both came up to me—very powerful people—and they came up to me and the director didn't say anything. But the producer said, Now, listen, Heather, you've only done theatre. Just remember, don't do anything. Just don't do anything. And I didn't know what it meant. I didn't have the courage to say, What do you *mean*? Don't *do* anything? I just took it and thought about it. Don't do anything. And I became so bound up in this whole thing of not doing anything and I didn't know what it meant. But I guess he meant that in film you don't have to do *much*. He thought I was going to perform it or describe it, facially and stuff. But I thought he meant *don't do anything*. So scene after scene I thought, I'll just say my words.

Early on you were talking about an acknowledgement of what we might call the dual consciousness of being both the monitor and the intuitive 'experiencer' at the same time. And then a little while after that you talked about the dangers and unhappiness of becoming self-conscious. Is that just a thing of degree, when this monitoring thing takes over and the doing of it recedes?

Yeah. Well, you're still doing it because your body remembers it, so you still do it, but the monitoring becomes overwhelming.

It's the same dual mechanism that's sometimes balanced and sometimes not?

Yeah. I think so. I think so. And it's almost like you've gone back into rehearsal. You've gone back in, you're observing yourself again. You can be so prepared some nights, thinking, I'm so prepared. And go on stage feeling really free and open. And it can happen to you, something can creep in.

I don't feel comfortable in an organised belief system. I'm not keen on organised religion, acting, parenting. I can't see how any organised belief system, whether it's in acting or anything, is foolproof and works all the time.

And yet, you've talked about employing the elements of a number of different things that might fall beneath the heading of acting systems.

In Australia we don't do classes. We tend not to. That's what I find really strange. You spend three years at NIDA or a drama school, or just doing courses or whatever—concentrating so much on technical things, also on exploring things, exploring yourself, observing things—and then it all stops and you're in the profession.

I think if you're not going to go and do classes, then you need to at least—not *need* to—but it's *helpful* to become aware of all sorts of different techniques and read as much as you can, see as many films, see as much theatre as you can, observe other people's work as much as you can, and enjoy it as much as you can. Try not to be cynical, particularly when you're out of work. Try to keep positive. I really think that everyone's success is great for everyone. If you don't get the role because someone else you know got it, then that's great. It really is, as long as the work is done well. It's so easy when you're out in the profession to stop learning. Really easy just to do it as jobs.

The industry has changed enormously. It's become so much more about results. And about money, a lot of it, because we don't have the government support as much, and the theatre companies are feeling that they have to get big names and they have to get big money. And same in the film industry.

Actors have to diversify. You used to be able to say, I'm an actor, and I'm not going to diversify. Somehow to diversify was a lesser thing. But in fact it's all part of the same thing. And the more actors who, like you, can write, the more actors who can direct and write and learn editing or learn any other skill, I think is not only fantastic but essential. I think it's becoming essential.

It is engendered

JOHN GADEN

The first things that John Gaden did when he arrived in Adelaide at the end of 1985 to take over as Artistic Director of the State Theatre Company of South Australia were, one, chock open his office door, and two, turn the desk around so his back was to the nice river view, and he faced the company. The door remained open for all of the three years that I had the privilege of working there during John's 'regime'.

When you work with an actor—day in, day out—for a fair period of time, no matter how good he is, you usually feel after a while that you have the measure of his acting capabilities. When I went to see John as Leontes in A Winter's Tale *in 1986, I knew he'd be good. I thought I knew how good. He surprised me. Twelve months later—twelve more months of working with him and for him—I went to see his Lear. Again, he far and away surpassed my high expectations. He did it again years later when I went to see him as Falstaff in Bell Shakespeare's* Henry 4.

John taught me what a leading actor is. A leading actor is not an actor with the most words, but an actor who leads, who sets the tone and pace of rehearsals, who describes—with his body—how high the bar is set. One of my great Gaden moments was after just one week of rehearsals for the premiere production of Stephen Sewell's brilliant and unwieldy Dreams in an Empty City. *We'd spent a couple of days discussing the play, and a few days on our feet. We'd blocked the first Act. The director, Neil Armfield, thought it would be a good thing to come in on the Saturday morning and consolidate the work we'd done with a stumble through Act One. I'm sure I wasn't alone in expecting this to be a pretty tame, technical 'reminder' session. Gaden came in that Saturday morning and tore the cat apart. His energy and passion were extraordinary. It lifted the whole production, stayed with us all for the rest of the run. Everybody wanted to match it. It was a perfectly judged act of leadership, and that's how John continued to lead that company through some of its best years: with intelligence, passion, his famous humility and generosity, and his wonderful humour.*

John began acting with the Young Elizabethan Players in the mid–60s. In the early 1970s he was an integral part of the landmark Old Tote *and* Nimrod *seasons, and has been a leading man with the Sydney Theatre Company for its entire existence, as he has been—for 30 years—a leading actor with every major theatre company in the country.* Travesties, Kold Komfort Kaffee, Amadeus, The Secret Rapture, Moby Dick, Racing Demon, Death and the Maiden, Who's Afraid of Virginia Woolf, As You Like It, Waiting for Godot, Cloudstreet *and* Major Barbara *are just some of the prompts for Australian theatre-goers' memories of great Gaden moments of their own.*

We spoke at John's home, overlooking Bondi Beach. I was well prepared for his erudition and his self-effacement, but with his emotional openness—unsteadiness even—he surprised me yet again.

Increasingly there is one thing that I look for. It happens very early on, and it's the connection you make when you first read—or first read aloud—the words you are going to do. It might be the first reading, or it might be the first time you read it for yourself. It might be the first time you read it with the thought in mind of doing the role. I mean, with Shakespeare, one has read most of the plays. But there comes a time when you start thinking about yourself as Jaques, as Lear, as Hamlet, whatever. And it is the moment when you make an absolutely involuntary and intuitive contact with the words.

I want to read something to you I just read the other day, that Robert Frost said about writing poetry. 'A poem begins as a lump in the throat, a home-sickness, a love-sickness. It finds the thought, and the thought finds the words.'

Now, I think that's pretty central to what an actor does. And it may sound terribly simple and simplistic, but I think it's the basis of everything. And I've come to trust that, really, above everything else. Because, if something doesn't happen to you, something quite lump-in-the-throat-y, something visceral, if some little seed doesn't start to engender—and I've always thought it wonderful that that's what Iago says when he hatches the plan, 'It is engendered'—if that little seed doesn't start to engender, then there are other things you can start to fall back on. You can do tricks, you can do voices, you can do make-up, you can rely on a certain chutzpah and authority that you acquire, but the essential quality won't be there.

As a young actor I played Lear, and for the first time I got in touch with this huge wellspring of anger that I didn't know I had—it was extraordinary—because of Lear's anger. It was a time when I was struggling with a whole lot of things about myself—about my own view of the world, my own sexuality particularly, a number of other things—and there was an enormous amount of rage which I had never allowed out, and which I touched on. But I couldn't have said that to you clearly and coherently then, because there are so many constructs that, as a person, as an educated person particularly, you have in your life, and it takes a long time to find the simplicity.

I found it when I was in a production of *As You Like It*, playing Jaques. I was doing the 'seven ages' speech. I'd read it a few times, and I thought it was really a fairly slight piece of doggerel, actually. There's nothing to it. It's not great thought. It's a direct pinch from one of the fathers of the church—I can't remember which one—and it's probably written to allow Orlando to go out and get Adam and bring him back in, which is underestimating Shakespeare—something one should never do. But I started to work on it, and I learnt it, and I came into rehearsals and… I had a bad back. I'm sitting on a little stool on stage. And I had just gone through the process of putting my own mother in a nursing home. She was not demented or anything like that, she was just very frail and old and couldn't look after herself any more. But against all our better wishes, we had to do that. And all those things were in my head as I started doing the speech. And when I got to the end, 'the final age', I started crying. The tears just came from nowhere. And the connection on a couple of specific words in the piece—and I remember it so distinctly—that having said the words, my voice began to wobble. And that was a very graphic example. You don't always get that.

Once you've made that connection you know what to do. It's extraordinary how it unlocks everything.

You feel like you're kind of at home then?

Yes. Yes, you've made it. You've made a contact which will be real to the person watching you.

Because for so many years, what I'd tried to do was *perform* the text. If it was an emotion, try to perform the emotion. And I had some success doing that, particularly with Stoppard. Not that I think Stoppard isn't

John Gaden as Harpagon in the 2004 Sydney Theatre Company production of *The Miser*. (Photo: Tracey Schramm)

capable of other treatment, but you can play that role in *Travesties* with an enormous amount of bravura and so on, and not always make contact. You can also do it, and *make* contact, and it will be better.

I'd been feeling more and more that I wasn't actually doing anything very creative. It was kind of decorative. Quite nice decorative art sometimes, quite good fake-real, but not real. And what I learnt was that in some ways—and you can't generalise about this—but in some ways the *less* you do, the more you are totally *inside*. The more the audience are watching you at a *remove* from you, almost like someone watching a person who is unconscious of being watched. The more that is happening, in a sense, the less you do to *demonstrate* to some generalisation called the audience, the more they will get. The more they will come to you, the more they will imagine for themselves what is going on. And it took a long time to learn, because you want to get up there and *do* it. We want to show off our homework. We want to show off all the things we know about the text.

So all those things start to come together. Then, I think, you're in a position to actually do something that will have an effect on an audience, deliver to an audience that feeling, that contact, that meeting you've had with the words. Any number of people can read something and be moved by it, but not be able to transmit it. So there is a step beyond that. And that, I suppose, is what you call technique.

Or art?

Or art. Yes. Perhaps. But it's the ability to turn that feeling into the beginning of the growth of a character.

But the difficulty is, Okay, so what do you do when you're doing soap? Do you have a moment of contact with the words? Well, you can kind of push one. But it won't be the same. So it's not an infallible or reliable process.

It's a chaotic process to a certain extent?

Yeah, it can come out as chaos. It can also come out—as in the example I've just given you, or two examples—it can come out of an edge of anger or sadness or unhappiness. And that may be good for your art, but may not be a good way to live your life. Some of the work that I've found most interesting—God knows what anyone else thinks—but in the last few years some of the things that I've done that are probably informed by that edge have been good, and have had an insight to them which I don't think

I've had in the past, and an emotional depth to them which I don't think I've had in the past, but it's not infallible.

I'd rather be happy than have a good edge to my art. And if being a good artist means being unhappy then I'm out of here. I'm going to join the Public Service tomorrow.

But you're not going to because–?

I'm not going to because there's something in me as an artist—as an actor, safer word—that does live on a bit of an edge. I mean, I think most actors I know do live on a bit of an edge. Not because they want to, but because it's the kind of people they are. That's why they're actors. And it's what makes them both interesting and exasperating. And difficult to live with, I suspect.

Well, I guess it's a fine line between that thing of personal equilibrium, a capacity to compose oneself, and also the capacity to de-compose and to throw those things to the wind.

Yeah. Well, that is a problem. You never cease to wrestle with that.

The other thing, of course, in my case—and I suspect with a lot of other actors—I love words. I've always loved languages. I studied Latin. I studied Greek. I studied a bit of German and French, a bit of Italian—I can do menu Italian—and I love it. I find a great contentment in looking at words. I love the way words are spelt. I love their appearance on a page. And each word has a little kind of biography contained in it, and I love that. That helps me. That's why this process works for me because I have this love affair with words.

So the process of making some kind of emotional, intuitive 'connect' with language is a useful one. And I think it's probably the basis of what Stanislavski was trying to say.

I think what Stanislavski has hardened into as a series of processes, has probably killed it to some extent—that early, intangible 'connect'. And I think he tried to find, in looking at what he thought good actors did—and that's what he set out to do—he tried to codify something that can't be codified, because everyone will come at it in their own way.

I have to say that I've been through the Stanislavski mill, and perhaps it wasn't put to me very well, but it didn't work for me. Because what I found was that it was crushing spontaneity. I mean, it's a much more complex thing than that. I found a lot of it very useful. I found the seeking of an active rather than a passive or decorative voice very useful, but for many it's a much more intangible thing. And it doesn't always happen. It's something that if you try to *make* it happen, it will resolutely *not* happen. A bit like erectile dysfunction, really. The more you think about it the less it will happen.

And the kind of epiphany-type moments that you've described, of doing *Lear* the first time and doing *As You Like It*, they surprised you?

Surprised me totally.

And when they do surprise you... The first time that happened, when you were in your 20s playing Lear, you weren't able to intellectualise it?

No, and I meant to say in a great hurry that I wasn't very good. I mean, apart from the fact that I was way too young to be playing Lear. But I remember making the first contact then. Some years later I did *Richard the Second*, which is a role that I make contact with on every word, I have to say. Every single preposition seems appropriate and beautiful, but I was shockin' in that too. The point I mean to make is that having made the contact, and then happily saying it shows you the way—it doesn't always. You need a whole lot of other stuff.

You say you know what it feels like to act badly. What does it feel like?

It feels like you're walking around with lead boots on, basically. You know it's heavy-footed. You know it's causing tiredness in the audience, tiredness in yourself, and you just wish you weren't there. It's a terrible feeling. And one's response to it is usually to push harder and go faster, which is probably the worst thing you can do because everything then turns into a huge, generalised mass.

Can a performance–that's at some point in the evening felt leaden-footed–find its wings later in the night?

Oh, it can. Indeed it can. You can do a shocking... Say, on opening night, because of extraordinary nerves and extraordinary pressure amongst everyone else—everybody's too high—you're not relaxed, so the work is kind of pushed and squeezed, and it won't work. Then maybe at interval you sit yourself down and say, Well, I've stuffed it now. The reviewers have probably gone. I might as well go out and enjoy the Second Act. And it's quite often better.

I saw Bryn Terfel the other night. Absolutely wonderful. He is the quintessence of stage relaxation. He just walks out. He stands there. He knows he's good. He's not up himself. He just stands there, opens his mouth and sings. It's heaven. He has a great gift, and he's worked on his gift. And he looks after himself on stage—you can see it—he doesn't push, doesn't force, doesn't work too hard, but it's wonderful. You go into it. And he's a good actor. Watch him doing Falstaff. It's fantastic.

When you know that it's working, how would you describe that sensation?

Well, you're the last person to know. That's how you describe it. You *don't* know. You come to the last word of the play and you kind of... blink... and the audience start going ape-shit, and you think, Oh, goodness. And I'm really not trying to be cute about this, but it's true. You might get little glimmers, you know, somewhere along the way, and you think, Oo, oh, we're rolling. But that's quite often followed by a major crash, or a dry. You get too smart, or too cute, or you get self-conscious or something.

So to self-congratulate is as dangerous as to self-admonish?

Shocking. Absolutely.

But when you're beyond all those things and you're into that thing I was talking about before, when you're really unconscious of being observed... Very, *very* difficult.

There can be 500, 1,000 people, their phones are going off, they're coughing, they're opening bags with enormous quantities of velcro on them. And they don't think you can hear them. And you can. It can be terribly difficult. But it happens. And when it happens, it's good.

I suppose the last element that I'd want to admit—and I'm talking about things very much at random here—is the quality of imagination. And it's vital. It's part and parcel of making the first 'connect', because your *imagination* makes the 'connect'. But if you don't have that ability to... It's childlike. Watching my grandson at play, you see the immersion of children in play when it's at its best, at its deepest. It's total belief, but it's playing. Two things so wonderfully combined. It's not turgid and it's not like life. It's play. And that's the way to unselfconsciousness.

And that's very difficult. You play *Copenhagen* for six months, it's awfully difficult to remain playful and unselfconscious, and totally immersed in the thing. But you can. I found the best way was to think, I still have no idea what quantum mechanics means, but I've got to talk about it every night, so I really do have to find it afresh every night. And it worked.

Well, talking of specific roles, you say you played Lear poorly in your 20s. You played it very well in your 40s. Were you able to take the lessons from the previous–a previous life–and apply them, or did it surprise you again?

It did surprise me, as it always does, I think, because it is *such* a dark play. I have to say that I think you would play that play differently almost every year of your life.

That's the other thing that happens, you change enormously. The difference between me at 27, and me at whatever I was when I played it again—early 50s—was huge. I think I got about half of it the second time. I didn't get the later years, the later part of the play, I don't think. It's both more exciting and more moving than I let it be. Because I suspect you do have to have the energy of a 50-year-old and the body and mind of an 80-year-old to do it, because there's a kind of an edge and a frustration, but also, a resignation that you really have to understand and be able to be inside. So that when he's finally looking at Tom and says, 'Is man no more than such a poor, bare, forked creature as thou art?', there's a huge, crashing realisation going on that, What is all the fuss about? A man is just flesh and bones and blood and shit and saliva. And, What's to get? What's all this fury about? And then, when he finally realises that he couldn't see the goodness in Cordelia because of all the constructs that he'd put around it, when he does see it, there's this wonderful, Let's go and live in a cave, and just talk to each other, and we'll be in this beautiful, golden light, and it will just be us. That's all I want to do. That is such a changed world. It's very hard to get that speech.

So each time, each year you would approach these same words, it's like different windows are going to open? If you were to play it today presumably you believe that there would be insights or ingress or bridges to your life relating to different elements?

Yes.

So once it gets discovered in a rehearsal room, this lump in the throat, once it comes, how do you remain the master of it?

Well, the text. The text does that for you. It's this complicated equation: You're the vehicle; you're the instrument; the text is moving through you; but finally the text is what the character *is* for the audience, and you can't play the text inappropriately.

You have played an extraordinary number of–and no accident, given your love of words–but you've played a lot of great rhetorical roles, and a lot of great emotional roles. Lear and Leontes are roles of great rhetoric and great emotion, roles from which we inherit expectations of great emotional stuff. What do you do when you know you are inheriting those expectations?

Yeah. It's a good question. You can't take any notice of it. You have to go to the text and say, Well, what does it do to me? What does it do *for* me? And that's what I'm saying about the Jaques thing. I'd looked a lot at that role. It's a role I'd wanted to play forever, and I thought, I don't understand this man. He's just kind of cynical and… There didn't seem to be anything to get hold of until you start, you know, you go into it word by word and start making a connection.

With Leontes, very much the same. I mean, I defy anyone to say a line like, 'Inch thick, knee deep! O'er head and ears a forked one', as if they're on some kind of a picnic. You can't. All those monosyllables do something to you. They affect you. They move you. They force you to speak in chunky, aggro syllables. And if you're alert to anything, you'll get that. Then it's really easy. But unless you allow that to happen, and unless you allow that particularity then it won't happen. You'll be forcing something. You will generalise.

Generalising, I think, is the big enemy. You have to find so much detail, and the detail has to live, and then you have to forget it. Which sounds like a whole lot of contradictions, but it's true. And that's the extent to which the text—particularly in something like Shakespeare—will do it all for you.

It was interesting doing *Cloudstreet*, which was, you know, something else I've done a number of times over a period of time. The thing with *Cloudstreet* was that we did it over a period of nearly four years, and the difference between the first time and the last time I did it was amazing. I think I got the early Lester very well the first time around. I didn't get the later one at all, I don't think. In the later re-stagings of the production, I think the later Lester was really good. I think I really got onto it. Because I'd started having grandchildren—a grandchild… Well, it's not just because of that, it's because of a whole lot of things. But the father quality of Lester became much more significant to me, and it meant a great deal in terms of the performance. It had to be much more real than I'd let it be. I'd thought more about people who have children who are in some way damaged, and really are just operating on unconditional love—which was something I didn't think I'd exhibited greatly in my life. And so all these things happen—and I knew it was different. I think it happened to others as well. We never talked about it greatly, but I felt a change, and I think I *did* change.

So these emotional links will come. They might come when you least expect them, but can they also be anticipated or plotted into the preparation of something?

No. I really don't think so. And that's the tough part. That's where I have a problem with what has become the Stanislavski method.

Or the Strasberg-type–

The Strasberg–Stanislavski, indeed. I think it's important to say that Stanislavski was probably trying to get at something like what I'm talking about. I don't know, but I suspect he was. Something far less tangible than it has been made to become. All you can do is keep yourself open to what's happening to you, and not be afraid to use it because it's a text. And when the text stops, it can stop. If it goes on into the after-show party, then it's gone too far, you know?

But you've got to be able to touch it again the next night. And there is no foolproof method for that.

But what you give a shot to, in terms of trying to touch it the next night, is the physicality of your approach to the words.

Yeah. With me, that works. Nearly always. Well, physicality and the memory of the first contact. The first time you had that gorge-in-the-throat feeling about something you were reading, or the first time you laughed, or felt the… whatever… happen. That will be a more sure indication of what the timing is, what the delivery is, than anything else.

As I've got older I've got more cautious. I used to do anything people offered me, and I felt confident about being able to do it. I don't have that any more because you know the pitfalls.

You also know what works. That's one of the few advantages about getting older as an actor. There aren't many. It's cruel but your memory starts to go. I recently did a piece called *The Fever*, which is an hour and a half monologue, and that's an hour and a half of hugely idiomatic, idiosyncratic writing. Wonderful, but not a way my mind works. I couldn't learn it for so long because I kept going, What? Why is his mind working that way? And, of course, you can't do that. You've got to say, Hang on, *his* mind works that way. You have to acclimatise. You can't try and turn things into something they're not, because then you'll fall over. But the point I was making was, you know, an hour and half monologue is quite a big ask for a 60-year-old mind.

You have to work smarter. You have to. It's survival. You've got to find ways of doing less, and having more impact with the little you do. I guess that's something that I'm learning.

One of the points of contention about acting is—it seems that one school says that having discovered the emotional connection to something, you observe how it is manifested, and subsequently you imitate that gesturally and tonally.

Doesn't work. Look, some people can do it. But it doesn't work for me. I can't imitate. I can sort of ease myself into the same position emotionally and physically but it has to find a link to the same process as the original 'connect'. That's all I can say. It doesn't always work, but it's better when it does. You get smart enough to be able to fake it. You have to, because it's unreliable. It's not ideal.

So some audiences get the real McCoy, and other audiences get your best simulation of it?

Sometimes you can't tell the difference.

Do you think they can reliably tell the difference?

I think some. They may not even know it consciously, but they can tell. I mean, if you are in the presence of genuine emotion you recognise it immediately. Immediately. We seem to be able to telegraph that. There's really no choice.

We're talking about empathy. Two separate empathetic experiences: the first is between you and words that were written by another human being however long ago; and the second is when you stand up in front of the tribe, an empathy between them and you?

A purveyor. And the less you're aware of the people that you're conveying these emotions and these feelings to, the more it will work. That's the paradox of what we are as actors. The way we do the thing we do is to go in the opposite direction. You are my client, as an audience, and now I'm going to forget you. I'm going to go over here and make a telephone call and you're going to watch me make the call and get involved in the call. It's such a hard thing to do.

What about when a role has you manifest behaviour—physically and vocally—that is other than your normal realm of behaviour? When you're playing someone who is markedly unlike yourself. Is there a pattern for how those things enter?

They tend to come as intuitions rather than as plans. I think, in terms of it being outside your normal boundaries of behaviour or patterns of thinking, quite often the things you imitate best, the things you speak about most forcefully, the things you think about most cogently, are the things you don't like.

It's very interesting to look at the way people imitate each other. They often imitate people they don't like very well. There's something about what they don't like that's impinging on them and printing itself on some kind of template, then it comes back. But if you ask them to do an imitation of their best day-to-day buddy, their friend, they probably couldn't do as good an imitation as they would do of, say, a politician that they hated, or a school chaplain. It's very interesting.

To an actor, the exotic—in the strict sense of the word, something that's outside their range of behaviour—is what's fascinating. I've never been a murderer, but I've played a lot of them. I've never been a woman, but I've played a few. And it's wonderful. It's amazing.

I remember, years ago, in a company called A Shakespeare Company—that Rex Cramphorn was behind—we did *The Two Gentlemen* in which I gave my Sylvia, the most beautiful woman in the known world.

'At first I did adore a twinkling star / But now I worship a celestial sun.'

That's the one! Well, the costume I had to wear reminded me of those photos you used to see of women playing at Wimbledon in the 1920s. Very long tennis dress, Chinese shoes that had been whitened. No attempt to do make-up or long hair or anything like that. But I had this kind of generalised tabard that we all wore because Rex's thing was: The text will clothe you entirely, so what we're going to wear is something that will say, This is a person who is not wearing the insignia of that character; this is a person who is simply appearing as a cipher for the words. And it was amazing. Most of the time in rehearsal I thought, Well, I'm just being me, and if that's a woman, well then, that's a woman. But it's amazing how it worked. I didn't change my way of moving. I didn't alter the pitch of my voice. I suppose it was my first lesson in responding to a certain measured and gracious quality in the writing, beyond that which is rough and male. It was very hard but, boy, it was an interesting acting exercise.

You see, I keep coming back to Shakespeare. Shakespeare does it *for* you. In a sense it's very easy with Shakespeare. I mean, if you do *Twelfth Night*, and you get to speak Olivia or Viola, you could be, you know, a front-row footballer, but if you spoke it with any attention to the text, it would have to be female.

I have a theory about the role of Hamlet. That one of the reasons that it's arguably the most famous role is that it's kind of characterless. That anyone can–

I think you're right. And the mistake you see when people make quite visual decisions about what Hamlet looks like, is they're immediately excluding 90 per cent of the possibilities of the text.

I say Shakespeare's easy to talk about because he does it *for* you. But when you come to texts that are more, I suppose, closer to us and less descriptive of the character and require a good degree of construction of an emotional and intellectual life for the character that's not contained in what you actually say and do, then it's harder.

Recently Kerry Walker and I did a piece called *The Unexpected Man*, by Yasmina Reza. It's a series of monologues, really. It was extraordinary. He's a man who's very embittered. And I had just had a rather bitter relationship break-up—or it was actually happening at the time—and I found things. Things started happening for me in the role that I was not prepared for. They just happened. Suddenly a phrase would get bitten off, and you'd think, Where did that come from? And this is my predicament. I mean, I got an award for that!

It's another way of saying what I've been saying all afternoon. These things come unbidden. I didn't set out to do those roles and to use what was going on in my life. In fact, if anything, when those things happen to you as a person you are often in denial about them. So, you know, the connections come just by saying the words in a certain context. And that's back to my real conundrum. It goes back to my original conflict, which is that there seems no doubt that the best things I do tend to be informed by emotions that I am either having or have remembered vividly. Now I don't think there's anything odd about that, but I don't seem to be able to retrieve them at will. So the process is hopeful rather than purposeful. And I certainly don't want to live my life on the edge so that I'll be able to do my homework better!

To play a murderer or to do something that is outside your experience, do you do imaginative preparation to allow yourself to do that?

It's hard to generalise. I looked at Eric Bana doing Chopper Read. I thought he was fantastic. I don't know Chopper. I've seen him interviewed a couple of times, and it seemed to me that Eric Bana isn't particularly like Chopper Read, but he was fantastic. I suppose what he did was take whatever was written down—which I presume was reasonably documentary, but I don't know that either—and process it for himself. I suppose he did some imitating of Chopper. However, if you're going to do Macbeth—a *fictional* murderer—I suppose you look at the lives of some of the great murderers. But, finally, the text will tell you what to think anyway, and it will give you the psychological links between what's happening in the world and what you're doing.

I made a big mistake, early on, when I was doing *Richard the Second*. I read everything about the real Richard the Second. Big mistake. Because I wanted to find out something about kingship. But the play's not actually about kingship. It's about a whole lot of things that happen to be uttered by a king. And that's a very different proposition. What I was playing a lot of the time was my research, which was meaningless to the audience and actually meaningless to me. You can't act research which is in a history book but isn't in the play. I mean, it's such a basic mistake I should've been shot. But there you are. You do it.

I do less and less of it because I find it more interesting to approach the role as if I've just picked up the paper and am reading the news for that morning. Oh, there's an appalling incident in Redfern where an Aboriginal child has been killed. The Aboriginal people say one thing, the police say another. What's going on? And, you know, you read that with the whole flood of information from your general knowledge of the world, then you start to apply your thought processes to a role you might be playing. I think that's more important.

Look, I'm about to do *Victory*, the Howard Barker, which is set at the time of the restoration of Charles the Second. It's a wonderful piece. Now I've certainly done some reading about Oliver Cromwell and the other people, and Charles and the Restoration, but, truly and really, you could do that play without reading any research at all.

So why do you read it?

Well, I read it because I would like to get a bead on why Howard Barker has taken certain things and changed them. Or whether he has. I'd like to see what his stance is. It probably won't affect how I play the role. I don't know. But it used to be terribly important to me to do all those sort of things because I couldn't enter the rehearsal space without them. Then I realised I'd probably have been better off to have just read the play another couple of times.

What do you think are the specific demands of taking your acting process and putting it in front of a camera?

I don't think I'm very good at it, so I'm not sure I should speak about that. I always feel I'm caricaturing whatever I'm doing when I watch myself back. But I don't think the basic principles of acting for a camera are very different. You physically have to make a big adjustment, I think. You have to do less. And if ever there was a need to *be* what you're doing rather than *demonstrate* what you're doing, then film makes you do that. You can't demonstrate. You can still do big acting—look at Geoffrey in *Shine*. Huge. Wonderful. Totally complete and perfect. But big. He was *in* it. And, boy, you can tell on film when people aren't. Much more than in a play, I suspect. So I suppose that's all I would want to say.

He's bloody good, this guy

ROBERT GRUBB

Robert Grubb was among the first people I thought of for this book. One of the reasons for this is the breadth of his experience. Here's an actor who was part of Jim Sharman's near-legendary Lighthouse acting troupe, and who has worked in television in over 30 different shows. Way out on another limb of the industry, Robert can be found pursuing a career as one of Australia's leading actors in musical theatre, with roles in Sunset Boulevard, Into the Woods, Company *and* Mama Mia!, *among many others. When one full career would be enough for most of us…*

Above these impressive credentials, there is another reason why Robert was a clear target.

Among the ideals spruiked by acting teachers all over the world is one which suggests that actors should spend all of their time in rehearsals trying new things. We should embrace failure, be unafraid of looking silly, discover all the wrong ways of doing things in order to discard them. Invent, invent, invent more, constantly tossing out what doesn't work, and retaining the ten per cent of ideas that do. This is one of the mantras with which idealistic teachers annoy the hell out of acting students. The ego-less actor! The actor totally without fear of failure! Such an actor doesn't exist, and the harping guilt-trip of pretending he does can be put in the same useless category as the 'Why-don't-you-sound-like-John-Geilgud?' school of voice teaching.

In 25 years I've only ever seen one actor come close to fulfilling this mythical process, and that's Robert Grubb. I've never worked with a more playful actor, nor one who tries so many new things, nor one who makes so many welcome, joyful mistakes in rehearsal, nor one who whittles the bones of what remains so finely. He is a consummate pro. Well, nobody leads a long-running TV show or a long-running musical without being a thorough pro, but he is also a great searcher. It's an inspiring combination.

The important thing is to be believable in the role, I think. I suppose that often comes down to the minutiae, and the character being comfortable with himself. That's difficult to say if you're playing someone who's a neurotic load of nerves or something like that, but I think the job you've got to do as an actor is to… When people sit down and watch it they've got to absolutely believe that you are who you're meant to be.

Usually when I'm doing a play I read books that are to do with the time. I mean, if you're doing a play set in the 1760s or something, you go and find a book that's set in that time. It's great. And that'll kind of tip you off with a few little bits and pieces, you know? And those little bits, those little minute things, add to the foundation, so when the time comes to go out there and perform, you know you've got a solid foundation underneath you. You feel comfortable.

I've worked with various people where each night it's just a little bit different, and some nights it's hugely different. I actually like that because I feel confident about where I am.

Because of this research you've done?

Partly that, yeah. And if I get a little bit of something different back, well then, Hey… You've just got to be able to work with whatever you get.

I worked with Gillian Jones in Adelaide a couple of times. When I originally went to work with her I said to somebody, What's she like? And they said, Oh, I didn't like working with her. Or something like that. She was different all the time, with everything. And I went along thinking, Oh, this could be a bit touchy here. But in the end I really loved it. Most of the time it was just subtle nuances which were slightly different. And then every sixth night or something, there'd be, bang!, a big change in the way she delivered something or meant something. To me it kept it really fresh and alive, and I just responded to it. If you're well prepared you should be able to handle most of those things, because the lines are going to be the same, the blocking's going to be pretty much the same, you know? It's just—

The instantaneous dynamics.

Yeah. Occasionally the blocking might change a *bit*, but I didn't mind.

Most times I find you lock into something—that's what you do each time. And yes, the lighting guys need to know that, and all that sort of stuff, and that's what's been directed. But she felt confident about her stage craft and what was happening and so did I, so we actually had a really good time.

At that point in your career you would have been in your early 30s, working at Lighthouse, which was one of the most esteemed ensembles in recent Australian theatre history. I'm interested to hear you talk about that being a learning experience, learning from other actors. Was there a fundamental change in how you saw the whole business of going on stage? That you saw it suddenly as a more fluid thing?

Probably, yeah. With most of the people I'd worked with up until that stage, you'd rehearse, and you'd do all of your exploring in rehearsal. Once you came close to going on, everything would be locked down, in a way. I'm not saying you did things exactly the same each night—

It's a thing of degree, isn't it?

Yeah. You're working with an audience too. They play a huge part in all that.

I'd come to drama rather late—I was in my mid–20s when I started acting—and here we were—early 80s or mid–80s, something like that—doing this thing at Lighthouse. I'd come through drama school where they like you to be extremely creative but then tend to lock you down for performance. Then when I first went to Adelaide, I was under Colin George for a while, and he was from that sort of older school of English training where everything was—

Setting things.

Setting things. Exactly. And here we were, we'd come to Lighthouse, and there was a lot more freedom to try so many different things. Jim Sharman had picked a bunch of people he thought would constantly bounce off each other. And it was true. We'd been given the right to bounce off each other, and that made it that little bit fresher every night. So when I started working there—especially with Gillian—I found that this was something that I really hadn't been bold enough to explore before.

I was still pretty much a novice. I'd only been in the industry three or five years or so. Here I am, out there, doing this stuff. Previously, I'd felt pride in making my performance pretty much right on what had been directed. You know, strong, comfortable, as believable as I could, and just doing things as they were written and directed and set. Not wavering.

I take a lot of things back to sport. I love sports of all descriptions. I especially love team sports. And here I am, in a play, and it really is a team effort. Look at a football team or something like that. The backline might be falling apart but there's that one character who's doing his job and holding it together. That was *me*, in my own mind. I've never said that to anyone else really, but that was partly what I was trying to achieve.

I think about hitting a golf ball. To hit a golf ball you need to be relaxed and focussed. And it seems to me that's precisely what you need to act with too.

Yeah. A couple of years ago something dawned on me. I'd always been pretty relaxed about things. And someone came up to me and said, Oh, God, you're just so relaxed out there. This person was quite nervous. How do you achieve that? And I said, Well, you know your lines and you know where you're meant to be. You feel confident in working with the people you're working with. There's no real problem. Look at it this way, you're going into a situation where you know exactly what you're going to be saying for the next two hours. You know exactly what all those people are going to be saying to *you* for the next two hours. You know what's going to happen, where you're going to be at almost every particular point in time. So what have you got to be worried about? It's more stress, in a way, to just walk across the street.

It sounds to me like you're talking about a journey where you've recognised that not everything has to be set, and the fact that some things are set is a security, but some things can remain fluid.

Absolutely.

And now you've grown to a point where there's a security in the fluidity as well. You're not afraid of the *play*.

Yeah. And that comes with time.

I think all this stuff about getting to keep certain areas fluid is only because I've reached a point in my career where I feel so confident about all the other stuff I know I can handle that. I *like* it when things get a little bit fluid. But I don't know if I'd have had that confidence when I was just kicking off.

I find sometimes you get—it's usually a young fella who's just out of drama school—suddenly they're out and they don't have to keep the structure or whatever and they're exploring with a little bit of freedom. And that can just spray everywhere—trying to be Brando, but it's just going on everywhere. You need moments of focus, because we're the instrument that leads the audience, and points out all those little bits and pieces that they need to know to get the story.

Well, sometimes, there can be a lot of misinformation coming from what actors are doing, and people go out at interval and you hear them saying, What's this about? So you can get the odd young fella who's out there and just throwing it to the wind. That's a different sort of fluidity to what I'm talking about. That's just... I don't know. And you've got to ride with it. It's a young person just having a bit of a fling. It might only be a transient thing. But unfortunately it might last for the whole run of the play, and then in the next one they get they might go, Oh, I don't think I'll do that this time. I probably made it a bit hard for myself.

Is that a failure to recognise the moments that work and put the pins in the board, sort of thing?

Sometimes I've worked with people who... You can see they aren't recognising those moments that work. Because a moment between you will work, and you know it's worked, and you can feel the audience go, Yeah. They're right with you. But then you do it the next night with that same person, and it's not there. They're trying something else.

This happy balance between what needs to be set, and what level of fluidity you employ around that, how does that affect the way you actually rehearse?

I do like to explore. I do try to *use* the rehearsal. Any idea I get, I like to go in big. Not expansive, I don't mean that, I mean go in... If I see the character being depressed, I like to go in and give it a real full depression thing. Or if I see him being happy, give it a real full happiness. In certain sections, though, not all the time.

To test it?

Yeah. So, therefore, the director can see what I'm doing, what I'm aiming for, and he can say, Yeah, that was good. Go more that way. And you've got to trust that he's out there looking in. He can't get a full appreciation of what you're going to do unless he can see the full thing. If you're only giving him a little pissy image of what it's going to be like, then he's got nothing to work off.

And I feel also that by going bolder early on, you cut through a lot of things quite quickly. Then you get to an area where you can—in those last couple of weeks before you open the play—you can spend a lot more time on all the other smaller stuff, which I really, really enjoy. Starting small and just fiddling around for a while, that sort of works for me in some areas.

You can actually make huge strides in the first week, when the director says, Ah, nah, nah, we don't want to go there. Or, Yeah, that's really terrific, let's explore that. You've already got something coming back from the director. Already we're starting to talk about stuff.

I came to acting school... I was an electrician one day, had a bit of a holiday, and next thing I'm flying up to NIDA. So it was all new to me. I was the only one there who hadn't been to a drama class. At NIDA they'd give us a play in first year or something like that, and we'd be doing bits and pieces, and I'd be real quiet in rehearsal. Then I'd go home and get the book out, and I'd be practising at night. Then I'd come in the next day with what I'd practised and the director would said, Where did that come from? No, no, no, no. You've got to do your rehearsal on the *floor*, in *here*, where we can *all* put in, you know? So I changed.

I was still a bit nervous about not knowing as much as the other people. But funnily enough, there were other areas I felt really confident about.

Like as soon as we got in front of people. I felt a great confidence because, you see, yes, I'd been an electrician, but I'd also had five or six years singing in a rock band and doing a bit of MC work down in Hobart. You know, what works in that environment is real energy. Energy that you're focussing into your performance. You've got to turn that switch and turn yourself on when you walk out in front of people. Even if you're just playing the guy who's going to stand in the corner and do nothing much. You've still got to radiate some sort of energy. So I had that down.

There's this other kind of energy—I call it the Ninja Performance. This has happened to me a couple of times. You work with someone in rehearsal, you go away, then come opening night, you walk out on stage and this other person brings out something else entirely. This fabulous performance that they've just sort of concocted, and it's like they sneak up on you and get you. I call them Ninjas. I hear it happened to Phil Quast over in England when he did *Sunday in the Park with George*.

Which is very different to the kind of surprises you were talking about working with Gillian.

That's right. Gillian would be doing something because she's, like, giving her soul to the show, the script. She reads me. If she does something really big, well, what am I going to do? I react to that, and that therefore gives her something to go with.

But the Ninja, I think, is downright selfish.

We've been talking a little bit about what not to do between rehearsals. Don't go home and rehearse.

Well, you'll always do that. You'll always go home and do this, do that. But don't go home and concoct this whole scenario that you're going to do. Because you're already negating stuff that is going to be put in.

So what *do* you do between rehearsals?

You use that time just thinking about your character, what he says about who, and who says what about him. If it's a period piece, then reading about the times. Because you've got to be absolutely into everything. It's no good coming out, looking like the King of France, if you're uncomfortable in all the gear. You've got to realise that, yeah, people had nits in their hair and that gives you the chance to... You can still talk to the other person, but you can bring out a stick and start scratching your head under your wig. All these bits can be a nice little touch. The director will say, No, or he'll say, That's great.

But what are such things doing for you? Are they kind of having an internal effect on you?

Yeah. Exactly.

Because you're talking about believability. Are those things helping you believe yourself?

Yes, it's putting down a bigger foundation. A nice, solid foundation. You can launch yourself off it or you can stand steady on it. You make a strong foundation. You build on it.

Richard Wherrett gave us some tuition when I was at NIDA. He said, Look, give yourself an objective each day. It can be as simple as, I am going to go home and I'm going to turn up tomorrow and I'm going to know all my lines between page ten and page twenty. Or something like, I'm going to look at every time I exit, and think about if they're all the same, or if I can take a different door, or whatever. Some little thing. Even if it's something weird, like, I'm just going to see if I can take my shoes off during a scene, and put them back on. Something. Give yourself some objective and try it. Think about it and try it.

What do you do when you feel like you're stuck, either in a role or maybe just in a moment, in a beat of a play?

Robert Grubb as Robert 'Bob' King and Felix Williamson as John Alderston in the 1994 Playbox Theatre production of *Sanctuary*. (Photo: Jeff Busby)

Oh, this happens quite a few times. I'll find I'll be going through a play, and there'll be some point where I lose concentration or stumble over my words. I often go to whoever's on the script, the stage manager, and I say, You know when I'm doing this speech, or this scene? Can you just put a little pencil mark wherever I stumble or wherever I forget my lines? Then later on I'll go over and see the pencil marks—it might only be in about one or two sentences. Then you know that in that area, your subconscious is saying, Uh-uh, something's wrong here.

Like a wonky floorboard or something?

Yeah, yeah. So you've got to really look at it, really focus on that little piece, and really try and solve the problem.

Of course I've explored the script to find out if I'm saying something that's not quite right in the script, or I'm saying stuff that I've just gone along with. But I haven't sat down and said to the director, Hang on a minute. Did this really happen this particular way? Or I might be saying stuff that I don't really know about, you know? I might be too shy to say, Oh, I don't really understand that word, or something like that. Or it might be that something's wrong with the whole direction for that section.

Maybe it's the attack, the dynamic of it is—not all wrong but slightly wrong. I just go and try and—

At first I explore the whole script and take it down to thoughts. Every sentence. Why does that lead onto the next sentence? Then I look at it over a run of six sentences. What's the string? Where is this person's mind going? I might look at it and say, No, he's not angry, he's defensive. He's hurt. He's sad. Maybe it's not attack, maybe it's defence. A perfect example is standing or sitting. You're in a situation where you're doing something but your whole body wants to get up. You might be sitting and the director wants you to stay there because the vision looks good. But you might say, Wait a minute. Can we just try it this way? And we might try it and it breaks his mould. He says, Yeah, it *is* better. It's more confronting or something like that. It adds to the drama.

You've got to get the microscope out and look at every little bloody thing. And try things. Some little thing, like the position of your body, can be the thing that solves the problem. See, your memory of lines, even, that's connected to your position too. The point I'm making is, if things aren't right with your head—things like lines and how you deliver them—well, it's more than likely because something's wrong with your body, where you are on stage or what shape you're making, what position you're in.

Shoes are very important. I like to get the shoes right. I don't know why, but it's like building from the feet up, in a way. I get the shoes right, and then I feel... The first time we go into costumes I get a little bit particular about shoes, you know? I want something good to work in. Often they're trying to bung you in some daggy old shoes that haven't been worn for seven years. And that's okay, you realise they don't have a huge budget. But ask if you can take them home and wear them around a little bit at home, whatever. Usually I'll put the shoes on and feel, Yeah, this is right. I can see him. And that starts to get all the juices going, because costume plays a huge part.

I want to ask a question about the idea of your emotional life and your emotional history as a person and how and where that sits in your work. How do you deal with big emotional challenges in a role?

Honestly, I just get there any way I can. Yes, if you can bring up things from your past, your history, that are going to help you get into the zone, then yeah, do it.

Have you done that?

A couple of times.

Does that mean that your focus has an instantaneous shift to something else? To bring it in?

Oh, that's a funny sort of thing. You've almost got tiers. You've got this person almost organising it all, organising the feelings, manipulating the feelings so that the actor person can portray it out there. It's, like, the mind goes, Okay, I've got to turn *that* key now to get *that* result to push *that* out. But that person at the back has always got to be in control. He's got to know when to use that little thing and when to put it away. And it's got to be put away because the play must go on, the scene must go on, or the film, or whatever it is.

Some people can do it just like *that*. I've worked with people in TV—especially in TV—who are just brilliant at banging it on.

Lenore Smith—when we were doing *Flying Doctors*—she had that wonderful ability to just… Okay, Lenore, we might need some tears. She'd go, That'll be all right. Then she'd go and take a moment for herself. Okay. Ready? Rolling. And you'd be doing the scene, and something would be said, and bang!, she'd be there. The tears would come or whatever it is, and then, Cut. And she'd just take a moment and she'd be right. And sometimes she'd have to do it seven, eight, nine, ten times, but it's always there, and she always gets into it okay and comes out of it okay. That's difficult for me, I can't… There are many other actors and actresses who can just do that, and it's an amazing talent in itself.

That brings us to the whole business of what happens to you when you shift to TV. What adjustments do you make to the way you work? Are there any?

Oh, God, you've got to try and keep yourself well because, if you've got a lead role, you're working every day, just about. You're getting picked up at six o'clock each morning and you work until seven, eight at night—you have that little bit of family time or whatever, and then you've got to be into your books to learn what you're going to do tomorrow. Try and get some sleep before you're getting up early in the morning again to be picked up. And that constantly, day after day. I don't know what happens, but it's like you gird your loins. Everything's condensed, in a way. Your concentration becomes bloody good. You can look at a scene and you don't think you're going to even get it down, but somehow you do. It's a tough bloody business.

You get a lot of great rewards out of it, but you've got to take your hat off to people who are doing it week in, week out.

Learning the lines is torture sometimes. When we did *Flying Doctors* there was no walk-through, because of the pace of it all—they had to get a certain amount in the can each day. So you'd drive to the studio and do a scene there, jump in a car, drive out into the country to a location and do a scene there. You're learning your lines in the car. You've just got to take what you get. Like we were saying with working with those people who bring things out of the bag—you've just got to take what you get and work with it.

You work amazingly quickly. Luckily, when I was doing *Flying Doctors*, I had people who had worked in TV quite a bit, so I learnt very quickly from them.

I also learnt that you're often *talking* about stuff because they don't have the budget to *show* it, you know, to *film* it. So you've somehow got to make all that stuff interesting. You can just say the lines and get on with it, and that's the end of the scene. But we always felt it was better to say the lines and also have another layer of something going on. We'd have these scenes where we'd have all this crap to say, and before we'd start the scene we'd work out a little joke to put in there, a little visual joke. Therefore you've given them a laugh *and* you've told them a story. We used to do that all the time.

It's dealing with basic exposition in a creative way.

That's it.

Can you talk a bit about the corresponding challenges of being in a musical? I mean, so much of your performance is set in a musical, isn't it? You're going to sing *these* notes. And the character *is* what the character *sings*.

Musicals are a very different bag, in that from the moment you start, you're almost going to a beat. There's a timing to everything. Even if it's 'Send in the Clowns'. You're going to a count, almost, and that bleeds all the way through, even in the scenes where there's no music. You've got to keep moving forward.

Musicals are all about heightened reality. And there's usually a stylised thing to it, however subtle it may be, so you've constantly got to be aware that you can't really dilly-dally with anything. Everything is concentrated. You've only got certain moments before the musical flicks onto someone else and all of a sudden they're on a song and they're doing that for the next four minutes. And then you're back onto some other thing. So you probably have to point things just a little bit more. You take your moment a little bit more when you get it.

Like a follow-spot?

Almost, yes. Whoever that follow-spot's on, you allow them to do it. And there's another thing. When it's not on you—much more than in a play—you tone it right down. The audience just has to know, Who's speaking? What's he got to say? Who's next? What have you got to say? Okay. *Song*! If you have problems with that, then you probably shouldn't get involved with it. You just sort of cut through a lot of stuff. Be that little bit bolder about the presentation of that little bit of information you're giving.

It's all part of the contract, isn't it?

Yeah. All part of the culture of that sort of thing. When you go in and pay and sit down for a musical—whatever it might be, even if it's Sondheim—you accept that—

Presentational style?

Yes, in a way. The reality of it all is just extended. Heightened. It really is. And don't be shy about it.

Embracing the artificiality of it?

Yes. Yes. You go along to see a little bit of artificiality.

Because there's artificiality in every kind of theatre, right? It's essentially artificial.

Oh, it is, yes.

But degrees of artificiality exist in different types of theatre.

Yes.

Do those degrees of artificiality also affect the degree of the controlling going on inside you? You talked about the actor-at-the-back earlier, who's kind of making decisions while the wilder beast is off the leash. Is there more control in doing musicals?

I think there has to be because it's not all about you. You have to work with the conductor. You have to work with, well, with what the whole show is about. You have your time in the sun, you've got to grab it. You've got to do something with it before you hand it over to someone else and there's a song. And the bits in between the songs have to be crisp and clear and moving forward.

Not muddied?

That's it. With a play you can afford a few different things. You can get into a scene and if you know the audience is with you—you can tell, you can hear that pin drop, you know that they're there—you can ask that question, and you can hold back on the answer just that little bit longer. It's not a technical thing. It's just feeling it.

There's more licence for elasticity.

Yeah. In a stage drama there *is* more elasticity—a very good word.

You find, with film, the technical does come in, but it's... Usually a good director won't be saying, Turn your head on that line and look up at such and such. Usually a good director would be saying, And right about the time you're going to talk to her, you hear a crow on that tree over there. Just register the crow. And *that* speaks to an actor much more than, Turn your head.

Because you're being provoked rather than instructed.

Exactly. He's put the image in your mind. I've worked with both kinds of directors. You get the type of guy who says, Oh, we want you to come in, walk two paces then stop. Then I want you to count to about five, then move on. And that's the only direction he gives you! Now, you can do that, but in your own mind you've got to relate it to, Okay, I've come into the scene, I walk in, I smell something's burning. You think, Have I left the friggin' iron on? I'd better go look. In your own mind, you've done something, and the director doesn't need to know what. He'll still keep coming up with all that technical crap, but you've—

Translated it.

Yeah, you've got to be able to.

I wanted to ask you about one role. And the reason I want to ask you about it is that, a little like in a musical, it was a role where you knew the expectations, you knew what you had to do before you started. And that's when you did the little Jeff Kennett turn in *Mercury*, where you didn't have the licence to decide, I reckon this guy behaves like this, because he's right there in front of you, and he's on the front page of the papers every day. Talk about that challenge.

I went for essence, in a way, more than trying to just copy. I didn't want to go out there and… I knew they were doing my hair and—I didn't say anything about hair or cozzie—I just knew exactly what they were on about. From reading the script. It was all about this government and that government and the newspaper. I said, Right, I don't want to get out there and try and *do* a copy of Jeff Kennett. It was all there—the costume, the things I'm saying—I don't have to worry about all that stuff. I just had to think about the essence of this character. So I started to think about the type of qualities that I figured Jeff Kennett has, along with the things he does in the script.

Everything I put out, I tried to make as a positive. Like, he was forceful. He was forceful because if he was wishy-washy things wouldn't get done. He wanted things to be done and didn't want to hang around. Push 'em through! If he was a bit bellicose, pushed people around a bit, so what? I kept thinking of things like Dermie Brereton. These tough footballers who go out and are stars on the field. They're stars on the field because they get out there and push people around and make a statement. They kick goals, they take huge marks and they dominate everyone else. They put their stamp on the game. And that's the sort of the thing I was doing. That was my Dermie Brereton. I was out there playing. I took those sporting images, and all the things from the script, and just spoke to myself in positives.

And you trusted that the externals would be looked after by everybody else?

I didn't touch any of that. I just came in and they did my hair and whatever. They did this, they did that. I just went out there, I said things the way I wanted to say them, and I treated my fellow actors as if they were—those who were on my side—as if they were lesser beings, like forward-pocket sort of characters. And those others who were against me, I just treated them like Dermott Brereton would treat the Essendon characters. That sort of stuff.

One of the challenges of that gig I suppose was that at the same time you could turn on the TV on any given night and see a sketch-version Kennett. But there are different levels of presenting something, aren't there? Like, if you were doing Kennett on a sketch comedy show, you'd be interested in different things. A different agenda?

Yes. Because if you're doing a take-off of this guy, you're doing it with the wisdom of… It's almost as if there's another person on top going, Oo, take the piss. You know? And I knew that was not the way to go. If you're doing a character, in a way, you have to care for him. You've got to love that character. You've got to care for him.

Which relates to the word you began with: 'believability'. Believing yourself.

Yeah. And to do that, with this guy, I had to take the character's negatives and do them as positives. How many actors have done a great performance, and then the crit comes out and they hated the performance because he did this and this and this. And you look at it and you think, Shit, they didn't understand me. Well, in the case of Jeff Kennett, people didn't like what he was doing. But from his point of view it was, Oh, they don't understand the big picture. They don't understand what we're trying to achieve. So you could love him. I could love him. I'd say, Nah, he's bloody good, this guy. He's kickin' arse.

And is that the key to that believability? Achieving that empathy and that love? Turning all the character's idiosyncrasies or peccadilloes into positives?

Yes. I think so. I think we all know we've got faults, but we constantly excuse ourselves, and get around things. We've got to like ourselves a bit just to get through the day, to get through our lives. Well, with whatever character I play, I try and find the things I really love about them. It might be difficult sometimes, but you eventually find them, and bang!, that's the little kernel. That's the seed. And from that seed grows this thing. Find that little bit you love and you'll find others. Eventually, in a week's time, you'll find all these other bits that you like about them, and then you like that whole character. That's really good. I love him.

The unseen character

HELEN BUDAY

Many fine actors have an exotic quality about them as people, something other-worldly, something that makes them intrinsically interesting and magnetic. It is a discomforting fact that the lack of such a quality often keeps the diligent, earnest 'workers-in-song' from greatness.

Helen Buday has such intangible and bloody unfair gifts. This 'specialness' was evident to those of us who were lucky enough to see her as a teenager at NIDA, where her Juliet acquired some small fame for the intensity and depth of her breaking heart.

Twenty years later, Helen's power held together the odd chords of Rolf de Heer's challenging film, Alexandra's Project. *Alexandra must—for nearly the entirety of the film—keep Gary Sweet and the audience spellbound. Spell-binders don't come by the dozen.*

Helen has played leading roles with all of Australia's major companies. She has played Shakespeare, Chekhov, Ibsen, along with Eliza Doolittle in My Fair Lady, *and an almost frighteningly perfect Sally Bowles in* Cabaret.

Helen has won Best Actress awards from the Sydney Critics' Circle and the Variety Heart Club, she has been twice nominated for Mo Awards in the Female Musical Theatre Performer category, in 1992 and 1995. She was nominated for a Glug Award in 1999 for her Lady Macbeth, and for an AFI for Alexandra's Project, *the role for which she won the 2003 Best Actress award at the Spanish International Film Festival.*

I interviewed Helen at her Coogee flat, with her young son, Kasper, playing happily around us. Helen was among those actors who spoke passionately about the hardships of an actor's life. She actually recommended a coffee-table book—photo-spreads of actors' houses—as a means of dispelling any remaining myths of glamour. She was bemused by my description of her career as a success. I understand that. An actor can do a week's work that gives people an impression of constancy, then be unemployed for months. But the success of Helen's career is as much about quality as quantity, quality to which we all aspire.

I don't think there's anything common in my approach to every role, because the mix is always different. It's a different director, a different design. For me, I guess it's text first.

What about it?

Sense. Just the sense, really.

I've often been accused of being a slow burner, of not really coming up with much in the rehearsal room. The performance part of it, though, that's a whole other chapter. But in rehearsal, I just like being really, really clear—with the blocking, as well, the shape—before it can lift and take off. I think that's something to do with my dance training, the sort of dance training where you're used to blocking things first. Marking it. I've never been very good at not marking things in rehearsal.

But it's such a multi-layered thing as it grows, and everybody else grows with it, you know?

You say you start with the text, but how much of the text can be absorbed before you go to rehearsals? How much pre-rehearsal work is useful?

The more the better. But once you get into the room and you see the other people involved, and there's interaction, then a lot of things fall into place. Your responses to the text feed into it, make it easier.

How do you know when you're starting to get somewhere?

I don't know that I've ever tested it or wondered at it. I've just taken for granted that there's an accumulation going on.

You're someone who's played Nina, and spoken those words about how it feels to act badly. What is the feeling of acting badly, and what's the feeling of acting well, and what's the journey?

Self-knowledge. But there are lots of people who act badly and don't know they're acting badly. Surely.

I can look back—on Nina—and know that I might have got close to something in the Second and Third Acts, but I had no idea what I was doing in the Fourth Act. None at all.

But I do remember—that was the first time I worked with Jean-Pierre Mignon—I do remember that thing of getting up quickly. Usually you have a read-through, you have a look at the designs, and then you sit around reading it for a couple of weeks. Jean-Pierre spoke about the body not being bent, so we stood and read. We walked when we wanted to. I remember being quite shocked by that.

The body not bent. You mean bent in contemplation?

Yeah. In reading and analysing. He wasn't too fussed about that. It all happened on the floor. And I remember that being terrific. Because it was a physical thing. If you're standing up, there's so much more energy, and you realise, Ah, there's *this* many people in the space.

Would you go so far to say that you can't really trust your impressions until they're embodied? One of the things that's clear about the American books, a tendency in those 'System' or 'Method' books, is that they seem to rely on a 'conditioning' of the self, and *then* taking that 'conditioned' actor into rehearsals. They do this conditioning–indeed what we might call character work–in relation to the text, but in isolation from the group. That seems kind of anathema to Aussie actors. We tend to think of characterisation as something that happens along the way, don't we?

Yeah, and that smells of maybe being up yourself or something.

Or being not as open to experiential things as one might be?

The group, yeah.

What else happens along the way to make you start to feel good?

Something will lock in, something will, 'tt'. Something will lock in and just feel right. And then that becomes a reference point.

What's the physical experience of that happening?

Well, something just... works. There are people watching, in the rehearsal room, and something is received, I guess. Something just... 'tt'.

You feel that you've transmitted something?

Yeah. Yeah.

And does that moment–the first of those moments–become like a hook? That it informs other things?

Yeah. I'm thinking of when I was doing *The Importance of Being Earnest*, and the moment when Cecily learns that Earnest's name is Algernon, or Algy, and I remember that Wilde's line is, 'Oh'. And I remember doing an 'Eerrrgh', because to me that's what it would be, not an elaborate, 'Oh'. And that worked. That was sort of fun. Oh, *right*. I can go down *that* track. Oh, right, so we can go a little bit askew with this. And that opened a door somehow.

That's sounds like a moment when you allowed yourself to be yourself.

Yeah, yeah.

You allowed or accepted *your* reaction rather than your concept of what a Wildean character would do when you see 'O-h' on the page?

Yeah, I guess so.

And you said it felt like fun.

Yeah.

Is it so that what you discovered then was an invitation for Helen to have fun in this play?

That's true. It becomes the tunnel *in* then, I suppose. Otherwise you dance around in circles—and I've danced around in circles in a lot of roles.

Stage is such an organic thing because it doesn't realise itself until it hits an audience, until you're well into the run. And it's usually the last week or the second last show when you go, Oh, *that's* the one! And you need to work at that level. I mean, just having done *The Threepenny Opera* with two weeks' rehearsal... I think even if we had six weeks' rehearsal we wouldn't have been ready enough for that thing of having to come into a remount of a show. You need to work at a level that is up against a house, up against an audience. And then go away and think about it. That's where out-of-town try-outs would be great.

Yes, we're not afforded many of the things that the theorists fantasise about. I mean, Stanislavski was talking about a situation where actors have a year to rehearse. The first thing you think is, What the fuck would we do with a year? But then you think, Okay, well... If you had to project that forward, imagine the kind of... Then the idea of wedding your life to the role becomes inevitable.

Oh, it would be brilliant. But it's also the thing with the group. I find when I work at STC that the first two weeks are lost with—even if you've worked with someone before—just familiarising yourself with the smells. The *Threepenny Opera* company that came *back* from Bogota—after sharing eight different planes to get there and back—is a different troupe to the one that left. The shorthand is there. Things are understood.

There's an intimacy?

Yeah.

And we don't have companies. We *don't have a company*. We don't have an actors' company in Australia. It's appalling. Directors and producers and designers get to work with each other again. There's a familiarity.

That's my dream or my soapbox, to work in a company.

So you think that that intimacy and connectedness—in a professional social way—can be taken on stage?

I don't know about taken on stage. It just enriches. Because, you know, there are safety nets—cautiousness and politenesses—and it's not until those have been broken down and tested, and you know the ground is safe, that you know you can go somewhere further.

You've played some pretty big and famous roles—Nina, Lady Mac, Sally Bowles, Juliet—they're big roles, with big history attached to them, and an expectation that your life is going to change, that you're going to go through big, life-changing stuff. I guess I'm asking what those expectations do to you. Or not even when there are expectations but when you nonetheless have to deal with big emotional stuff.

That was the thing about *Seagull*, not understanding the role. Because I would stand backstage going through: my dead mother, dead father, dead sister. Horrific things. To the point where, by the end of the run, I could have watched my whole family burn alive and not reacted—trying to conjure up real tears.

I remember seeing some show—this was a few years out of NIDA—and thinking, She faked it! They're not real tears. And thinking, Oh! That's good! That was so releasing.

And then with Sally Bowles, I really got right into the music of it and the sound of it and the story and the researching of it.

Skylight was very interesting for me. That's the first time I—this notion of researching—I'd never… I think I'd been to London once but… I took myself off to London for three weeks before rehearsals, because it was so heavily London-referenced. I took myself on a—

Helen Buday as Sally Bowles in the 1991 State Theatre Company of South Australia production of *Cabaret*. (Photo: Xiao Xiong Zhang)

Reccy?

Yeah. And it was the best research I've ever done. It was fantastic.

So what did it give you when you hit the floor?

It gave me temperatures. It just informed everything. It gave me confidence so that I was much more relaxed in how I approached it.

Is that to say that relaxation is an important part of the process for you?

Yeah, relaxation that gives you energy. High energy that's coming from a place that's not stress or mania.

I'm interested in the fact that you made direct reference to a text-book exercise of Affective Memory, that that was your perception of how to deal with emotional stuff on stage.

Yes, something to do with personal recall.

And now you've rejected that?

No, I haven't rejected it, but perhaps I'm not willing to put myself through the amount of angst that I used to.

But also, in that experience, you said that it didn't work anyway.

It didn't work. It didn't work.

So what would you now do instead when you're seeking to portray–?

If I was going to do someone crying, I would fake it. I would act it. I would demonstrate it. I would manifest it all. I would borrow the experience and demonstrate it. I would *present* it. Yeah.

Present the physical and vocal, temporal and tonal manifestation of it?

Yeah.

And believe that that's enough for the audience to go with you?

They stand very close, side by side, those two versions, I think. And you can travel through each of them, because even if you're really emotional, you can still recall your lines and you can still know where you are in time and space. But you're travelling through—it's hard to articulate—but travelling through a different mode, I guess. One that's a bit stylised. I'm talking here about acting for the stage where you have to come up with the goods eight times a week, rather than film which is a one-off.

You make reference there to the fact that even while pursuing this presentation of emotion, the memories of real life and real life experiences still exist in you. The two approaches are not mutually exclusive.

They inform it. But you're not left to feel as *used*. It's not as masturbatory or something. It becomes a sort of a choice. I know personally that when I'm watching someone on stage, I don't actually enjoy watching real tears rolling down their face. To me it just—I don't know—it doesn't disturb me, it actually offends me. It just feels like a betrayal. There's a suspension of disbelief. Yes, we're all sitting here travelling into that world but... I like artifice. I like detail and technique and artifice, because that's what it is. It's not *real life*, it's a *reflection of*, which is much more interesting.

You're talking to the distinction between what Stanislavski said about people's real emotions in their lives, and what Strasberg made of it. Because the idea of dredging up your history while you're on stage in the moment is not a Stanislavskian idea. Or at least, not an idea that he stuck with. His idea was to recognise the connections between the role and your life. His word was that it gives the actor *enthusiasm* for the role.

That's nice. That's good, yeah.

You don't actually pull something off the shelf in the moment. That's the American idea.

You're saying it's been misinterpreted?

Yeah.

And in a way it's become some kind of indulgent psycho-analysis.

As a trained actor, how do the things that you learnt still live in you? Do they live in you in a general philosophical way or are there actual practices that you sometimes or always employ?

Both.

What are the broad philosophical points that have stuck with you?

I guess it's related to going through NIDA in the early 80s and the people who had gone before—an inheritance, I guess, it was back then. A little bit exalted, I guess. This *fantasy* that one should never do a commercial. One would never lower oneself to do a commercial. That, of course, has been discarded a long time ago.

But I think that's what's severely lacking. To have a philosophy, there has to be a tradition, an inheritance to pass on. There has to be something proven that works, and I don't feel that... I don't look back and feel like I actually have a philosophy. I'm very glad I went to NIDA at the time that I went there. And I think it's more to do with putting a band of people together for three years than it has to do with any of the teachers' techniques or philosophies that come out of that school.

The seminary factor?

Yeah. It's insane. The juxtaposition with the year ahead and the year below. All that sort of hothouse stuff. And I was really young when I went there, I was only 18. And from interstate.

Are there specific practices and exercises that you still employ?

Well, I adored Betty Williams and the voice work because I'd done singing at school. There was this whole thing that maybe I'd become an opera singer. I went to the Con in Melbourne before I went to NIDA. And I loved the discipline of Doreen Hogan, and I think that comes from dance.

I remember when I first worked with dancers and singers, when I did a musical—*My Fair Lady*—how refreshing it was. It really impressed me that—for a dancer and for a musician—you *know* when your technique is off. Your leg can either go that high or it can't. Or you're a bit flat or a bit sharp. And the discipline of practising, getting up and doing your scales, getting up and doing your stretches. As an actor, though, I guess I've been lazy. I didn't know what to do. I needed other people to do it with. I needed to do it on the job.

It relates to what you were saying about artifice. That there are certain elements of performance that you either do right or you do wrong. Where you can actually judge. I mean, I'm either hitting this note or I'm not. And in acting, we don't often have such precise indicators or guides.

Yeah. Yeah.

Or maybe there are such things but we don't always know what they are or don't always respect them.

I think that's right. I think that's true. Because there are shit-detectors in the audience, and they know who they're going for. And your leg can be as high as anything, but if you don't invest it or fill it with something then it doesn't mean much.

But with NIDA, I think the intellectual part of the acting discussion was beyond me at the time, at my age. I didn't understand it. I didn't understand Stanislavski. I didn't understand character-building. I didn't know how to start.

Does that mean that the work now is based on something that you've built since?

Yeah. I guess the character thing's still in the back of my mind really strongly. I mean, I don't really *make* characters. How to put it together—it's still a mystery, how to do that well.

I hear what you say about your general feeling that you didn't get the acting instructional stuff, but–

That's not to say it wasn't there, or wasn't offered. In retrospect I think I was just far too immature. It's that thing: you need the experience to absorb it but how can you get that experience unless you… I'd actually auditioned for NIDA the year before, and Aubrey Mellor came up and said, Go and observe life. So I went out and looked at things. Really took him literally. I *looked*. I had no idea what he actually meant. I just… looked.

But that is at least part of what he meant.

I suppose so.

I want to talk a little bit about *Alexandra's Project* because acting teachers like me would look at that and gamely say, Only a trained actor could do that.

Why?

I guess because it's so… To be at the heart of something, and to so gamely carry it, and yet not look like an actor while you do it. Because that is so skilful as an exercise in unselfconsciousness. Did you find yourself employing particular skills to achieve that level of unadorned intimacy?

Every job comes with its own sort of context—ingredients, I suppose—and you're at a particular stage of your life where you've never been to before, so you're going to bring that into it too. It's the combination of all that that makes it what it is. It can't actually be anything else. Can't be any better or any worse.

With that one I was cast on a Thursday and started working in Adelaide on the Monday. And straight into the video bit first off, so there wasn't much choice but to plunge. I'd worked with Rolf before, and as far as the nudity stuff—I mean, I wouldn't go topless on a beach—but I went for that.

I went off to read the script the week before. And I was standing so close to the person in front of me at the station so I could get through the turnstiles, because I couldn't afford the train ticket to get to the casting session. I was so broke. And I thought, Okay, this will save me. As long as there's no sex scenes in it I'll be fine. Then I find there's masturbation and piercing nipples. I was weeping about it. It was personally horrifying for me.

And when I read the script I didn't understand it. I'm not good at reading scripts, and I still feel, in retrospect, that that film could have been workshopped, although, in effect, that's what me and Rolf did. He gave it to me, we had a week's rehearsal, then we had two weeks to shoot that video.

Also, I was pregnant. I was 16 weeks when we finished, and about 12 weeks when we did the video part. Because your body is embarking on this extraordinary transformation anyway, I think that something physically kicked into me, hormonal-wise.

Rolf filmed it in a huge set with a big curtain between us, so I was virtually in a room by myself. He would watch it on the screen behind the curtain, and after a take we would stop, I would put on a sarong, come out and we'd have a chat, then I'd go back in again. So he made it as easy as possible. He was terrific.

Being pregnant, being so aware of the changes going on in your body, that's a really obvious example of the thing you hinted at earlier. The fact that we're always changing anyway, and that a role meeting you at a certain time is all part of the art, isn't it?

Yeah, you sometimes feel that synchronicity. But I still didn't understand it. I didn't really understand what Rolf was writing. So I would just trust and walk the line, because in my stance there was always, Why doesn't she get a fucking job? Why doesn't she do a uni course? Why doesn't she *better* herself? Afterwards people would be really surprised that it was written by a male. They couldn't tag it as a dyke film or a feminist film.

But then having Kasper, and going through those first three months, then I understood that the experience he was writing about was incredibly accurate. So I had that perspective of going through it, then going, Oh, *that's* what the fuck that was about! Then going, Well, that serves it too. It's not as though you have to do-the-water, play-the-water. You don't have to actually experience it—or even fully understand it—to play it. People's imaginations do the rest.

You put your faith in the moment-to-moment thing?

Yeah, I guess so.

It reminds me a little bit of working with Rhys McConnochie on *A Midsummer Night's Dream*, when he refused to talk about what the

play meant. He said, Let's just do each moment, and let the play mean what it means. You're saying there's something of that in an experience like *Alexandra's Project*? Where you might not understand the whole but you—

Yeah, definitely. If you don't understand the whole... That's really interesting, actually, because that would frustrate me because I always want to *nail* it. Otherwise, what are we doing? How can I do this if I don't... *But*, just lend yourself to it moment by moment and it will add up.

I guess it will work if it's working. I should add that was, no doubt, a very particular episode, and informed by a respect for the fact that we happened to be dealing with the *Dream*—perhaps the most 'perfect' play ever written. There was that sense, though, of knowing that you're in something special right from the start. Everyone starts in a play with such expectations, don't they? And then so often you get those little signs when you think, Er, this is not going to be heaven.

That's terrible. It's really terrible. Yeah, the heart sinks a bit.

What keeps the heart afloat? Are there signs that make you think, Wow, this is going to work?

In the theatre, there's always a chance. But in film, you can give so much, but then it's given over to others—you're just a cog in the wheel. But with theatre, the first day—or certainly the first week—I know how it's going to land.

It's to do with the way a group of people come together—which is an extraordinary thing—from all their different... They come to a still point, and they have a test. A piece to come through together. And they've got to join and link into that somehow. It's human beings together in a space and how they adapt and adjust. I think it's usually who's at the helm that guides the group, and the group dynamic adapts around that. Because if you've got someone like that at the helm—

As an actor?

Yeah. I think so. You tend to rely on it. You refer to it to take your bearings in the room. I've been in companies where it's incredibly factioned, and that's interesting too, but that gets pretty much sorted out in the first week. You feel where the status thing sits and lies, whether or not it's going to be fun.

And that's the beauty of working in a company. You don't waste time sorting those things out, they're already sorted out. I guess I think a lot of things are only 30 or 40 per cent explored, and they could just go so much further when you *know* that person is capable of so much more.

I remember working with Jean-Pierre and *at last* being able to argue with people in a room and not offend anybody, and not be bitched about because of it. You know, this culture of politeness and niceness? But being able to disagree, vehemently and passionately, and then go and have a drink after it!

People do confuse social nicety and professional cooperation.

I think so. Yes.

But that's also to do with the pressure of short rehearsal periods, isn't it? It becomes a time-management thing. How much can I afford to explore? How soon must I find and keep?

Yeah. Well, again, with *Seagull* and Jean-Pierre, he insisted on seven weeks' rehearsal, which was a pioneer thing for Sydney Theatre Company at that stage.

Is there anything else you want to say?

Just my soap box. About actors. How actors should be more than just objects used to make the designer's and the director's 'vision' work.

There is this other thing that I sometimes call, to myself, the unseen character.

What's that?

It's hard to explain, but it's a thing that's always there, that must be there for it to make any sense. It's the heart of the piece, the key to it all. It's like a key in music. Once you know what key the play is in, you know what's going to work and what should be chucked out. Gags, business. All this stuff can accumulate, but if you respect the unseen character, then you can gauge—

So it helps set the parameters of a performance?

Yeah.

So you know you can't play a G-sharp if this play is in a different key?

Well, you can play a G-sharp, but you have to know that it's a discordant moment.

It's the style. But it's not just the style, it's the content, the message. Like, there's usually one line in a play that carries everything—the key line. Are we serving that? Are we delivering that? Because the theatre should be fun and all those things, but we should also be *delivering* something, *giving* something. And being tuned in to this thing, this unseen character, helps.

So it's like a personal guide for you. In the way that we might have a central idea that serves us as a moral guide in life, this unseen character is something we can test our behaviour against on stage?

Yes. Absolutely.

You give me this and I'll give you that

JUDI FARR

Australian television's first success in that most difficult and elusive form of the sit-com was My Name's McGooley, What's Yours?

In McGooley, *Judi Farr played Rita Stiller, John Mellion's dry but loyal wife and partner-in-gags. I loved it when I was a kid. I just loved the way Mellion cruised into the cheap little McGooley kitchen set, and cracked open a tinnie. And those mysterious, adventurous, weird scenes with Nancarrow down on the wharf brought a flicker of fright to the comic dream.*

When I was a first-year NIDA student in 1982 I scored tickets to a production of Arthur Miller's Death of a Salesman. *Miller's name resonated just a little for me, as did that of Mel Gibson, who played Biff. I was most excited about seeing Alf Garnett (Warren Mitchell) and Rita Stiller (Judi Farr). These childish investments left me totally unprepared for the gut-wrenching drama that unfolded in the hands of this great cast. Judi Farr was breathtaking as stoic, suffering Linda Loman. It was the night that I realised why I was spending my days in boring voice and movement sessions. It was the night I made the link between such tedium, and the kind of acting I wanted to be able to do. Both Mitchell and Farr were 'wired', from their toes to the hair on their heads, every inch of them involved in the action. Judi's work was inspirational, and has continued to be an inspiration to me over the last 20-odd years.*

Judi's CV is remarkable for the indelible sense of adventure in the theatre work she's achieved. There are the commercial productions and the Marian Street comedies, but for all the 'nice nights out', there are also the bold strokes of Tartuffe, The Man from Mukinupin, The Women of Troy, Angels in America, *and so on, over 50 productions, over 30 years.*

It seems that some great comic actors have a flipside, a particular edge when it comes to drama. Deborah Kennedy has it. Judi Farr has it: guts, integrity, timing, a lightness of touch when needed, a tight-bound, neurotic frenzy at other times. She has the grace to play graceless, the humour to play humourless, the heart to play heartless, and the intellect to play dumb.

I met Judi at her agent's office in Surry Hills. Like many, she began with humble apologies-in-advance for how little she had to say about the craft that—it was hinted—rescued her from an uneasy childhood.

When I started I don't know what I thought it was about.

What attracted you to it?

Being someone else, I think. I'd done bits of drama at school in the strange way that people did drama in the 50s, at a catholic girls' school, where you weren't allowed to wear pants if you were playing a male role. But in the odd thing that I did at school I think I felt comfortable. At home.

I had a strange sort of up-bringing, and I think it was to do with that. I suddenly decided I was going to leave school a couple of months into my final year. I just thought, Nup, I'm not going back. I saw an advertisement for a drama school, and went without telling anybody. I was there for three months. I worked at how to close a door without turning my back on an audience, how to kiss without actually touching—and neither of those things have I ever had to use.

But I knew I loved it. I didn't really learn anything but I made some good friends with whom I went on to do revue work. Then I went to The Genesians. I had some great roles there, and someone said, You should be a professional actress. Oh, what's that? Really, so naïve.

Then NIDA was starting, but I got a job and it sort of went on from there, and so I didn't ever get to NIDA. In one way I'm sorry. Just for that camaraderie and that basic knowledge. Whereas my knowledge was all gleaned from this one and that one and you do this and you don't do that, and that looks awful doing that so I won't do that. Or looking at people and thinking, I don't think they're very good, I don't want to do that.

I'm interested in the kind of experience that you had when you started doing revue stuff.

Yeah. Great training.

Well, can you talk about in what ways the things you learned there still inform the way you do things?

It was adopting a character very, very quickly because you went from something—with maybe one musical number in between—to something else.

This is doing sketches?

Yes. A lot of it was topical so you had to learn new text very quickly. As a young person—because then it was a bit of a game—it was what I loved doing. But now, well, you know the pitfalls, I guess, as you get older. When they're younger it's just, Wow, I'm on the stage. And they're *paying* me. Isn't this fantastic! I was very gullible and naïve. But I worked instinctively. I think I still do. And I think revue honed that quality, because none of the stuff we were doing was particularly in-depth. You just had to grasp something from the ether and create a character.

Gordon Chater was one of my greatest early teachers. I learned a certain amount of confidence from him, because he took me under his wing and said, You have an innate timing, which is something that can't be taught. And I still go along with that. You *cannot* be taught comedy timing. You can be instructed, but if you haven't got it, it's not going to work for you. And some people are not good at comedy, for that reason. Still, that instinctive comedy timing had to be honed as far as an audience laugh was concerned. These were things that he taught me. And stage presence, which I don't think I had at first.

How did it feel to go from having no stage presence to having it?

It's not something I've really thought about. It's just that now I *do* know—I think I do, I must. I must have acquired a technique, without really having been taught it—this is what you do.

I just loved being somebody else. I loved dyeing my hair a different colour for a role. I loved plonking on different hats. But I'm not a dress-up person. I never really liked dressing up. I mean, it's a bit of a joke in wardrobe departments now, because I just hate fittings. Oh, just give it to me and I'll wear it, whatever it is. Whereas a lot of actresses particularly go, No, I don't like that and I don't like that. I just go, Yeah, okay, it's fine.

I think—no, I don't think, I know—I work from inside out. Whereas a lot of actors go, I must have the shoes and I must have this. Because they work from the outside in. It's just a different process, whereas I would really rather go through an entire rehearsal period without wearing any of the costume, and then put it on the week before.

I'm working *inside* and creating something from the inside. I think whether it be comedy, sketch work or drama, it has to come from—an old clichéd word—truth. If you believe in your character and what your character is saying—it doesn't matter what you're doing—it's going to have the same quality of truthfulness.

I do fear that I could slip into that thing of being facile and getting up there and just saying the words, and you know that, because you're experienced, you'll probably get away with it. I see it in other actors. I think they're acting from their head, but nothing's happening in their body or their heart.

So where does it start–the process of making it truthful? What is the process of getting to know what you're doing?

Sometimes I don't ever know what I'm doing. It depends on the play. On the production. I went through a play once—did it for a couple of years—and I was never quite sure, never really quite comfortable. That was hard because I had to sort of put myself into a world and hope that some power out there… I had to make it work.

What was missing in that experience?

It was partly the writing. It was an adaptation of a book, and the character—this particular character—didn't actually adapt as well. The director—I wasn't his first choice and I always felt insecure in what I was doing—he never seemed very happy. So I think there were all these external things. Once I got on, I'd make myself forget all that. But actually getting there was never easy. Whereas other things, like *Death of a Salesman*, are just a joy, every night.

I'd been doing television, *Kingswood Country*, and my agent was determined that I was going to do *Death of a Salesman*. I had to see the director, George Ogilvie, three or four times and I thought, He'll never take me because I've been doing this ridiculous comedy thing, but he did. It was a magic experience, the whole thing, and working with him.

But when he came back to check on the production—we all wished we'd taped what he said. He's an amazing man. He came back and said we were all doing very fine work, but because we'd become familiar, we were denying the audience the full truth of the play because we'd suddenly become *knowing*, and none of these characters were *knowing* people. They were simple people who didn't analyse anything.

Well, of course that's an actor's job in rehearsal, to analyse and psychoanalyse and do all that. But then you've just got to forget it and let it happen, which was what was happening when we opened. Then four

Judi Farr as Hecuba in the 1992 Sydney Theatre Company production of *The Women of Troy*. (Photo: Tracey Schramm)

weeks down the track, we'd brought in all this, Why am I doing this? How do I do this? He said, Everybody knows what they're doing and why they're doing it. This is all very good, but the audience are missing out on the heart and the soul of the play. Now that was 20 years ago and I've carried it with me. You cannot ever go on *knowing*, because your character works off moments, works off the other actors. It was fine advice.

And that knowingness can creep in without you noticing it over the course of a run?

Yes. Which is what happened to us.

It's the one that was a complete experience. Wonderful director. Wonderful play. We all, as a cast, adored each other. We all loved what we were doing and it was a huge success. You can't ask for more than that.

Talk about—in professional terms—the importance of that sort of social angle of a show working. How important is that, that the community of workers is a harmonious one?

It's a very important element, I think. Because it means you respect each other—you haven't got to all love each other. But if you work well together—if there's a closeness—you're aware that if somebody says something differently you can reply in kind. Instinctive, once again. I don't think there was a night when we weren't all 100 per cent involved with each other, where we were and what we were doing.

Is it true to say then that the kind of sensitivity to other people that creates a good social-professional environment is then able to be taken on stage?

Yes.

Is that to say that when a show is socially less successful that there's something missing on stage?

Oh, not always. But that was a magic production, I think.

Early on—and this brings to mind the amount of times I've counselled young acting students through the 'problem' of being offered a job—you talked about being offered a job and that ended up meaning you pursued the profession as your training ground rather than a formal training experience, and you said that carried some regrets. What are the regrets?

I used to say something about religious training, that if a child is given some religious training, they can get to a point when they can make up their own mind. They can say, No, that's not for me. And jump away, or hang onto it, or go down the middle path, or whatever. And I think that about all types of training.

Whereas I still feel there are certain things... For example, I look at a text as a piece of creative work, not as a piece of academic work.

Which is only proper, surely?

Of course, but I'd quite like to be able to... I realised when I started directing, that I was actually reading the script differently, more academically or more fully, somehow. If I'm going to be performing in it, I'm looking for other elements, I think, whereas if I'm going to be directing it I have to look at every single character, and the structure of the play. Whereas I don't think I worry about that if I'm performing in it.

The two weeks I had in Adelaide with the Playwrights' Conference, I found just so stimulating and exciting. My involvement with the two plays that I was assigned to—acting-wise—were no great challenge. They were just stereotypical things that I'm often given to do. But because I had to work on the play with the playwright, and with the director and the dramaturg, and we were encouraged to give our input, I treated it as a totally different exercise to one where I just take on roles. I thought, I love this. Whereas years ago I wouldn't have enjoyed it. I get bored at rehearsals. I want to act. Let's get up and do it! I think you learn more as an actor on your feet than sitting over a text book, or listening to somebody talking at you. If you get up and *do* it, you learn more that you can hone, put away or build on.

What do you do when you can't find the at-home-ness in a piece? What resources do you call on?

The powers that be.

Prayer?

Yes. Hand it over. Yeah, I do actually. I just say, I can't do this. I've done that with lots of things, and it's actually worked, I think. I've just handed it over, said to the universe, I can't do this. You do it for me. And something happens.

I can't leave it at that. What happens?

I don't go to church and pray.

No, no, but in doing that... Does it affect a change in the way you go about the work?

Yes, I think so. I think—and I'm not sure—I think it frees you from pursuing thought processes that are getting you nowhere, and instead of doing that any more, you just let it happen. And I think that's what it should be.

And if somebody says, That was wonderful. You always say, Good. Thank you. Because there's nothing worse than an actor saying, No, I was terrible tonight. I was terrible. You think, Oh, I'm sorry I spoke to you.

You will get nights when you feel really disconnected, but the audience are not really going to be aware of that. They're only going to see what they've received, and if it's worked for them and it hasn't work for you—if you haven't *felt the pain*—it doesn't necessarily mean that *they're* not going to. And it takes a long time to accept that you don't have to go through every emotional high and low for an audience to grasp it. That's not giving credit to the writer. It's *there*! And all you have to do is just let it happen.

So you don't seek to be as emotionally involved as the character? Is that right?

Sometimes, you don't. Other times, you will. It's one of those silly things where sometimes you can do a play where tears will be pouring down your face but you haven't really affected anyone. And I don't know what that is. It's magic. Theatre is magic—and sometimes magic works and sometimes it doesn't—but I don't think you can turn on a knob and say, It's magic tonight. You've just got to trust that what you're doing is right for that moment, and live in each moment, and if you can come away and be analytical of what you've done and not like it, then it's best not to think about it. I wasn't happy tonight but somebody else was. I don't have a process where I can help you on that one.

When you talk about giving it to the universe... Really, when we dug into that, it's true to say that you're kind of giving it to a different part of yourself. That you're taking it out of your head and giving it to your body, to your gut.

Probably, yes.

Which is something a lot of people talk about. Coming to a point where you have to shelve all the analysis and the thinking about it in order to

achieve the sort of thing that George Ogilvie was encouraging you to go back to achieving.

Yes. Just let it happen. Unfortunately, that's more difficult when the writing is more superficial. With superficial writing, you more easily fall into the trap of sitting back between smart lines and thinking, Oh, missed that laugh, or, Didn't do that. Just don't worry about it. Just let it be. Trust that even if you're not mad about the play or the role—and I've played lots of roles where I hate the people I'm playing—you have to find a way of loving them. Or understanding them, coming to terms with them.

I've played some horrible women, but I can usually find someone to remind me of them. It's actually harder to do those sort of roles but you have to—once again—just stay in that moment.

A lot of the women I play remind me of my grandmother, who's been long, long, long dead. But I just remember tones she used to me as a child, and her philosophies, which were pretty awful. They fit a lot of these characters, these women. Which is probably why I keep being asked to do them.

That's a very interesting thing. Family members tend to be such a resource for actors, don't they?

Yes.

Because of their proximity to us, the way that we are part of them, and they're part of us, and so they can be summoned so readily. Is that true, do you think, of you and your grandmother?

Yes, I think that's probably true. When I played Gwen in *Away*—even some of the stuff she says—I can remember my grandmother saying to me as a child. She was that sort of character. She was horrible. But to get into it, you have to find out why she's horrible. And I have developed over the years a great deal of sympathy for my grandmother.

It really can crack difficult moments, can't it? This strange conjuring act. It can really open things up?

Yes, you can sort of *give* it somebody you know. It comes instinctively. These things come to you. You don't just look at your brother and think, That's what I want. It just hits you, and you go, Oh, my brother does that. Or, I can remember that being said to me.

Yes, or you just find yourself in certain patterns and you know where they come from. So do you have the experience of finding yourself on the floor and thinking, Oh, here comes granny again?

I have done on a couple of occasions, yes. Here comes that woman. Stuff from your own life that you've been through. You don't plan for it to happen, but it does.

How do you know when you're touching on that? Does it just occur to you that you are? Or do you ever go digging it up?

No, I don't go digging it up. It might hit me in the middle of a speech. A visual thing. The images I'm creating in the moment. I don't think, I must recreate that image, because it doesn't always work. But I do work with images, and they'll be different images every night.

It's a kind of organic or lateral or incidental version of the American stuff about Emotional Recall, isn't it?

Yes.

Talk more about how you use images. Because to this point you've implied a great investment in the idea of reading the other actors, being alive to them and kind of improvising the play every night. So how and where and when do these images fit in?

It's during monologues, I suppose. It's certainly not if we're working as a group, because that's purely characters connecting. You haven't got time for anything else, just, You give me this and I'll give you that. But, no. No. It's in monologues—and I've had a few huge ones to do in my time—that's where the visualising of images crops up.

One of the interesting things about that is that it tells us your focus as an actor shifts from one thing to another. And I don't just mean the changing focus of the content of the scene, the character's changes of focus, if you like, but changes in the way you are acting. You employ different mechanisms at different times?

I suppose so. I did *Buried Child* a couple of years ago, and Halie has this huge monologue which is then broken by somebody else talking to her. She has to connect it all in her weird madness. And along with whatever images came to me during the monologue, I knew exactly when I had to be at a certain point on the stage, with very technical aspects, lighting et cetera, relying on that accuracy. And then I had to connect with somebody interrupting the flow of images, which also had the technical things woven into it, and yes, something different happened. Because it has to become—at that point I was also serving the images the director wanted to create on stage, and I had no problem with that at all.

That was another wonderful experience. The rehearsal period was wonderful. I loved working with Gale Edwards, and it was a great play.

I think you go over it in rehearsals or you go over it when you're having to really grasp the words, and technically you know where you have to be at certain points, then you can forget it. It's what you've practised. Then you can let everything else ride or float.

The element of practice is important, isn't it? Because you're training your body to be at ease. Like learning a dance.

Yes. The dancer in the rehearsal room is going through the movements—one step here and one step there, and then there's a lift—they do it technically. Okay, let's do it with the piano. And then when they get on stage with the orchestra and the lights, they have to forget all that. But it's been programmed into the body, so you feel comfortable, physically comfortable, and you can just… It happens. And everything else, the imagination, can go. You just become the character.

What about when you do something like *Kingswood Country*, something that is undeniably slighter writing than Arthur Miller or Sam Shepherd?

Undeniably.

Do you actually do anything differently?

Oh, it's hard, hard work.

Do you focus on different things, and in what way?

Once again you're still trying to play a character truthfully, I think. That goes back to the group of actors. If we hadn't all liked each other, I'd have left much earlier. We have to *make* it work. And we were all—apart from Ross Higgins—we were all theatre actors. So that we had that feeling of responsibility to the fact that we had contracted ourselves to do a show, and therefore you do it to the very best of your ability.

What for you are the differences between working on television and working on stage?

Well, television's much more technical. I never have learned the craft or art of which camera is on me now, because I think I decided quite early that it didn't really matter. I just have to do the performance. Unless the director says, We want you to look this way, I just play the scene. Otherwise the technicalities get in the way of actually doing the scene.

We did *Kingswood Country* to a live audience which was probably quite good for those of us who had come from the theatre. Because you had an audience to work to—although you had to keep the performance back for the cameras—you had live laughter as well. And there were people there who came week after week after week, and sat in the audience and watched it. Same with *Mother and Son*. We used to do that to a live audience, and it just gives it that pluck of 'a show to do', and I think that probably helped.

It's unlike film or a telemovie where you might do the last scene on the first day, and all over the place. Those shows were done in sequence.

So, with the technical demands—even though you work at not being daunted by them—nonetheless you have to hit marks and so on. Is this where the analogy of the dance comes in?

Yeah. I often think that young actors think, Oh, I've got to find that mark. You sort of learn how to find it. You stand back from it, you see where it is, you hear, Action, and you just know how far it will take you. And that's the dance thing again. Going through the process. Coming on stage in a blackout. I will probably work that several times in the light, work out how many steps and what furniture I have to move, and exactly where I have to go.

It's like an identification of anything that might stand as a hindrance to acting in the way that you want to act?

Yes. But it all becomes organic—that word again—with the process of what you're doing. And that takes practice, I think.

Just like falling off a log

PAUL GODDARD

Paul Goddard's CV depicts a career that has rolled forth in even, measured and classy links. Every year, another couple of stage productions with major companies, another couple of TV appearances, another film. It's the kind of career most of us hope for and few of us build. Paul has built it through immense natural gifts—including a terrific brain—and a cast-iron commitment to professionalism.

I've known Paul for over 20 years. Few people talk about acting with his passion. Like all of the best actors, Paul avoids that safe, seductive, plodding 'netherworld' beneath inspiration. He dislikes treading sluggishly ordinary water. He swims for the deep.

Paul won a Sydney Critics' Circle Award in 1993 for his work in Angels in America, *and a Glug Award for his MC in Richard Wherret's 1997 production of* Cabaret.

His films include Billie's Holiday, The Matrix *and* Holy Smoke. *He spent five years, on and off, as Stark in* Farscape.

We spoke in the back garden of his house in Sydney's inner-south. Having just completed the final series of Farscape, *Paul was re-focussing on the original music he has written and recorded for over 15 years.*

Acting is just like falling off a log if you've got a fantastic script that tells you what to do.

But, philosophically and intellectually, the most fundamental thing, I suppose, is that acting is acting on other people. That's the thing I've taken away from my training. That seems the best approach, and the best way to avoid what I consider is basically a crime—which is self-indulgence, just acting on oneself. And emotive acting, which is something that we're all guilty of, to a degree. Emoting and mistaking acting for emotion.

Emotion is a by-product of interaction in the context of two people working together.

So the idea of interaction, there are two ways one can look at that. One is the concept that is sometimes sold to acting students that one is always trying to affect a change in someone else. And the other way of interpreting what you're saying is more loosely as an investment in the space between two people. Is that a better definition of what you mean?

Yeah, just being aware that you're in this situation with another person.

When I was an acting student at NIDA, I would go through the text, look at each line, sometimes break the lines down to beats within lines, and see what I thought I might be doing to the other person. You know, I'd go through it all systematically. Decide what my objective was, and how I might go about trying to achieve that objective. Then I'd give myself actions for each beat. And that was a great way to practise this methodology. But there are problems with doing this outside of the context of rehearsing with another person, and I've worked with directors who've insisted on sitting around doing this before you've got on your feet and played around. And I ended up using it as a means by which I made sure that I hadn't missed any moment. Or a means by which I might resolve uncomfortable moments by making it *active*, because it always feels better when you figure out, Yes, I'm doing this to the other person, rather than feeling self-conscious about what's going on. By taking it outside of yourself, it takes away the self-consciousness, as in life.

So I'd do it beforehand, and I'd do it during, and gradually, at some stage, I'd do it after the fact.

You're talking about the stages of your career?

Yeah. And I'm really simplifying here.

But *now* you would be more inclined to do what, in relation to that stuff?

In theatre I leave myself open initially during rehearsals to see what's going on and just feel my way around. I'm a fairly cautious person. I carefully build things up.

What I've absorbed is the strategy which I suppose I built up at NIDA—which came from Nick Enright, mostly—which, basically, is to begin with linear sense, figure out what the fuck is being said here, make sure you understand what the words are and what the lines mean on the first level, and then to personalise it, to endeavour to make it feel like you've got some connection with the lines, before trying to do something with it. Understanding what the line means, then trying to develop some connection with it. That can be a process of dropping-in a line, and building up a pyramid of connections to it.

Let's say there's a relationship in your play that's been going on for a number of years, and that relationship's breaking up. In order to try and rekindle that love, you start talking about your honeymoon 15 years earlier—the beach and the evening when the waiter dropped something over the table and it ruined the evening. Well then, if that was the basic text, I would lie down and imagine the resort. I'd go, Resort. What does that mean to me now? And I'd get an image for that. Then I'd make it more specific, and the strand going off resort might be beautiful ocean, and another strand going off ocean might be scuba diving—it's like a branch—the beautiful fish that we saw together, and another strand going off the beautiful fish was that later on I decided to buy her an aquarium and I managed to find her one of these fish, and another strand going off that is looking for this fish and I only had two hours during my lunch break, and when I brought it home she was... You know what I mean?

And that could go on and on, and that's just from resort to water to scuba diving to... And so then I'd go to beach, and what I did at the beach, and I bought a book of poetry, and so you keep going like that.

It would then be useful if you could share some of these things with the other actor so that they're shared imaginative memories. So that when I say to her, Do you remember the poetry on the beach?, having done all that, I'm getting images of the fish tank and the day and all that. Because when you initially read it, it's just resort, and it just doesn't... But now I've got a whole lot of other... Just as in real life if I said, My mother, I'd get a whole lot of memories fire off in my brain.

So really, what you're talking about is creating a fictional complexity that's as detailed–or somewhere near, like a tenth as detailed–as the complexity that underlies our every moment.

Gradually imagining more and more and more and it becomes as real as if it were really happening. That's your aim as the actor, if you're trying to recall past events. Ideally, they'll be there in front of you, the stimuli.

This part of your process is relatively autonomous. I mean, a bad play, a bad situation, a bad kind of collegial set-up with other actors and directors can seriously inhibit the other aspects of your craft, but it's true to say that no one can really take this part away from you.

No.

Have you found that in bad situations? Have you been in bad situations?

The only bad situation with regard to this approach is when you say to the other actor, Look, I've been thinking about that line about our honeymoon, and I've got some imagined stuff. And they go, Oh, yeah, yeah, I'm not interested in that sort of stuff.

They don't play the game. But still, that doesn't stop you, at least. Perhaps it lessens the effectiveness.

Yeah. Especially if you look at them and there's just this blankness when you talk about the tropical fish that you know should be real to them! How do you say to them, Look, don't you think this tropical fish should have greater meaning?

Would you say that?

No! I'm not that kind of… I would say, Look, I've been thinking about it. And generally the other actor will go, Oh, that's good, yeah, let's talk about it.

What do you do when you feel that no one is playing the same game as you? What do you do when no one else is investing in you what you're investing in them, in terms of wanting that connectedness to them?

Well, it's never happened that *no one* else is doing it, but there'll usually be one or two people in a cast of six.

So in the moments when you would otherwise be relying on their sensitivity to you, and you don't feel that it's there, do you confront that?

Not directly. I might do it as the character.

I'm thinking of a difficult moment when this actor decided that he needed to generate a certain emotional state, related to guilt, and—for the scene to work for him—he cut himself off entirely from me, so he was not at all open to what I was giving him. And I thought, If you'd just fucking open your eyes, and listen to me, and receive what I'm giving you, I will give you everything you fucking need to have to feel guilty. But that wasn't happening and so I upped the ante a bit to try and break through, to try and get him to open his bloody eyes. But I suppose he was an actor who came from a particular school of thought—which I think is erroneous—about generating emotional states. It's just bad acting.

With the pyramid of connections, is there a danger that the line is *bound* to resonate with those things that you've associated with it? At what point are you able to discern that some of those resonances may be inappropriate?

I guess I'm starting with an imaginary stimulus—going back to the honeymoon idea—so I can be selectively creative as I go. I'm guiding this 'visualisation', if you like. If my character has chosen to recall this memory in the scene to try and rekindle their love, then it's appropriate to create a memory that was by and large a positive experience. So my mind is not going to come up with images of a shark-attack or eyeing-off others on the beach. If anything starts to appear that's not appropriate, it will almost automatically be replaced by something that is.

Sometimes you create memories that you have to tweak later on as you discover more about your character and the needs of the scene, but if you have a handle on what's needed in the first place then you guide it appropriately.

What does that process do for you?

It helps me to not over-act.

How?

Well, my experience is that often when people resort to over-acting, they're not connected. If they are connected then all that resonance stuff happens, and they can say the line and get that good feeling of being connected to it. Because I know that all this stuff's happening, my brain's firing off with all these memories—and it might be unconscious—but there's a richness, there's a resonance to it. Whereas, say for instance if I had the line, I love you. When you say that to someone that you really love, it's often said in the simplest way, and it can be said simply because you know you truly believe it.

You're trading on the real history.

Yeah. And you know you really believe it so you don't have to convince them that you really believe it. What often happens, I think, is that actors feel they've got to convince the audience and the director that they really feel the love for this person, the other actor, and so they overdo it. But if you've done all that personalisation, and it's given you a great sense of love for that person, then you simply articulate the words.

How does that relate to... I'm thinking about when you've got to play that line and embody that feeling for a relative stranger? Presumably this resonating of an idea is going to bring out, in a kind of Strasbergian sense, *your* lover, or previous lovers and things like that. That's going to be part of the depth-sounding, isn't it?

Or chocolate ice-cream. But, yes, most likely.

So how do those things live in the moment when you're talking to the stranger? How do you reconcile that with your commitment to being affected by the other person, and the space between you, and all that?

I don't know if this is exactly what happens, but as you're asking me, then I think what I'd be doing is looking at the other person and taking them in, taking in things that… I suppose what I'm doing… I mean, if I'm thinking of *you*, what I'd be doing is taking in things *about* you and attaching the feeling of *love* to them. If we had to go and do this scene and shoot this in a minute, I'd be—

You'd be looking for things to love?

Yeah. And attaching a feeling. I'd be generating a feeling of love inside me and attaching it.

So it's a combination of both looking for those things in the other person, in this case, and mixing that up with the fact that you have deliberately remembered what love feels like.

Yeah. On a kinaesthetic level I'm generating a particular feeling state, and on a visual level I'm taking in something, then I'm adding the two.

I think the ability to manipulate your emotions comes with a lot of practice over the years. And it comes with the maturity of having experienced a lot of emotions, and having learnt, as you get older. I think it's much easier for me to do now than it was 20 years ago.

You described that when you were studying acting you really bought into a very methodical—and I don't mean large M, necessarily—a very methodical process of script analysis and personalisation.

And actions.

And action-playing and identifying. Are those things less methodically applied now?

Yes. Yeah. To a great extent they're absorbed. The lack of practising them diligently and consciously is partly a function of the business. I'm thinking of TV again, I guess. But in theatre I would still diligently work on things like that, to a degree. I was going to say it's part of the function of being in the business and finding that you don't get rewarded for doing this kind of background—the diligent part of it. Maybe my acting would be better if I *did* do it diligently and mercilessly. You just get a bit lazier, for one thing.

So partly you're getting a bit lazy and partly you're coming to trust yourself a bit more, maybe, so that you can skip a few steps?

Trust myself, and sometimes you get to do these steps.

In film or TV there's no room to play with these things, to explore. I've just been doing *Farscape*, a sci-fi TV show, and the character has an emotional condition—a psychological condition, if you like—that means that his response to stimuli is actually inappropriate. He's a bit crazy. But even in that case, I'm still absorbing from other people. And some of the best, best, absolutely best moments during the shooting of it have been with several of the other actors who are there with you, and you're bouncing off each other, and trusting each other implicitly.

It's interesting, the stunt guys in film and TV are always the gentlest, nicest, best communicators on set, in my experience. In the 20 years I've worked on things and I've done lots of fights and stuff.

Why might that be?

Because the idiots—the guys who are just there for the buzz—they get weeded out quickly because these guys are relying on each other for their physical safety—in literally life and death situations on occasions. Those who can work together and are not hotheads and who care for each other, they're the ones who remain in these teams, the ones you can rely on.

What can you do, in a practical sense, to contribute to the building of those best moments?

Always be available and listening. Being prepared is another thing. There are some actors who rock up and haven't even read the scene for the day. The first time they see the scene is when we're about to do a little read-through rehearsal before we shoot.

Does that give you the shits?

Oh, yeah. And they advertise it and celebrate it as, I don't know what. It's a double-edged thing. Partly, it's saying, Look, I'm this good, I can just rock up and do it instantly and be fabulous. And the other part is this aggressive thing, where they're jacked off with the situation and the script and so this is their way of demonstrating. I find that frustrating.

Well, it could be—I'm just being devil's advocate—that someone might say that the reason they are not prepared, the reason they're doing that is, firstly, because they know the character, because they're in a long-running TV series, and they have a set of conditioned responses to things, a sort of Pavlovian idea; and secondly, that it's facilitating an openness. But you don't find that to be the case when you work with such people?

Oh, no, those two things can be true. But what they don't know is the new information that's in the scene, and how that relates to other information in the episode, and how the very words might be picked up and referenced in subsequent scenes and subsequent moments. I've seen people go, Oh, well, this is the meaning of it, so I can just paraphrase it, I don't have to learn it. And yet, one of the words they've left out has to be picked up by someone else later on. I've seen gags lost because they didn't read the big print that describes what's going to be referred to later on, and so the scene is changed because they haven't read the big print. You know, the stage directions.

That reminds me of the limitations of the Practical Aesthetics stuff, which might more accurately be called pragmatic aesthetics, because the aesthetics of the work—in this case, the words—are not high on the agenda.

Practical Aesthetics. What a funny name. I'm always suspicious of schools of teaching that have funny, highfalutin' labels. They often appear reductionist, cultist and narrow. The mystifiers love to mystify so they can then get paid to demystify what they've mystified.

But in this instance, you're talking about putting your investment in a basic component that you've always put a great investment in, and that's textual analysis?

Yeah, exactly. And on *Farscape,* people often go, Oh, you don't read the big print. Some directors say, Oh, don't read the big print. But people in the sound effects department, make-up, everybody else has to read the big print.

I don't believe in reading the big print and going, Okay, I have to literally follow this: 'Picks up gun and waves it in the air'. You don't have to do that, but 'Picks up gun and waves it in the air', while saying something or other, gives you an idea of what the writer was imagining and thinking, and you can interpret that, give it your own thing.

Doing something like *Farscape*, that's something that one might describe as a highly fictional circumstance. It's not like life.

No it's not.

And the acting is usually not like life, because the characters are obviously hyper-fictional. What does that do to the personalisation process? Does that make it more or less significant?

It makes it quite significant, actually because... When you say it's hyper-fictional, the thing with *Farscape*, as opposed to just a straight sci-fi action thing, is that it's quite character-based, and so a lot of it's about dysfunctional relationships. So if you take away the sci-fi element, and the constant threat to our lives, then you just have these people—

A societal drama?

Yeah, you have *Friends* or something. In outer space. So, on one level there's this personal interaction that's all very human-based. And that's what the actors endeavour to bring into it, some truth in the interactions. Given that, it's still basically a sci-fi, adventure, action show.

If you're sitting in a chair and you've got electrodes strapped to you, you just have to imagine being there in the moment. You don't have to go away and do research on this, you just have to imagine in the moment your fucking muscles are spasm-ing with electric shocks. Those things are easy to personalise. If you've got somebody pointing a gun to your head, you'd think that would be easy, but I remember Ben, the lead actor, pointing a gun at me one time, and I recoiled. He said, I can see you've never had a gun pointed at your head. And it just made me go back one step and think, Okay, what would it be like to really have a gun? You know? Sure, I acted like I had a gun at my head, but it wasn't the deep terror that comes from really having a loaded gun pointed at you.

That's an interesting distinction, isn't it? That at any given point in a piece of work one is offered the choice of either *impersonating* someone

having an experience, or of imagining that one *is having* the experience. And I guess you're saying that you swung from the former to the latter.

Yeah, yeah, and I felt the difference, because suddenly I looked at the gun and all that it implied.

I want to tie up this action thing, because to me it's the holy grail.

Do you believe that we're always actively seeking to achieve something from someone else?

I've tested it. I've tested it a number of times.

So you believe that it's true?

No, I don't believe it's true. I no longer support the idea that we are *always* trying to affect somebody else in a social context. I think it's a useful, reductionist approach to be able to get a handle on the text and the situation, but sometimes you watch people's behaviour or you do things yourself and you think, That was just for *me*.

And even though you might retrospectively be able to analyse it, construct it, describe it as seeking something from someone else, that wasn't your *focus* at the time. So in terms of acting, how applicable is the idea that you're always trying to affect someone?

I think it would be true that whatever you do in a social context has to be influenced by the fact that you're *in* a social context.

You can retrospectively analyse anything and say, You're talking to me now in order to impress me, or in order to appease me, or in order to shut me up, or in order to continue a friendship; but that's unlikely to be what's actually in the middle of your head, in the middle of your being, at the point that you're speaking.

Mmm.

Even though a Stanislavskian performance analyst could say later, Well, yes, it does work, because this is what he's trying to do. But how useful is that, to play 'to please Terry', you know? This is where the late-Stanislavskian revision relating to the idea of the Object comes in.

What I'm saying is that if we were to act this scene—this conversation we're having—and there wasn't the same connection between us as we talk, and I was directing it, I'd be saying, You guys have got to connect more. Paul, you've got to look at Terry when he's speaking to you. And

Terry, you've got to have a bit of active listening, a bit of nodding. Because even though I'm not doing this to *do* something to you, primarily, it's a dance between the two of us.

Sure. But that's putting the focus on a different thing, isn't it? Because in that case, you're investing in your sensitivity to me, and to–

Well, I think why I'm doing it—and it would take us a whole day to analyse and to throw up possibilities of why I'm doing it—maybe why I'm doing it, what excites me about this, is an opportunity to talk about acting, and to get that buzz one gets in talking about acting, which one rarely gets to do. So I wanted to get the buzz of talking about acting, and feeling like I know something about it. It actually makes me feel good. Now, what I want from you, in this context, is your affirmation that what I'm saying is intelligent, is clear and is useful. So, like, if you were shaking your head at me I'd be picking up on those cues, going, This is not what you want me to discuss? I'd be shifting around, so—

So you're *investing* in me?

Yeah. If that's what you call it. I'm *needing* something from you.

Exactly, and you're alive to my presence.

Yeah, but that's me, Paul. There's another character who doesn't give a toss about you. And that's a choice. I know people who just... You have it in life. Somebody just wants to talk to you, and you're giving them—you think you're giving them—cues that you're not interested, that you want to move on. You've stopped asking them questions, yet they carry on. It appears that they are completely oblivious to you and the situation. And there are lots of very narcissistic people. So it's a mistake to think that all characters are eyeballing the other actor, because there *are* these narcissistic people.

But initially it's just connecting, and seeing what's happening. And then the director may throw in other conditions.

So one day in rehearsal, this scene might have a very singular focus for you. You'd be trying to achieve a very particular thing. Is that so?

With a good director, yeah, who knows where they're taking the piece.

Well, when it's not a good director and perhaps you've lost faith in the director giving you that quality of feedback and cooperation and partnership, do you make those calls for yourself when you can sense

Glenda Linscott as The Angel and Paul Goddard as Prior in the 1993 Sydney Theatre Company Production of *Angels in America*. (Photo: Robert McFarlane)

what's missing or what's wrong?

Yeah. I've been fortunate. Most of my theatre career I've worked on classic contemporary texts. Only on maybe four occasions out of 25 at the STC have I worked on texts that are really lacking in guidance for you. So the majority of my texts have been in plays where you read them and you go, Well, this is clear anyway. Generally, I think I've got a very good facility for getting the linear understanding and quickly being able to figure out what the dynamic is in a good text. So most of my work has been guided by the text.

And you don't need strong direction if you've got a strong text. Trouble comes when you haven't got a strong, clear text, and you haven't got a strong director. And that's the case often in television. Television actors have a strong facility for going, Well, this is about nothing much, or, This is just exposition but I'll make it very natural by being myself, using my personality. And that's where I used to feel at sea because there was nothing to hang onto.

I guess you're saying those people are hanging onto different things, things you feel less comfortable finding or selling?

Well, I think they have a stronger sense that their personality is intrinsically interesting.

That begins to get close to the—I was going to say the discrete area, but I'm interested to know how discrete it is—the area we refer to as characterisation. What does that mean to you?

Once again I go back to Nick Enright and characterisation. He managed to separate character from the whole of the mix by getting us to do an exercise where we would personalise the text and the character for ourselves, stopping short of characterising.

I was playing a 70-year-old grandfather who had dementia. He'd go raving off about things and talking about the past. That character was so strong in the piece, and I was itching to become an old man, to do old-man-acting. But Nick stopped me and said, You can't go there.

I spent a hell of a lot of time personalising the thing, trying to make it sound as if these stories were just coming out of me, off the cuff. I'd wander around parks and talk to people. I remember telling somebody the story of the play, hoping that he'd just think I was telling him a true story. That was the test I gave myself to make sure it sounded like it was just coming out of *me*.

That's a basic personalisation exercise, isn't it?

Yeah. And I'd talk while I was eating dinner, just so it distracted me from acting and made it feel like it was just me talking. And when it came to do the play, what I discovered from the process was that—and I didn't do stooping acting, as I recall, I really was diligent in not going the next step—but what I discovered was that the character was there to a great degree in what he *did* rather than how stooped he was or whether he had a funny old voice. There was a 70-year-old way of thinking.

Yes, the lesson being that personalisation *is* characterisation.

Yeah, it is if you really personalise.

Making those words your own is a surer way of putting an audience at ease with you, perhaps. When an 18-year-old actor paints lines on his face to portray an old man, he's actually just screaming to the audience, Look at me. I'm 18! I am *not* this character.

Yeah. And you've personalised the cognitive process as mapped out by the author in the words of this person, and the way they're sequenced, the syntax of the thoughts, not just the grammar. This character flipped off to another thought, and then to another, and then to another—that kind of cognitive syntax revealed not an 18-year-old but a 70-year-old.

I remember Nick's advise with regard to characterisation was always along those lines: Believe the words as you say them. Own each word, moment by moment, and that will characterise you.

I'm thinking of another play I did where I was playing a prostitute. One means of personalising it was to go out and seek some clients so I could actually have genuinely experiential stuff to draw from. I didn't end up drawing on it. But I got some very useful things out of the experience. And some that weren't so useful, because I got really paranoid at one point, and that wasn't useful for the character at all.

That's an exercise that would have you referred to as an ultra-Method Actor in the pages of any magazine. Does that mean anything to you?

Well, labels are ridiculous. They just help people understand things, but they're very reductive. I would say that it was an ultra-Method *strategy*, but at the same time I was doing other things that would put me in another camp, if you like.

Did you feel that you endangered yourself in doing that?

No. I was there with another actor, and we went across to the fountain and sat where the rent boys sit. We sat there and contemplated taking this Method approach to its ultimate conclusion. I thought what I would discover—which I'd already discovered to a degree—was that the line between being a prostitute and not being a prostitute is very fine. If the price is right, and the context is right. And that's what I wanted to find out, because I'd got to the point where I was ready to do it. I thought I'd crossed that line psychologically.

I never saw it as dangerous. Psychically I did, though, I got the shivers. I'd misrepresented myself—that was the danger. That's why I was shaking, because I'd misrepresented myself to this guy, and he was going, Okay, let's go. And I had no intention of going through with it.

The funny thing was that the prospective client who came and talked to me was a very well known theatre critic!

Another time I was playing a junkie and I asked a doctor friend of mine, What's the closest thing I can do to get the feeling of heroin? He said, I'll give you a prescription for a couple of Panadeine Forte. Now, okay, that Panadeine experience wasn't as intense as a heroin experience might have been, but I offer it to demonstrate that there was a line there I wouldn't cross because it was dangerous. But I found some kind of alternative experience, safely, with the advice of an expert.

What makes a good actor? I used to think that you could learn to be a great actor. Having worked with what I consider great actors, I now realise that a great deal of it is to do with who they are. Fascinating acting comes out of people of a particular temperament, with a certain inner energy and tension. And they have it in real life, it's not something they just generate.

Is there a variety of types? Or are you talking about a specific–?

One thing they all have in common to me is that they are generally direct, they have strong intentions. And that fulfils the criterion of acting on other people.

I think people's acting styles come out of their personality too. I've talked a lot about being open and listening to people, and that's how I am as a person. There are other actors who work just as successfully who don't do that. Just as successfully from another perspective. I'm thinking of someone you and I trained with who we couldn't stand working with because their work was entirely self-focussed. Yet the audience used to love watching this person on stage. It was bizarre, and we couldn't understand why, given that we'd all been taught that acting is about interacting and acting on other people. This person was breaking all those rules and just having a love affair with the audience.

And I remember going onstage with another actor I admired enormously, and I was so disillusioned to find that perhaps one of the reasons I admired him so much was that he was giving to the audience more than he was giving to the other actors. And from an audience perspective that is satisfying.

Cruel. Sad but true.

Sad but true. But there has to be another way or else I'd just give up and say, Well, I'm just going to do it for the audience.

Except that *you can't.* That's the point you're making, isn't it? That those people are playing to the person that they are.

No, no. I'm saying you have a penchant or a predisposition to approach the work and do the work in a particular way, but direction and teaching can alter that. Experience can alter it too. If the director had said, Listen, don't worry about opening it out to the audience so much, just focus on the other character and try and get them to understand what you're saying, then that scene would have been quite different.

Working out what your strengths are is useful, and accepting who you are. Knowing yourself and accepting. And even when you're getting away from yourself—playing characters—your essence is always going to be there.

Would you go so far as to say that your essence *must* be there? Because we're back again to the idea of character, and what is a character. Is a character a particular pattern of behaviour that is either more or less similar to your normal pattern of behaviour? I asked you a question about *Farscape*, and playing 'a character', a big character–

The interesting thing about *Farscape*, because it was sci-fi, from my perspective the actors who worked best were those who had a fair degree of theatre experience. Even if they were young actors, they'd done a lot of theatre at drama school. And they knew that behind the rubber and the prosthetics they had to be bigger than the rubber and the prosthetics. You can't do your minimalist, reducing it to the who-you-are-and-nothing-bigger kind of performance that you can do on a telly soap or on a police kind of thing. When you're covered in all that stuff, you've got to be bigger. That was part of the joy of doing *Farscape*. There was a good feeling of theatricality about it.

It's a version of knowing what play you're in, isn't it?

Yeah, absolutely.

Because you can't do Shakespeare by picking your toenails either.

No.

Is there a point in a rehearsal period where the personalisation process might bring it down in energy, or must all those things co-exist all the time? Is it possible or useful to knowingly sacrifice the aesthetic, the form, in order to personalise it for a day or a rehearsal session?

Oh, definitely, yeah.

So you'd be quite happy to say to yourself, I know this is *not* how it's going to end up, I know this is wrong, but there's an element I'm trying to get. Would you do that?

Oh, I'm a huge believer in that. A great believer in not trying to go for the end result. Unless you've got opening night looming. Then I'm a great believer in trying to fulfil the requirements and not indulging yourself endlessly.

That perhaps implies that there's a point at which you fake it, or a point at which you do the best version of the complete story you can, whereas before that you might have hoped to have pieced things together more carefully.

For me, at the start of rehearsals, there's the excitement about the role. Then I'll start off and try and—I've already done some preparation—try and feel open, initially. Just try and understand the words—personalising. Then there'll be the struggle on the floor for the next three weeks. And I nearly always get to the point where I think, I'm not going to crack it. I don't feel the character. Sometimes there's pressure then to start coming up with character, just acting out stuff, and fulfil what I think are the requirements of the director and the audience. And it's hard to resist that. But inevitably—at least on stage—I get to a point, maybe in the fourth week, where suddenly, clunk, clunk, clunk, everything falls into place. I feel that I've got the character, and the character's coming from what I'm doing rather than the external. It may have come from an external change, like getting a haircut or… And I usually wait right to the end to put on the costume because I like an extra kick in the final stages. So it's partly about getting to that stage where I know it's not going to happen, but I know it always does, so I've just got to let go, and it's the letting go, trusting—

Letting go of what? Worry?

Yeah, letting go of the worry and letting go of all the diligent stuff like: I should go back and personalise this; I should go work out what my actions are; this isn't working. It's just, I'm going to get up there and trust that all that stuff is going to feed in. It's getting out of being self-conscious. That's why I think being active is important, because it gets you away from—

On film and television that's so important, especially in the action stuff I've done. If you're running from an explosion, the stimulus is really… You just have to ramp it up there and say, If I get caught, my arms and limbs are going to be blown off. There's a real stimulus to respond to.

And that stimulus in that situation of running away from the exploding building is so great, that if you play that, you don't need to be playing anything else in that moment, do you?

No, you've just got to do the action of—

Stay alive.

Yeah. Get away. Get away from the threat.

There's this whole other side, of course, about tricks. And about camera angles and hitting the light. All that technical stuff. How the camera captures what you're trying to reveal to the audience.

Have you come to a point where that's no longer an inhibition?

Yeah, I love it. It was a terrible inhibitor for years.

You know, I really think acting for the camera should be taught extensively in acting courses, because that's where the majority of people's work is going to be done, on camera. In the same way that people are taught stagecraft, they should be taught camera-craft.

For years I felt fantastically comfortable on stage. I knew where the audience was. I knew all those things we'd spent a lot of time on. At NIDA we actually did a class on curtain calls, which I thought was ridiculous at the time. I thought, If anybody doesn't know how to fucking get out there and take a curtain call, they shouldn't be here.

Well, there have been plenty of shows where I wanted to throw things at people because of the way they've taken the curtain call, I must say.

I agree. Curtain calls are often terrible. I think it comes from the Australian thing of going, Oh, it's just a play, we shouldn't be getting thanked. But you should fucking get out there, like in opera, and go, Yes, I've fucking worked my arse off for the last two hours, and now I'm going to humble myself in front of you and accept your thanks. Even if you didn't like the fucking production or the play, I will accept the applause because I think it's right that you thank us. I've always applauded actors strongly for getting up and doing it, even if I hated what was being done.

But this camera-craft thing... So for years I felt extremely comfortable on stage because I felt I had a really strong grasp of those skills, and I could just focus on the acting and focus on the other actors. But every time I'd go for an audition for television I'd feel terribly uncomfortable because I didn't have camera skill. And I kept *reducing* everything because I bought that idea, you know: The camera never lies! Which is bullshit! You can lie to the camera through your teeth, and if you do it in the right way, it'll be believable! So I used to unnecessarily reduce things for the camera.

It took doing *Matrix*, where we had video splits all around the place, screens practically everywhere. If I was pulling out a gun I could see myself on screen—out of the corner of my eye—and I knew technically to raise my arm a bit higher so it was perfectly parallel with the bottom of the screen. If I tilt my head slightly it looks stronger, whatever. Those kinds of things. *Matrix* was such a technical exercise because the acting brief I had in my head was not to act, because this was a character who had no emotional investment in what was going on. I was hidden behind glasses. I just went, This is a fantastic opportunity—18 weeks of it—to work out the technical aspects of hitting your marks. And I had to do some physical stuff that required… It was like a dance, in a way. One time one of the directors said—this was in the opening scene when Trinity gets away from the agents—he said, You know, Paul, maybe you should, like… And I said, Act, maybe, a little, in response? Because this was in huge close-up. And so I thought, Okay. And I reacted to it, like angry or upset at the fact that she'd got a way. And they looked at it and said, No, you're right. It was so much easier to be cool by making no response to what was going on.

Then going onto *Farscape*, when you're doing a television series that's shot like a movie, you've got all these opportunities to explore that—practise hitting the marks and altering eye-lines. You've gone from a wide shot and now you're in a close-up or a medium close-up, and your eye-line is completely different to how it was before. Now—coming back after a year of not doing it, and coming back to do this mini-series for ten weeks—I discovered that I'm saying to the camera operators, Is that a good new eye-line? And they're going, Yes. So that represents all the technical screen-craft that's intuitively happening for me now. I don't have to consciously work it out.

That sense of where you are, what environment you're in, what culture you're in, which most of us get on stage through going to an acting school, you've acquired in front of a camera.

Yeah. This time there'll be times when we're having to shoot stuff in a rush, and there'll be three cameras, and you find out how big they are, and then you'll be running through the place doing stuff, acting, dealing with obstacles, but knowing exactly where to place yourself in order to hit that mark, hit that camera, so you're there for that one moment. And it's such a buzz when—it's like improvising, in a way—but knowing that you're hitting *that* camera and *that* camera, and you're getting into *that* light so the light is hitting your eyes in a certain way, and to not have to worry about those things.

When you start out, those things are enormous. It's like not knowing how to drive a car, and somebody suddenly saying, Okay, play this scene, but I want you to drive a car at the same time. You think, All I can concentrate on is how to drive this friggin' car. Once you know how to drive the car you can play any scene driving a car. And that's very important.

I've got a few more things to talk about. One is 'indicating', which is a pet hate.

When I did *The Club* I was playing somebody who was a sleazy, slimy bastard, and everybody else just got to act angry and over the top. And I thought, This is going to be very boring because I'm just going to have to be nice, truthful and trustworthy in every moment. And generally, that's what I did. And it *was* boring because I *was* nice, trustworthy. But afterwards, people said, What a slimy, sleazy cunt you are. Because they'd witnessed somebody being really trustworthy who'd avoided giving a nod, *indicating* to the audience what was really going on. I hate that kind of conspiratorial thing between the actor and the audience. I think, Listen, if you did this in real life, I'd be going, Excuse me, what are you doing? You're lying to me.

Taste is another thing. Good acting is, at times, a matter of taste.

You mean in the discernment of the actor, or the way that it's received?

The discernment of the actor. The actor exercising their taste. And that's something that can be developed. I can look at something and look at the person and think, Now, that's your taste. That's your good taste. Whereas another actor might make different choices. Taste is maybe not the best word for it.

I know what you mean. It's tricky though, isn't it? Because you're processing it through *your* sense of taste. And what you find distasteful somebody else might find tasteful.

Yeah, and that's always dismaying when you go and see a performance that's been reviewed as brilliant, and you think, That's just cod. I do think there are some—it *is* a matter of taste—but I think there are some constants. Some things we could all agree on.

Well, we might nod and say, That person's acting is shithouse, yet be in a hopeless minority.

Yeah.

And they seem to be adored from all over, including the papers, yet we might sit there and agree that they're not doing–it's that funny

hegemonic thing—we might sit there and say, They're not doing anything *right*. But what they're doing right is that the audience is loving them. So it's us who are wrong. It's difficult, isn't it? It's not a science.

You'd like to legislate against bad acting, but then—

You might find yourself in court!

Yes.

I think the final thing is that truth—whatever it means—is a constant concern for actors and directors, and I think, however you pursue it, it's a very important thing to pursue.

Acknowledging its slipperiness?

Yeah, and acknowledging that in some instances it might even be a matter of taste. In other instances it might be a matter of using a trick in order to create something that reads as a truth.

You feel it should be somewhere on the agenda?

Definitely. And high up on the agenda.

Get up and jam

PAULA ARUNDELL

Australia is currently stacked with fantastic young female actors. I wanted them represented here, and decided to ask Paula Arundell to do the job.

Paula has had a wonderfully rich and varied start to her career as a stage actor, with leading roles for Bell Shakespeare (Hero in Much Ado About Nothing, *Ariel in* The Tempest, *Cleopatra in* Antony and Cleopatra *and Joel Edgerton's prize Katherine in that company's luminous* Henry 5*).*

She is a young actor of impressive emotional and imaginative range. It's the imagination that has excited me as an audience member. I've seen her apply it to the Queen of the Nile and to the character of a dog with equal conviction and success.

She has been nominated for numerous Green Room, Glugg, and Sydney Morning Herald Awards, winning for Cleopatra and for Katherine. In 1999 she won a Glugg Award for 'Best Up and Coming Actor'.

I spoke to her in Melbourne in the middle of a season of Night Letters, *the stage adaptation of Robert Dessaix's popular and celebrated book.*

If the career pans out the way she projects it here, I look forward to a dazzling decade ahead.

I walk in with very little except myself, and the play under my arm. I hope to find the easiest way possible to get the deepest version and the most explored version of the text onto the stage with this group of people. To have a lot of fear, but to be very courageous. I hope to find people who I can do that with. I hope to find a director and group of people who will constantly question what we're talking about and what we're saying. I hope to play like crazy, but I play very seriously. I hope never to be satisfied, even though it's the thing about me that drives me most crazy.

At times I've tried to read up on everything and get as much research done as possible, but then I've got so bogged down by the *right* way of doing something. I like to start with just me, and listen to what goes on in the room. Because, even though we've got this play, we've also got a group of people who have come into this play. So there's the characters in the play that I've already read, together with this group of people who I haven't read before.

You're talking about the danger of anticipating what other people are going to bring, aren't you?

Yeah. Because each person's got their own personality that they're going to bring to it and that's what's going to make their character unique.

How do you prepare yourself to read others and to be read?

I think there was a time when I felt stuck, emotionally, because I *was* stuck emotionally. I'd lost someone very dear to me and I think that was my big turning point in a lot of ways. So it's hard—without getting personal in that way—to actually describe.

Well, you can perhaps omit what is personal about it but nonetheless describe the actor's body in the work before that life-changing event, and what it felt like to be you, the actor, after it. What was the difference?

Before—even though I felt like I had a lot of freedom when I walked into the rehearsal room and when I played in the rehearsal room—there were so many things that I couldn't tell between… I couldn't pick my instincts on things because I knew there were things in my life that were still hurting. Had this personal situation not happened, had I not lost somebody, I could not have felt grief, for example. And grief is just one of many things that I hadn't dealt with. Once I had, I was able to actually see it in other people. Before that, I found being in that kind of state depressing, very darkening. I could only see certain elements to a character, be they in real life or on the page.

You seem to be describing a situation whereby you grew out of a limited way of looking at the world and, through a significant personal experience, you came out the other end with a broader view of the world, and a broader view of an approach to the work. Because you now say that you're founding your work on this openness. Is it true to say that prior to this event you weren't as receptive to other people?

I was only receptive to certain things. My *instincts* about situations were very strong. And that's what I find difficult now, because I still get instincts about things when I'm doing a show, but I don't actually know where they come from. But I'm able to talk about it now and say, Look, I have a problem with this scene because I know what this is like, this bit. It doesn't necessarily mean we want to show it on stage. You can't go, I should trust my instinct just because I've experienced it.

So when you find parallels or contacts between what you're being asked to experience on stage and what you've experienced in life—which a lot of actors would welcome and think, Ah, this is a kind of security for me—you're saying it becomes a bit of an insecurity for you because you don't trust that it's going to work or that it's a good thing?

No, I know it will work. But I don't trust that it's always appropriate. No, it's not that I don't trust that it's appropriate, it's just that I question if it's appropriate for this person's story. That's when the director has to stand up and actually say to me, Let's go for this, then.

So if all modern drama is about bringing the actor into the work, acknowledging that it's Paula on stage and not anybody else, then you're aware of the dangers of taking that to its logical extension, which is that every impulse or every association you make is going to be the right one. And that's where you're relying on colleagues a lot to help create the parameters.

Yeah. Definitely.

You say you start with this kind of receptivity to the situation with the other people and with the text, and try to meet everything as baldly, and boldy, as you can. What comes next? How do you know when you're getting somewhere?

It's easy. It feels easy. It feels easy, and then I know I'm really getting somewhere when it starts to get hard again, which I expect it to do after about two weeks' rehearsal. Then something else falls back in.

What's happening at the point at which it starts getting hard again?

It starts getting hard because the flow starts getting stopped. It's like rocks getting thrown into a stream. When it's easy it's like... You know, first reads are always fantastic. We're actors! They're always brilliant. And then suddenly it just *goes*, as people start going into their heads.

Is it because you inherit responsibilities as you go along? You become more aware of the complexities?

Yeah, I think so.

The water gets deeper, in a way.

Yeah. Yeah. And it's like that thing of just growing up, isn't it?

Or, indeed, like a romantic relationship that can start off being just fun, but as you go on it must get deeper, or else that level of fun becomes just facile and not satisfying.

God, yes!

That's true of acting, isn't it?

Yes. Yes. Yes. Yes. Yes. And that's one of the important things to me, finding that depth of relationship, more so with the text. Of really getting in there and being able to deepen with yourself, the director, whoever you're playing opposite. To just ask the question, What is going on here? Because we know we can play it a thousand different ways. That's easy. But I always really want to *know*, to dig deep, deep, deep, deep, deep.

What are the mechanisms for going deeper?

Never taking for granted that I understand something at face value. I still sit and think, Why?, for a long time. Even into a long run. I'll still go, Is this really why you'd go to this extent? Why? Why?

It's like those 3-D pictures where you look at them and they just look like a fuzzy pattern. Then you look at them again and you say, Hang on. I've got it. I've got it. And you see the coral underworld or whatever. Then you lose it for a second, then you see it again. And that's what happens to me, the more I go, Why? Why? Why? Sometimes the question will drift inside my head. Then the answer will drift into my head and I'll go, Ah, that's why. Then it'll slip away again, and I'll be like, Nah, that's not it. And then it comes back again.

It's just something that's in me. I can't let it go and I'm very rarely satisfied.

Is that your mechanism for knowing when your intuition has kind of led you in a wrong direction? When these questions arise?

Yes. I think, Something's not working here. It may be myself or the other actor, one of us is a bit tired or one of us has stopped playing—but that's fine. But when the flow isn't happening, then the questions start happening.

Why? Why? Why these things that I'm stuck with in this play? It's all been going swimmingly then suddenly there's this one rock that I can't get past—even if it's only a sentence that either I'm saying or someone else is saying. It just stays there.

What other mechanisms might you employ to try and crack it? Are there exercises or things that you might have done at acting school that you might employ?

Well, if it's a problem with myself delivering lines, I'll go into dance a lot, and the musicality of it as well. If I'm not sure why this person's saying something, then I'll think things like, Well, when I say these lines I'm going to imagine that each one of them is going to tickle their way around my body while I'm saying the words. I'll play with imagery like that. And wait to see if the audience has got what I'm doing.

I can't tell you how I know it's working. All I know is that the audience is getting a chance to see two people dancing at that moment. It's all strategy. A game. It's all play.

When the flow is stopped, the current that travels between myself and the other actor, I feel it so strongly. It doesn't mean that I haven't already been using that kind of imagery, but it's effortless. I'm not thinking about it. Sure, I employ the conscious to kind of rev myself back up again. Then I go, Okay, I'm going to use that. It's like putting the music back on. It's a guide to doing what you were doing anyway.

How do you know when you're stuck? What's the experience for you of acting badly?

I get angry, because I know it's not always my fault. Acting badly is hard to do by yourself, I think.

Is it as hard to act badly by yourself as it is to act well by yourself?

Yeah. Because you need the other person. You need each other. When someone's stopped playing with you, seriously, that's the worst. I can be harder on other people than I am on myself. If I hear someone saying something that's off, I might think, My God, that line sounded so naff, the way you said that. But then straight away I'll go, No that's *my* fault, because I'm just not helping them to be not self-conscious.

So we're acting our scene and you're approaching it in your normal way that you have faith in, and I'm acting poorly. What are you going to do?

Paula Arundell as Cleopatra in the 2001 Bell Shakespeare production of *Antony and Cleopatra*. (Photo: Heidrun Löhr)

I once worked with somebody who wasn't very good. I never found a way of working with him. He wasn't very good because he was very afraid. He'd never really been on stage before. It was a big theatre. A huge stage. And I acted all over him, like, I literally did act on top of him. I almost put my paw down on top of him, like a lion's paw, because I was trying to overcompensate for what wasn't happening. Now I look back and go, Is this how I would handle it now? Now I would sit down more with him, I'd bring the scene into us, so that we could start—like in rehearsal—we could start so small, and then gradually build out.

I guess more commonly it's not that you're stuck with someone who's a problematic actor throughout, but that there are moments when someone's withdrawn from you.

Then I'll always ask, Why? That's what I do. Not necessarily ask *them*, either, because sometimes that's a really good thing to have happen in the scene. And so rather than trying to connect, connect, connect with them, I'll withdraw as well. Sometimes that's necessary. If you've rehearsed your scenes and you've both been going great guns, then it reaches a point when it's not—you know, a night happens and that person's just not there—then I'll never try and get it to where it's supposed to be just by *myself*, because that's impossible.

In a sense, I view acting like when jazz musicians get up and jam together. That's how it should be all the time. If I'm working with someone and they're a bit down here one night, and we're meant to be up here, then I'll try and go somewhere maybe in between, and hope that they'll come over there with me. That's how I prefer to work. When people I work with understand that about me, and I understand that about them, then it's just riveting. It's really good.

It's common for acting teachers to say, What we're giving people is a set of tools. All acting schools claim to do that for people. One can see clearly in what you say about your approach that you must have been helped, or conditioned to approach things in a certain way, but were you also given tools for when the car breaks down?

Yeah.

So what are some of the things that you might do?

Can you give me an example of a problem?

Well, when you don't feel that you're acting very well in a moment. When a moment's not working.

Doesn't ever happen.

It doesn't happen?

Not really.

But you said earlier that you were never satisfied.

I'm not.

So when you're dissatisfied, what do you do about it?

It doesn't mean that I'm not… I just keep going. I don't know how to explain it.

One of the things I'm interested in is what people retain from their training. They inevitably retain something of the kind of culture and tone of the experience they had, for better or worse. How much of the nitty-gritty, theory-based exercise-type stuff do you retain? For example, would you ever think, Maybe the key to me unlocking this is to really think about the given circumstances? Or to think in Laban terms? Or to clarify my actions?

No.

You don't do any of that stuff?

No. No.

So you would say then that you are almost entirely relying on your instincts?

Except I also do a lot of work on my voice. And a lot of dance and movement as well.

Do you feel that that other stuff is kind of absorbed and lives somewhere in you in the way that you read a text and the way that you go about working, or do you think it's just not important to you?

I didn't need to be taught things at a drama school like: Why would somebody do that? What do they want here? How do I go about it? I find it really difficult to answer all these questions, because nothing is ever set.

I'm realising how difficult it is to talk about a process that I find so hard to pinpoint. Otherwise I'd be bleeding my life away. It's a very hard thing to separate from me personally. That's why, when I was talking about a turning point in my life, it's very hard for me not to talk about the actual turning points in my life. The turning points in my life, for me, have taught me more about acting than any book, any class has taught me. It's taught me more about what extremes a human being can go to, and to what extremes a human being can think, and to what extremes a human being can move, or imagine. So it's kind of hard to actually set out: This is what I do or this is how I work.

What gets me passionate is *people*, and why they do things in the world, in all walks of life. The question of moral values is probably the biggest question that I have in my head, and it's still there now, so I talk more passionately about that than I do about acting.

I'm wondering about—because you're a young actor—in what ways would you like to grow? I'm not talking about ambition in a career sense, but do you have ambitions in an artistic sense? Are there things that you'd like to resolve further down the track? Or is there a slightly different actor that you'd like to be when you're 60?

I don't want to be an actor when I'm 60.

So when do you want to stop?

Probably in about ten years.

Why do you feel like that?

It's a feeling that I have. I'll probably write more. While I act, there's a psychosis about me that I'm still afraid to bring on stage. Even though I know I've played characters where I know they've had that.

I guess I'd say that over the next ten or so years I'll keep acting, and that's what I want to do, because it's so beautiful. It's such a gift when you see an actor do that for you, and you to walk away feeling, Someone's given me that. And they've gone to a place where they could be ridiculed, where they could be killed, where they could... And you think, My God, thank you so much, because I'm a person who has felt that way, and that really makes it easier to be alive.

That's what I want to do.

He's the holy fool

GEOFFREY RUSH

Geoffrey Rush has had a unique career as an actor. It has been a 30-year romance on the Australian stage, with two other significant journeys woven into that long adventure. The first of these was when he was given the opportunity—in his early 20s—to train at the illustrious Lecoq school in Paris. Jacques Lecoq was one of the great figures of actor-training in the 20th century. His aim was sometimes misunderstood as wanting to create mimes. In truth, he taught actors through mime, eschewing an American reliance on the psychological aspects of acting for a reliance on an intuitive, well-tuned, responsive and inquisitive body. The second 'interruption'—or concurrence—has been Geoffrey's engagement over the last decade with the world of international film. I guess I refer to these elements of his career as divergences or concurrences because of a deep hope that the Australian stage will remain—for decades to come—Geoffrey's home base.

I have a kaleidoscope of images of Geoffrey. They include images that the world shares, like the iconic leap for the stars as David Helfgott, the joyously nasty pirate of the Caribbean, the austere political monster of Elizabeth, *the outrageously pragmatic theatre owner in* Shakespeare in Love *(like a drunken politician at a perpetual Christmas party) and—possibly my favourite—the man lost and tangled in* Lantana.

I share with thousands of Australian theatre-goers many more great images:

- *Geoffrey as the lank-haired Sir Andrew in* Twelfth Night*;*
- *drolly turning to the audience in* The Government Inspector *to deliver the aside, 'What a cunt!' (a moment that simultaneously let us in, privileged us, and challenged us);*
- *as a kind of frenzied hybrid of every Mel Blanc character ever created in* The Alchemist*;*

- *perfectly nailing Chekhov's bizarre paradox of spiritual excitement, longing and torpor in* Uncle Vanya*;*
- *his Horatio, seemingly carrying all of human history in his heart, and anticipating all the sorrow of the future.*

Many more.

The stage moment that to me was most revealing was on the night I saw Geoffrey in Diary of a Madman. *At one point during his two hours alone on stage, he had to light a candle. No sooner had he lit the wick than the candle went out. He lit it again, and it quickly petered out again. When this happened a third time, Geoffrey said to the audience, 'Let us say the candle is alight', and accompanied this with a mimetic gesture of his hand as a candle flame, before getting on with the show. Geoffrey creates around him a refreshingly uncomplicated theatrical space. He gets on with the show. He loves the communication and the circus elements, all the fun of the fair. His great old mate, Bille Brown, talked to me about a love of the theatre as 'both high and low'. Geoffrey is the master of high and low. Watching him act is an event, a celebration of our having gathered together in this odd room, like being at a party at his house.*

This brings me to my third, most privileged set of images. I was fortunate to work with Geoffrey for a couple of years in Adelaide in the mid–80s. Just off the top of my head, the images include playing charades at the late, great Daphne Grey's house down near the beach; Geoffrey playing head-barman at after-show parties in the bowels of the Festival Centre, mixing the tequila slammers; MC-ing Theatresports, and entering on a pantomime horse, or dressed as a duck, a Martian or God-knows-what; sending his cast home from rehearsals mid-afternoon with instructions to not miss a minute of Bugs Bunny; letting me sit in his dressing room to watch him build his latex neck for Cardinal Bigge in Patrick White's Shepherd on the Rocks*; leading the company on an elaborate car rally to a cricket game in the hills. The life of the party, the heart of the company. Always full of ideas—high and low—to try and make the work better.*

A few years ago we worked together for an afternoon on the draft of a screenplay by a mutual friend. Someone said to me later, 'Was it exciting being with him?' It seemed a strange question, but understandable, I guess; Geoffrey was by this time an Oscar-winning 'movie star'. I reflected that, yes, it was exciting spending time with this guy, but then, it always was. It is always exciting being in the company of that great and articulate body and mind. That's why he's special. I'm sure you'll enjoy his company here on a ramshackle review of his career and his acting.

I never grew up thinking, Oh, I know I'm going to be an actor when I grow up. And yet a lot of my childhood play—even as young as seven or eight—was consumed imaginatively by having seen Sorlie's Travelling Tent Shows around Queensland. They were the variety shows that would tour, I think, mainly northern New South Wales and up through Queensland, and it was a Palladium-style tent, where they had a proscenium arch made out of canvas.

It was a built-in variety show by night, and pantomime for kids by day. So that impregnated me with something as an actor, by the very nature of seeing that kind of non-commercially-driven pantomime style. I think now when you say 'panto' it's what Julian Clary refers to as the sort of seasonal hell-house you're forced to go into because there's nothing else around. But there was something in the shambolic, rough and ready diversity and the magic and the fantasy of that style of theatre that would seem to go from far-away, fairytale, exotic countries, and suddenly it would be a ventriloquist doll that seemed to be just like we were: eight years old, scrappy, bit naughty, bit cheeky, bit irreverent. We'd squeal with delight. And in the middle of all that, he'd get two kids up out of the audience and say to them, When I press you under the ribs, I want you to open your mouth. And then he'd ventriloquise them. It was, like, *interactive*. Very, very powerful.

The equivalent of that was when we moved to Brisbane in the late-50s, and George Wallace Junior had been running the Theatre Royal there. Similarly, at night doing kind of lewd, risqué, highly excitable, nudie-cutey revue; then in the daytime he'd do a panto. People might say, Oh, I saw Helene Weigel play Mother Courage. I say, I saw Eddie Edwards play Dame Trott. He played a wonderful dame—I can still recall how centred and still he was. And foolish, completely foolish. And to see someone that you thought in your mind was the same vintage as your loving grandmother being a complete clown… He used to have dummies, you know, babies' dummies for earrings, and stuff like that. I love all that stuff. So, in lots of ways, the seeds of that guided me on a path towards Paris, rather than going to NIDA.

We did plays at school. For me, it was a really great antidote. I went to a fairly young high school in a pretty rough, suburban context. Heavy emphasis on sport. We happened to have a couple of teachers who were very good at galvanising the kids who wanted to do a school play. We did really classic stuff like *Charley's Aunt* (that was when I was in Year 10), *The Admiral Crichton* and *Arsenic and Old Lace* (when I was in Year 12).

Classic repertoire.

Classic repertoire, French's Acting Editions. And it was to do with having a great art teacher and having a great music teacher and a great English teacher. At one point we had a very camp locum teacher who happened to play Julius Caesar in the local amateur production of *Julius Caesar* that we all went to see. Probably my first proper encounter with an actor, and of course he was amazingly arch and witty and reptilian and flamboyant. He was—

An actor.

He was an actor!

We eventually took over the drama club when this particular English teacher left, which had a huge impact on us, I think, because we were able to take decisions into our own hands about what plays we'd put on and who'd be in them, and we had to convince the school that, yes, we could do it without the help of the teachers, and we could print the tickets and sell them and do all that sort of stuff, which was very good for us in a general landscape where theatre in Brisbane was amateur. You'd get the odd JCW musical coming through with the opera season.

We'd go and see *Oliver*. A friend of mine phoned up and—Richard Wordsworth, it would have been, who was starring as Fagin in that particular season of *Oliver* in the mid–60s—and invited him to come to the school and speak with us. And again, it was a man with a very crisp white shirt and a lovely suit, terribly English. He got up in front of us and, I remember, regaled us with anecdotes, and we Year 10 boys were laughing our heads off because he was telling us funny stories about when he'd been in *Julius Caesar*—

That he'd no doubt told before.

Probably. We just thought he was naturally hilarious. So everyone had this image that that's what an actor had to be. They were all a bit… *other*. But at the same time we were doing it at school, and going, Yeah, but it's also great *fun*. And in a funny sort of way it was also a great refuge from those elements of school life that we weren't particularly interested in participating in. We had a serious alternative.

That continued at university, and I happened to join the College Players, who were, I suppose, what you'd call a semi-professional group. They'd been going for ten years, based on campus, touring Gilbert and Sullivan and/or Shakespeare all around Queensland. Bryan Nason had this amazing carriage with bunks and stuff that they'd hook onto the back of a Queensland railways train. You might pack up in Bundaberg, strike the set, go down to the railway yard, go to sleep in the carriages, and at four a.m. you'd feel yourself being coupled onto a goods train and being dragged up to Maryborough or whatever, if my geography's right.

And also it was a pretty hefty time on campus. The Schonell Theatre opened, which was a new theatre. There was always some striking, pop-art, rock, stage imagery that went beyond the more conventional text theatre that the other companies were doing. This was the golden age of the Architecture Revues.

And again, we ran our own company on campus. Bryan Nason did a big tribal-rock-musical version of *The Bacchae*, called *The Bacchoi*, which opened the Schonell Theatre. It was a pretty huge production—Keith Bain came up to choreograph it for us, there was a 16-piece band in the pit, rock orchestra and all that. And in the third year we ran our own company and did things like *Spring Awakening*, which no one had touched. We'd read about a German revival. It was before a major English-speaking revival had happened. And *Peer Gynt* and stuff like that.

So that's sort of a preface to going to the QTC, because the Queensland Theatre Company was formed during that time, and there was a lot of controversy around the town about who would take it over. And, of course, to everyone's shock, it was an imported Englishman. And the feeling from a lot of my colleagues—

I had literally finished my final exam on the Friday, and I was studying academic topics like Modern Drama with Rob Jordan. He was a major influence because he introduced us very excitedly to an understanding of drama from the mid–19th century. You know, he took us through the Tom Robertson repertoire and through Victorian melodrama, and all those Symbolists like Maeterlinck. I mean, the great shift from Pinero and all the social conscious sort of stuff—Shaw and everything—right through whatever happened in Europe between the wars, pretty much up until Pinter and the whole 1956 thing. He made that a very exciting and lively journey. And it was still felt there was a great need to air these plays as theatre.

What do you think your acting was like?

Well, see, interestingly enough, that question comes up. People go—when I say *people*, North American press re film (they love the fact that I did theatre for so long because it gives me pedigree and it gives me *class*, you know, and gives me *quality*)—they go, You finally had *success*, with *Shine*, you know? And even here. *Sixty Minutes* pushed that idea. I was so resentful. When they did an interview with me the feeling was, Here on stage at Belvoir Theatre where, you know, the implication was, He was slugging away at it with half-empty houses, you know, desperately plumbing, probably indifferent audiences. And I'm thinking, You arsehole. People were queuing around the block to get into *Hamlet*, you know? *Popular Mechanicals* was the hottest ticket.

But also no respect for the essence of why you do it, either. No respect for the art.

No. No. It was the only point of conflict I used to have with Gordon Chater. He came in when we were doing *The Importance of Being Earnest* and was flipping through the ten-year history of the Sydney Theatre Company, which I think had just come out—'79 to '89, or something like that. And he was there, very facetiously going, Ten years of subsidised shit! He kept saying to me, You're playing Jack Worthing, you should have your name up as I did when I was in the Phillip Street Revues—I want 'Gordon Chater *in* ...'. He was of that school that says you must stake your claim as a commercial identity, and that's what people are coming to see. Whole different thing. But we overlapped on a lot of other great areas because he reminded me of Sorlie's. He reminded me of the Theatre Royal. He could sing a very funny song and pour tomato sauce over himself at the same time, stick syphons in his ear and smash boiled eggs on his head, and make it high art! It was fantastic.

And it seems to me that all those early influences—the tent shows, the fun of the fair—they survive in your work. I'm interested in how it got professionalised.

It got professionalised at that very point when I joined the QTC.

I think I developed the beginnings of my preferences and my style as an actor at high school. I think the moment I played Jack Chesney in *Charley's Aunt*, who is the most boring, straight... I should have been playing the *funny* role, the guy who dresses up in drag. I do recall there was a genuine sense of irreverence in the way we approached it. We didn't care that it was an English play. We knew it was funny because there was trickery going on in the plot—deception and a farcical outcome—so we were drawn to that. In *The Admiral Crichton* I played Ernest, who was a bit of a sort of boffo-twit, upper-class figure who gets his comeuppance on the island because he can't handle not being in class-bound Britain.

And then when I started with the QTC, we did a big Christmas show. What I'd call a thinking child's Christmas show, what you'd take a very smart ten-year-old to who reads a lot.

Bookish theatre.

Bookish theatre. Here, I can show you the photograph. Bille Brown gave me this. My professional debut. We were the witch's side-kicks.

That could be a photograph from Lecoq.

Kind of. In a way, yeah, the fact that I was playing a bird in a mask. So, suddenly, going from doing *Peer Gynt* or whatever to doing that didn't feel like a betrayal, whereas a lot of the more serious—

We'd joined forces with a lot of the on-campus revolutionaries. The politicos and the actors got together in 1971 with a common antipathy to the vice-chancellor who was the authority figure who needed debunking. So they all felt I was now working for *The State*, you know? The *State* theatre company. They saw it as though I had really sold out. And I had to weather that because I thought, I *am* actually working professionally as an actor.

And I didn't really know what I was learning because I already felt at that stage that I was already constantly looking for diversity and new, challenging things. To go from *Spring Awakening,* in which I played the headmaster of the repressive institution as a vulture. I had nose putty, a beak, and… A lot of bird imagery, wasn't there? Or the Troll King. I remember I used to paint myself yellow, and I made a wig out of rope, so I had very long, crazy hair. I was already working in a very physical way.

When I joined QTC, I got straight-jacketed for a while and did more conventional character work in—cop this for a repertoire—*Lock Up Your Daughters*. I played the inn-keeper, but I managed to make him out of Hogarth. He had everything. He had a limp, he had a West Country accent, he had rotten teeth. It was full-on.

The very first grown-up show I did, there was an element of Barbossa in *Pirates of the Caribbean* already being looked at. It only occurred to me when I was first shooting Barbossa. I thought, This feels very familiar to me. I haven't really played this sort of role on stage, but then I thought, Yes, Abanaza, Queensland Theatre Company, Christmas 1973.

What happens to a young actor who has not had any official training but has been on a couple of adventurous years, what happens if you say to

Bille Brown and Geoffrey Rush in the 1971 QTC production of *The Wrong Side of the Moon.* (Photo: Queensland Performing Arts Centre Museum)

them, Okay, present your scurrilous villain? You don't really start to analyse it in a technical or analytical way, or even in any kind of meaningful way, you just play it. I think I was probably more technically competent and skilled when I did it as Barbossa, but I know that the primal juice of it was back there.

I get flashes of it in my own kids, or their friends, if they decide for a moment to be a flesh-eating monster. I go, Yes, now all you've got to do to be a great actor is to do that a lot more, and with more finesse, and make sure you get a good agent. You know what I mean? That sense of play was always very strong for me.

The whole experience at the QTC was framed by the two men who ran the company, both of whom had been teachers at NIDA for a good couple of years, I think. Alan Edwards, who came from a very kind of Royal Air Force, British-background family, and RADA, and West End theatre; and Joe MacColum, who was a wild, irreverent, challenging, provocative Irishman. Between the two of them we had our sort of Maths teacher and our English teacher.

Alan would create shows with terrific rhythm and terrific precision. He got us to articulate ourselves as actors, physically and verbally. Joe would challenge us on passion, emotion, belief. With Joe we'd do things like *Juno and the Paycock*. With Alan we'd do Sheridan's *The Rivals*, and at the end he'd say, Now this is the Act where we tie it all up with a lovely, big, pink bow, and it would all end in a lovely, big, courtly bow in the curtain call. Whereas with Joe, he would push and provoke and make you look for areas within yourself. You couldn't fall back into any kind of comfort zone.

Joe happened to direct *You're a Good Man, Charlie Brown*, which we had a great success with, and took on a very long tour around the state. And I know that Snoopy and I were as one. It was just this simple, little, six-person musical with neat, witty lyrics and great little characters, very popular with an audience. And I can remember Charlie Brown—who was my good friend, Trevor Smith, who I'd done my first professional gig with—he'd be on stage going, Oh, that little, red-headed girl doesn't like me. Nobody ever writes to me. I didn't get a Valentine's card. Or something like that. Enter Snoopy, with a pile of 28 Valentine's cards, downstage, across the front of the proscenium, and off, to *huge* response. And I remember playing with that in many performances. It would always get a huge response because the dog has trumped his master. But I realised you could fiddle with it, and sometimes the journey of, I don't know why this is happening, it just *is*, would read on my face. Or other days there would be a devilish extra little bit just as you exited on the prompt side that would make the laugh treble.

I guess we have to accept that even though that's an intrinsically funny theatrical-literary idea, we have to assume that a person of–

You can fuck it up.

A person of no talent could fuck it up, couldn't they?

Yeah, but I think you do land... Certain people land on certain roles at certain points in their career, and if they're lucky, it sort of identifies and galvanises them in their own minds as to what sort of actor they are. I started to find out even before I left the QTC. I did three years there, maybe eight plays a year, so there was a good understanding of repertoire—and I wanted that because I'd studied that at university—and I loved being in the repertoire of Restoration and Shakespeare and—as we did at the end of each year—a pantomime.

And, each year, Alan gave me absolutely free reign in the panto. This season was only probably three weeks and I was playing the Idle Jack character, where I could just open up a rapport with the kids. And I remember going on stage thinking, I can change everything I did yesterday in these bits of the play, because it will depend on what the kids do. Some little eight-year-old might get up and run across the stage and run backstage, and you'd have to incorporate that. We had an old guy, Wilson Irving, who was playing the dame, and I always used to try and drag out old gags that I remembered George Wallace doing when I was younger. You know, I'd say to Wilson, Do you like my new dress? And he'd think, Oh, he's ad-libbing now. And he'd say, Yeah. I'd say, I bought it at Coles. It was Woolworth it. Terrible stuff like that. So I started to pile away all these bits of stuff. And the following year I did Abanaza, similar kind of thing because you had your solo bits with the audience.

I'd say that moment, all of the stuff at Lecoq, and then ten years after that, working at Theatresports as MC for two years in Adelaide, really shifted me a lot because I... There's an instinct in me that likes to be very meticulous and sort of distanced in the preparation and then once I've conquered that I can go in and try and bring it to life.

Can you talk a bit more about that process?

Well, I got more daring, I think. It probably started to come to fruition in the mid–80s. I was Director of Magpie, so I wasn't acting for two years and I sort of missed it. But I was able to, as the MC of Theatresports, sort of satisfy that urge in some way. And we got quite elaborate, I remember.

And I know that directly from that time, the sort of roles I did when I started working in the theatre again—like Autolycus in *The Winter's Tale* and the Fool in *Lear* and *Shepherd on the Rocks* and then *Diary of a Madman*—were definitely influenced by… I was sort of trying in a way to stake a claim to the kind of clowning and fool repertoire of Shakespeare, because I thought, This is where I sit. This is where I am Snoopy to Charlie Brown's Hamlet.

And I remember Philippe Gaulier… When I was a student in Paris, we used to go and have lunch every day because he loved to drink red wine—because he was French—and like Joe MacColum, he was the provocateur of that school. Gaulier would always—he'd never praise or flatter you as an actor—he would always define you. He would be able to say things that would seem hurtful, but you realised they were very insightful. It was a great time. I think he and Jacques Lecoq together… I just happened to strike two extraordinary, genuine pedagogues in the playfulness and the heritage of performance and acting. And I remember Gaulier saying, I always imagine you being a great company member, but on the *outside*, not the hero at the centre, you will play on the outside. That's what he said—I can't remember—*du dehors*, or whatever it is in French. But I knew what he meant, because in the conventional repertoire, I played the Fool in *Lear*, and I had a lot of fun doing Andrew Aguecheek with Neil Armfield at Lighthouse.

Later, after we did *Diary of a Madman*, Neil was talking about *Hamlet*. He said, I'd like you to play Hamlet. I think it would be a great kind of shift in how we perceive this play in Australia. And I said, No, it's just not me. I'm not that guy. I think the madman in *Diary of a Madman* was my Hamlet. So, in the sort of repertoire like *The Government Inspector* and, to a degree, even Astrov in *Uncle Vanya*, I was able to look at, How do I bring that into the so-called more serious roles? Because people tend to confine those roles and say, you know, Oh, Chekhov is supposed to be funny as well as serious. And it requires great daring and irreverence to find out how outrageously farcical and painful and funny it can all be.

And Chekhov is often done without a recognition that he was an iconoclast. It's often done overly-reverently. Consequently, it's rarely funny.

Yes. Neil and I first worked together in 1980, and all the stuff we've done together has been an accidental accumulation that's led to an exploration of that kind of high-school-ransacking and taking-over-of-the-school-drama-club energy.

How do you apply that, somehow, to the European classical tradition? It's been partly a rebellion against a lot of the English stage conventions that seem to be always rammed down our throats, or that our bourgeois subscription audiences tend to favour as being the benchmark. And that we're still colonials, even though amazing things had happened through the Pram Factory and early Nimrod and stuff like that. I mean, it still happens here, you know? They can haul out *The Hollow Crown*, throw it on a tour around Australia, and a certain audience takes something out of mothballs—

But Neil and I had hit a fun time together. Once we did *Diary*, we sort of felt as though... I remember Neil telling me that somebody had said during rehearsals, How was it going? And Neil said, I don't know. I don't know what we're doing. But I think it's amazing. Just extraordinary things are happening that don't follow our normal rulebooks as to what you're supposed to do in getting a play ready for an opening night.

It was just me and Lydia Miller, and the two musos came in later. So I was on stage a lot and it was a big learn. I'd never learnt that much. It's a full-on, two-hour monologue. And we'd said to each other, We don't want this to be done how it would have been done ten years ago. What we would have called A Very Brown Night Out in the Theatre: some poor fucker in a dark brown, unappealing, theatrically-unimaginative coat, on a bed. Bleak, depressing setting. With a glass of water, a sort of wry humour. I suppose we were sort of mocking what we thought the Pram Factory might have done with it, that it had to have a certain worthiness to it.

So, of course, Catherine Martin, who designed it, didn't go for anything like that. She gave us a sort of Van Gogh set with bright red walls and yellow floor and green roof, and there were pots and water dripping everywhere. And I remember when—we were in rehearsals and I went in to make up for it—Lech Mackiewicz, who was the assistant director, had given me this fantastic little Russian edition of the Gogol story, with these fantastic painter's plates in it. I thought, Wow, if I could get that expressionistic, abstract sense of the moulding and the make-up from these plates. And, of course, I did that and Neil said, It just looks like you've smashed a cake on your face or something. It's not reading as anything that you were working on in rehearsals, it's not letting anything out. He said, Go down and do a full West End juve-lead make-up. So I went down and put on green eye-shadow and eye-line and a beauty spot, and carmine on the lips and a little bit of blush on the earlobes as per a Leichner make-up chart. Then somebody found this rather good wig. It had a little sort of floppy bit and it was a real ratty wig, but it had quite a good lace to it, and we could never afford anything like that, and we decided to make it very red. Almost like a shock-clown wig or something. Suddenly the character just freed up even more.

But this was quite late in rehearsal?

Oh, yeah. This was like during the tech. I don't think we'd even thought about... We knew what the costume design was like. I think I was just going to have my hair, like, crazy, but then this wig idea came up. Once I knew his outline... See, because this goes back... I don't know how to wrap this in but—

When I was at university and when I started at the QTC, apart from all the grand English traditions, this was a time when Peter Brook's company was touring the world with *A Midsummer Night's Dream* and we're going, Oh, this is fantastic. And the very early Trevor Nunn production of *A Winter's Tale*, that involved that giant rocking horse with the young Judi Dench in it. With all that going on in the theatre and all of us studying the repertoire at university, there was also an explosion in American cinema. And I *loved*, I mean, I'd always loved that sort of... Which I realised the other day... I saw an amazing program on Michael Chekhov, whom I never really knew that much about. I mean, I'd learnt a bit about him because he'd left a brilliant notebook regarding his performance in *The Government Inspector*, which was one of his big *tour de force* roles. And I remember at the time reading it and thinking, Boy, I seem to have a lot in common with how you think, not so much internalising things on a psychological level, but finding an expressive, theatrical gesture or a sense of the silhouette of the character, or thinking of shapes in a bigger space as a way of where to start, or the locomotion of a character. But again that's all through Lecoq training as well.

It means you can play. It's a way you can play heightened realistic prose or dramatic prose writers like Mamet or Pinter. Or you can play the large rolling hills and dales of Restoration wit or the density of Shakespearean language. As long as you find what theatrical place you belong in to get an audience to come onto that plane with you.

But, you know, there were all these performances around with the new movement in Hollywood. I remember we were at the QTC and I came in to do *The School Mistress* or something, and I came in saying, I saw this film today with these actors, Gene Hackman and Al Pacino—I'd never heard of them before—doing *Scarecrow*, about two losers having most of their conversation in a bar. And just going, They were amazing. Yet I had no identification with them as actors, but I was really—as an audience—so deeply impressed. And that goes back to loving the great tradition of John Garfield, Shelley Winters, Brando, James Dean, that tough, American cinema that sort of reflected the theatrical tradition of Eugene O'Neill or Arthur Miller. You know what I mean? That kind of writing somehow found its way into serious text. And the *Godfather* movies and all that.

Yeah, but that was a very different theatrical road to the one you'd been on to that point, wasn't it?

Totally. I mean, that was just something that intrigued me. It's why I never really thought about being in cinema, particularly in the late 70s, early 80s, when it was really happening. I remember people saying, You're going to go to Adelaide for two years? But you'll miss out on a film. And I remember thinking, But that's such a long shot. I really cannot project myself into the idea of being in film, because the sort of characters I do don't exist in film. I remember thinking, Oh, I could be in *Cowra Breakout*, because I could be a good prisoner-of-war character, because I'm really skinny. So I was already thinking of a physical assessment. I used to look at things like *The Dismissal*, and go, I don't look like any Australian politician, so I can't be in something like that. Or they all ride horses and they've all got pecs and brawny shoulders, I'm not that sort of actor.

It was a dilemma for me because I remember when we were shooting *Shine*, which was really only my second major role in a film, I'd only done a spit and a cough. The spit was in *Hoodwink* back in the early 80s. I played one scene as a detective. I look about *nine*! And I remember then thinking, I am so unlike what a detective looks like in Australia. I had one day's filming, and I thought, I've got no idea how to be in a movie. But I had my two pages of dialogue. I thought, I get to do this great scene with John Hargreaves, and I get to be tough, which just wasn't in my repertoire.

I get to menace him and mock him. And Claude Watham was quite smart about it. He gave me four big, bull-necked guys around me who were the Queensland detective sergeants axing the door down, so suddenly I thought… It was almost like I was in a Coen brothers movie for a moment. I remember going in and thinking, I know what I'll do. I find it really funny the way certain people part their hair very low and scrape it over their head. So that's what I did. I was always looking for the silhouette or the mask that could bring it to some kind of vital life. The shape.

I was talking about that film thing. I often think about that. I still, in a way, don't belong to that. I got lucky with *Shine*. When I read it I thought, He *is* the outsider. He *is* the broken peripheral character. He *is* the fool. He *is* the clown. He's the holy fool. He's the idiot. He's the hermit. All those sort of areas. I'd never defined it that way. Somebody wrote to me after *Shine* about how Jung had defined all those types—the Joker and the Imp and the Hermit—and I thought, Oh, yeah, I can sort of understand that.

I'd had that conversation with Cicely Berry once. She gave us a workshop at Lighthouse, and I asked her, Do you find many of the actors within the company—? Because Lighthouse having twelve actors, we thought was an approximation of Shakespeare's company. You can actually do his plays with twelve actors and you start to see how—

The same twelve actors indeed.

Yeah. And if you look at how Jim Sharman cast them, ranging from John Wood to Kerry Walker to Peter Cummins to me to Russel Keiffel to Gillian Jones, et cetera, you get a pretty good cross-section of people. You have noble princes, kings, lovers, idiots, fools, drunkards, gods—

Braggards, cowards–

Yeah, yeah. And I said to Cic Berry—because she worked at the RSC a lot—Do you find that people make the cross-over very much between being at the centre of the play—not necessarily the lead role, because we know from Shakespeare's company that Burbage probably journeyed through Richard the Second, Brutus, Hamlet, there's a kind of maturation in the writing that's reflected because there's one actor there who's got the facility and the development going on in his company life to keep expanding into that repertoire—with the fools? And she said, No, not really. They don't. Alan Howard, in all the history plays, would play the king, but would be not terribly interesting as Pistol, or whatever.

And I think that's probably true. I've tried to do that cross-over a bit, but I've always known that I never would be, I'm never gonna be the Hamlet and I'm never gonna be the guy who gets the girl in the end. Oh, except now that I'm older I've become... There's one side of me in films where I become the older guy who mentors fascinating but troubled, powerful, young women like Frida Kahlo or Elizabeth. Or the Marquis de Sade with the laundry lass. I get to be the older dude who does that.

You've talked about looking for that mask and that shape and that energy right from the kick-off. But in *Diary of a Madman*, you say it didn't come till the very end? Is that to say you resisted your natural thing of looking for that earlier on? Were you trying to approach it in a different way?

We had a psychiatric advisor who came very early in the process—

Every production should have one.

Indeed. He said, Well, Gogol has written a definitive madman who's got mania, he's a depressive, he's schizoid, he's delusional, he's a literary creation of many, many things. I think it gives you licence to think of him as a theatrical clown rather than a psychological type.

That was very freeing, to go, Oo, we don't have to honour, in a worthy kind of way, all of the ticks and nuances of this condition. He's a metaphor now. He said, I'll tell you now, people with mania, when they're up, can be hilarious. And they know they are. They will hold court. They're on. And he said, There's almost a camp, bitchy kind of energy, where it just flies, and people are like, Wow. And we talked a lot about how Tony Hancock did that, and how Billy Connelly does that. So we started to think about the performance as being, I've got to find whatever is in me that just floods out, and so we started to sort of play it that way. I would just throw in things to try and make it more outrageous for Neil and Alan John and the stage manager sitting in the rehearsal room. Can it be *this* ridiculous? You know? And when you're playing mad—and this guy is so delusional and spinning away. It's a very strange area for humour.

We found Gogol to be so anarchically modern. It wasn't as though we were trying to dig something out of humour that was kind of buried in dust, and 160 years old. It felt to me that he was sharper than Leunig gets, more outrageous than Robin Williams on a flight of fancy, just *so* quick, you know?

It's amazing. I've probably done more talking about acting as an assessment of my film work because you promote films, and you get to do it to such a degree.

Like, if you do a press junket for a film in America, you might talk about it for 30 hours in a row over a three-day weekend, and 60 different people will ask you, Did you have *fun* playing this character? And you've got to come up with... Or, What research did you do? And you suddenly find you have to analyse and contextualise and formulate something, which in the theatre I wasn't that conscious of doing. I mean, I even think at the stage of doing *Diary*, we weren't that conscious of standing outside it and trying to pull the watch apart, and take all the springs out, and lose the fact that it could actually keep time. But you sort of occasionally would have those conversations. Neil's a very—as well as being very smart, his instincts are very astute as a director. Go and do a West End juve-lead make-up. And it's the absolute final key.

It's like when I did *Pirates of the Caribbean*, the moment I put the hat on, I knew exactly where this character had to go. The arrogance, the flamboyance, the pretension to authority, the romance is all there. The hat functions as a kind of a mask. A complete body mask. Penny Rose, the designer, was right on top of that. She said, Oh, you're a slim lad, I'll make you look a lot bigger than you are. And when I put the boots on she said, Yes, Geoffrey, well, you know, you've got to stand much wider than that to make that read. Which I did. You can't put on big thigh-length boots and stand like... You know what I mean?

Then I started working with the voice coach and we talked about, Why do pirates go, Aghh? She said, Well, they all go, Aghh, because they all come from Bristol or the West Country because that was the seafaring port of Britain. And you could easily see how my older pirate, in the golden age of piracy, probably ran away to sea with visions of, Nothing's going to happen for me at home, I'll go off on a life of adventure. Then suddenly he finds, Oh, you can earn much more money much more quickly if you actually steal it from people rather than do it legitimately.

So you start to make sense of the character, and we were trying to define not being the shiver-me-timbers, Aghh, kind of pirate. In fact I only go, Aghh, once in the movie, to frighten the girl. It was definitely a post-modern Aghh, in inverted commas.

When you're doing that, you're answering the question the American interviewers ask you about what's your research. You're talking about giving yourself an allowance to play, by understanding.

It is. It is. That's it. That's the whole Lecoq thing: *le jeu*. You know, the French say theatre is play. It's a rhythmically unpredictable build-up between either the performer and an audience, or two performers together and an audience, or a performer and a complete chorus and an audience, where almost anything is possible. It's not just bound to where the text takes you.

It's what a lot of sort of *diminished* theatre never quite realises for me. Case in point: Lear carrying in his daughter, dead. Five howls. Howl, howl, howl, howl, howl, is not the greatest piece of text in the world. But where it sits, it's telling you that a god-awful, horrifying wail has to just power through the theatre from some animal place at that point in the story. I suppose it's always from the text. I don't know.

Because people could then say, Do you always just find the shape and then go and play? Well, sometimes you can reach a complete dead-end on that.

The Marquis de Sade was one where, once I got over the fact that historically he was a very obese, buddha-type figure, a Marlon Brando-type figure, the director said, No, this is as if the Marquis de Sade has written his own screenplay. And sees himself as a very lively-minded writer. That's what we're doing. We're not doing a documentary.

Again, I had a great, open discourse with the costume designer. She was very concerned about finding the right wigs. I said, The one sort of wig we don't want to have is the Captain Cook look, which is just not attractive on anybody—those two horse-hairs in rollers on either temple is a shocker. She found this fantastic wig, or had it made or whatever, that had two tails and this fantastic, distinctive, interesting shape on top. And the moment I put that on with the rest of the outfit, which was like a fading glam-rock star from the 70s, made out of silk, with britches and everything, with these little pointy shoes with buckles. I could only walk like a mountain goat. It gave me these little pin legs. And there were these kind of little horns on the head. So there was something in there that I thought, Gee, this is quite interesting because he is kind of precariously balanced. So it starts to kind of become rich.

Mind you, in that, you also had self-consciously brilliant and rhythmic dialogue. It's a very epigrammatical piece and it plays out a fugue of arguments between four characters in a very musical way, so you've got to kind of match it. I remember Joaquin Phoenix had a lot of trouble with that at first because he thought he couldn't find the thing, being an

American. He was in awe of me and Kate Winslet and Michael Caine, wrongfully, because he thought we came from a sort of theatrical tradition and you needed that to be able to approach this language.

We were shooting the film in sequence and one day we were doing the scene where the priest in ransacking the Marquis' boudoir and stripping it of everything, all the furnishings, all the privileges he'd been given. I made this sly reference to *Love and Death*, this Woody Allen film, just when we were rehearsing, because it was one continuous take, this whole two-minute scene, a steady-cam moving around, so it had to be rehearsed and orchestrated, focussed, set-up and lit so it could all play in one long continuous movement. The strategy I took was, rather than bemoaning the fact that the Marquis' room was being emptied, was to encourage the priest, and say, Oh, don't forget this. And, By the way, you haven't taken this. And for some reason I said, And let's not forget the Virgin Mary, my favourite. And Joaquin said, What did you say? I said, It's like that old Woody Allen film, *Love and Death*. And then he just did pages from that film. He said, It's my *favourite* movie. And he had me on the floor because he knew absolute huge chunks of it. The bit I was doing was based on when Diane Keaton's character says, Boris, you must understand there are lots of different kinds of love between people, a father and son, the love between a mother and her child, and Woody Allen's character goes, And two women. Let's not forget my favourite! And Joaquin could do it. I said, Look, say this dialogue as Woody Allen and it all makes sense. So he had lines like, 'Marquis, you think you're the antichrist. You're just a malcontent who knows how to spell!' And so, even in rehearsal, I'd say, Say them as Woody Allen, it'll be fun. So he would say it, with an uncanny sense of Woody Allen's staccato delivery, 'Marquis, you think you're the antichrist. You're just a malcontent who knows how to spell.' How brilliant is that! And I said, Well, it's that but sort of more seriously appropriated. That's the rhythm of the line.

I remember Warren Mitchell saying that to me. That was another great turning point for me. Once I'd got out of Lecoq, QTC invited me back to play the Fool in *Lear*, with Warren. And with my experience at Lecoq's, I was into all of the improvisational techniques. I was looking at the concept of masks, of physically identifying with the rhythms of things, from nature, from substances, you know? The whole kind of catalogue of imagination devices that we were apprenticed in. Warren had been studying from the Stella Adler school, that American school. He was approaching everything that he was doing with action verbs, and endowments and objectives, and all these tools of the trade from that school of thinking. And we swapped a lot of stories about that. The Fool's got a lot of dense, now-defaulted kind of jokes. I'd say, This joke doesn't work anymore. This is filled with so many words that we don't say anymore. Maybe we should change it. Warren would go, No, no. If you have trouble with a comedy line, he said, Here's a great tip. Do it as Groucho. I said, What do you mean? He said, Well, you know, Groucho would say, 'Send two dozen roses to room 28 and write "Emily, I love you" on the back of the bill'. He said, What it makes you do is push through the whole line, give it its package, and let the audience catch up. If you try and analyse that line psychologically and feel your way through it, you're going to kill the thing. The old George Kaufman thing of saying, Dissecting a joke is like dissecting a frog. You may find out how it works, but you end up with a dead frog. There's something in that, and consequently I think the Woody Allen advice on the *Quills* set was useful.

That was like putting the hat on for you in *Pirates of the Caribbean*. It became one key which suddenly made things seem easy.

Totally. Warren would play scenes with me where he would say—and I started to do that with the Fool's lines, and in performance I would get massive laughs on dead language because what it helped me do, the attitude became really clear because Warren had given me great licence to do—he used to say, Make me laugh. In today's rehearsal, I don't care if you do everything different to what you did yesterday. You are my jester, you make me laugh. So I would go on and try and do everything to deliberately get a rise out of him, because he gave me, out of everyone else on stage, complete freedom to do whatever I liked. There's a great speech the Fool has about talking to the king about his crown and an egg. So I came on one day with a real egg, and broke it into my hat, because I just wanted Warren to be dazzled by me having this tricky bit of business. And it got incorporated into the performance.

He'd rehearse a scene with me and he'd say, Now, I just want you to say 'cunt' on the end of every line while you're talking to me. And it was fantastic to hear—I can't remember the dialogue—but I would come into the king, very kind of considerate and tender, Well, perhaps your daughter isn't happy with you doing that, cunt. Suddenly I went, Wow, if you sort of think that, or play two things at the one time, it just puts you into a different, unpredictable place that doesn't make you follow set, prerequisite constructions that the audience will understand.

Hollywood film-making would always have the right amount of signposts so the audience could follow the film, and not get worried or upset in any way. Curiously enough, the films that become the great run-away box-office successes that they never anticipate are the ones that set up worry and anxiety, where the audience goes, Oh, we didn't know what was going to happen next.

I wanted to talk a little bit about *Lantana*. I'm interested to find out whether that role was a challenge to your processes, when this character seems kind of naked, when it seems almost like a cipher, or seems so unadorned. Was that an unusual process?

Yeah. That was a happy accident because all the initial discussions I had with Ray Lawrence and Jan Chapman, the producer, were to do with playing Leon, the main cop. I read it, and I went, Wow. That script was on the page. I don't think they trimmed out anything. The dialogue would throw from one scene to the next in the most interesting way. Or he would start a scene with a curious line of dialogue that would pay off five scenes later or would echo. He had it all, the jigsaw of it, the psychological jigsaw of it, the puzzle of the thriller was very knowingly put onto the page.

We did a reading of it, and I said to them, Look, I can't do this role because it feels to me that the cop needs to be such a blokier kind of character when the audience meets him, so that his emotional detonation and cave-in through the infidelity with this wife, and the numbness of his mid-life crisis, and the nature of the case that he's solving, come as a real sort of shock and surprise in the latter part of the film. I said, I don't think I'm your man for that. In fact, I know I'm not. And I was also going on the fact that the last five films I'd done—well certainly *Shine* and *Quills*, *Children of the Revolution*—I cried at the end of each of those films, in some form. I said, I think they're going to see it coming a mile off that this guy's gonna have some kind of *cri du coeur*, but thank you very much. I think it's going to be an amazing project.

Then a week later I rang up and said, Look, I can't not be in it because I think it's ear-marked to be one of the great Australian films. It's just too well written, and the clientele—the director and the producer—is too interesting. Very rare to sort of smell that one, because you often never know what's going to happen with a project. Are we setting out to make a turkey here, or are we setting out to make a ground-breaking hit, or a modest success or whatever? But I sort of knew on that one. I just thought there was something in this that's fresh. It's a mature development in Australian film-making, on the page.

And, thankfully, Ray cast it in a brilliant and surprising way, and for Anthony LaPaglia, it was when a role and an actor collide beautifully with each other. How wonderful that this particular script and this career were in perfect alignment.

What about you and the role that you ended up playing?

Well, then I said to them, I'd like to be involved, so if you like I'll play the other professional guy, who at that stage I don't think was detailed as to whether he was a doctor or whether he was a dean or whatever. And I thought at that stage he was probably the least interesting character in the film for the very reason that he and his wife, they're the ones trapped in the situation of grief. And I thought, Well, they can only really work in counterpoint to the rest of the story. It's going to be a hard task to try and find a singular journey where you take them from *some* grief to *more* grief to a *shifting* grief. That was a bit of a challenge, but in a way Ray sort of knew, in his use of widescreen, which was, again, a very bold choice, I thought, for that film. You'd have thought it was going to be very tight. He used a two-thirty-five to one ratio with just single faces in it. The camera relentlessly on people. And Andrew Bovell had written a fantastic scene between the cop and him, where they talk about fidelity and sense of identity and all of that. I think that gave it some resonance.

What gave the comfort to you? What became the key, putting-on-the-hat moment? Was there such a moment when it all felt like it was inside you?

No. I was very reassured by Ray, though. It came after a pretty flamboyant batch of films in which I seemed to be jumping around inside the frame. It was a really interesting exercise for me to be disciplined, trying to do nothing, but not nothing to the point where you don't register, or you're not interesting to the story.

That's trusting the material, isn't it?

It is a little. I can remember when I did *Shine*, I had the conversation with Scott Hicks where I said, Look, everyone's told me ever since I started work as a professional actor, In film, you don't really do anything. It's all in the eyes. My implication being, David Helfgott is a very manic, physically effervescent character. There's not much hidden going on inside, it's all spilling out.

That's the nature of the disorder.

Yeah. Exactly. And I said, I'm a bit worried about that looking overly theatrical or over-the-top. And he said, We'll just work on that as we shoot each scene, and find the right sort of barometer. And I was next to Noah Taylor, who I think is an exquisite… who seems to do very little on the day. You think, Is this performance going to register on the celluloid? And then when you see it, you go, Oh, my God. It's just alive with all of these hidden nuances and flecks of fascinating meaning, up against which I always felt I was like a great piece of industrial, 19th-century, steam-driven machinery. That's what I think I do. And I still, to a degree, think that. But then I kind of try and justify it and go, Well, the Marquis de Sade *is* flamboyant.

I did go through a period… Going back to *Vanya*. I remember in the wake of the collaboration with Neil on *Diary of a Madman* and *The Government Inspector*, we felt, Wow, we've got this great… And Neil said, Oh, I'm thinking of doing *Vanya*. And I said, Well, there's nothing in that for me because it's such a serious play, and up until that point I really did define myself as generally being a comic actor. And my successes—as I've mentioned—were all in that line. So it was a fairly significant thing. I said, I'll have a go at Astrov. It might be fun to see if we can make him funny. Which became quite interesting, because Astrov spends a good part of the play drunk, sometimes very depressively drunk with insight, and sometimes rather devilishly drunk, sexily drunk, flirtatiously drunk, you know? So it became interesting to do that.

That planted a seed that became a kind of secondary strand to how I saw myself as an actor, in that I did end up doing things like Walsingham in *Elizabeth* that I would never have even thought about prior to that sort of experience.

I'd played Horatio in *Hamlet* which is a no-laughs role. It's the no-laughs, bridesmaid's role. That was informed by a lot of circumstantial stuff in that I'd had bad anxiety and panic attacks around that period so I was lessening the load, and not wanting to take on a big thing like Hamlet, but wanting, yet again, to be involved in the production because I thought it was going to be very strong.

I've got *The Life and Death of Peter Sellers* coming up, and already in some preliminary press, people have said, You play a lot of mad guys. And I go, Oh, look, if you're saying that David Helfgott and Peter Sellers and the Marquis de Sade are the same person, then I've really failed. And they're probably the only three clinically certifiable people I've played, but that becomes the hook. So you have to look at roles and determine, It's very advisable for me now not to play another psychologically aberrant character, or if you are, find a different way. Most of the great roles in literature are either drunks or mad. It's pushing people to an extremity, that's when it becomes really interesting.

I think acting does divide up into movie stars and film actors, and movie stars tend to have to deliver a pretty acceptable brand-product set of qualities that audiences want to go and see. They want to see someone be sexy and unattainable and god-like, so there's a whole heap of actors who fulfil that for them. Or they want to go and see actors who are very chameleon-like, and surprise them each time. I had the privilege of doing *House on Haunted Hill* because the offer came up, and I'd just done a whole lot of period-based films like *Les Miserables* and *Elizabeth* and *Shakespeare in Love*. I felt like I needed to freshen up my act and do things like *Mystery Men* and be in a sort of science fiction comic-book world, just for the repertoire challenge.

Because it's only occasionally that you get a whiff that, Ah, I'm lucky enough now to be in alignment with a role that is *mine*. I sort of felt that a bit with *Shine* even though I was overwhelmed by it. I never thought, Oh, I know how to do this. You don't. You go in working on a fear factor or a challenge factor, going, Well, if I don't do this, what would I be doing? I'll be doing a non-aligned role that will be in some ways not that satisfying.

But I feel lucky in a way because I seem to have struck a period of film-making internationally and in Australia... I mean, the year of *Shine* was the year of *Fargo* and *Secrets and Lies*, it was a big independent year in the Hollywood calendar, which quickly got absorbed. But in the aftermath of it, films like *Elizabeth* suddenly got made, and *Shakespeare in Love*. *Shakespeare in Love* is quite a literary piece when you look at it on the page, and now all that's been absorbed, audiences will take on *Adaptation*, for example. People will now accept quite disjointed time-frames, something that's approaching more a dreamscape. *Mulholland Drive*.

The *Peter Sellers* project was like that. I thought, Well, I've had a really good run for about five or six years of doing what almost felt like a fortunate film-land embellishment on the theatrical repertoire that I was playing with—through Gogol and Ben Jonson, *The Alchemist*, and all that—and suddenly I was getting to play rather strange and exotic character parts in films.

It's also true, isn't it, that it was—I don't want to use the word lucky, but, I mean, your conduit into that world was via *Shine*, something that did call for you to act in the way you were naturally inclined to act.

It does put you onto a very steep learning curve. See, there was no other screen performance that I could think of. I suppose I thought of *My Left Foot*. There's that British school that goes from Alec Guinness right through to Daniel Day Lewis or Gary Oldman that I always revered for bravura and daring. You look at Daniel Day Lewis—similar to when Dustin Hoffman first came into the radar being in *The Graduate*, then *Little Big Man* and *Midnight Cowboy*—and you think, My God, this guy's got... There's something thrilling, a very old-fashioned nature of acting. It's thrilling to see someone be so powerfully diverse in an entertaining and meaningful way. Not just for showing off. And Daniel Day Lewis had that. The guy from *My Left Foot* being in *Last of the Mohicans*, where he suddenly came thundering towards the camera with mighty pecs! It was great. Haven't quite seen that for a while, you know?

I think it's what we were saying earlier—off the record, when you first came in—about the notion now of how popular and widespread and carefully marketed everything is, and the notion of reality TV, et cetera. Actors have become celebrities, and they're often referred to as that. And I sort of say, Look, the winner of *Survivor* and *Australian Idol* and Paris Hilton are celebrities. I'm an actor who works in film and sometimes in theatre. I see a huge difference. But in the public's mind, I think the edges are starting to get very blurred.

It's a dangerous period. I think of the *Popstars*-type of things where, basically—in the mass media of television—the very urge to want to perform is humiliated and made fun of, or depicted as endlessly disposable. And then I think of that time when NIDA invited cameras in to make exactly the same kind of thing out of those students' training and ambitions: The Drama School Game Show. I think a lot of us were troubled by that, that it kind of seemed like a betrayal.

Oh, God, yes.

Where's the art in that? Where's the respect for art?

The motive behind all that is there's airtime to be filled, let's fill it with something, because that's what one does nowadays.

Sure. And as you indicated before, commercial television will do

whatever it likes with the 'material' it uses, sometimes despite the subject's intentions.

That's true.

But, curiously enough, out of this year's bunch of films, and even in the mainstream cinema—or what became the mainstream cinema very quickly, because it becomes mainstream when people go and see it, and spend money on it, and therefore it's worth promoting via the mainstream machinery—is how emotionally dark a lot of the work has been lately. And maybe that's the actor more as shaman coming back—an essential thing, because people will want to feel that the theatre can in a strange sort of way heal something, illuminate something, contextualise something, create a common bonding for audience and the participants, *as* theatre or film.

I hope so.

CONCLUSION

At this point, I feel like a Tonight Show host, thanking guests. So be it. I want to thank not only the actors themselves again, but acknowledge all the friendly ghosts that they brought into the story with them, the professional mentors and heroes whose words and deeds lie beneath those of the actors. It's an unlikely collective, but nonetheless a 'dream' cast: John Saul, Richard Wherrett, Joe McColum, George Ogilvie, Alexander Hay, Nick Enright, Betty Williams, Rex Cramphorn, Neil Armfield, Jean-Pierre Mignon, Sam Mendes, Doreen Hogan, Philippe Gaulier, Alan Edwards. Perhaps, more poignantly, I call for a bow from Judi Farr's grandmother, John Gaden's grandson, Bud Tingwell's children, and Paul Goddard's procuring theatre critic. The lessons for an actor are everywhere, and the great teachers are not those of us who stand before them in acting classes, provoking, annoying, exciting, daring, demanding, enlightening. The great acting teachers are the mothers and fathers and lovers and children.

For example, it's very tempting to read Geoffrey Rush's CV, note that he trained at Lecoq's school, see his work on stage or screen, and arrive at the easy decision that this actor is the 'product' of that school. Clearly, however, he is the product of his parents, his total education and his nature. He was always going to act in the way that he does because of who he is, just as surely as Michael Chekhov's technique grows directly from the flamboyant, athletic child that he was, Stanislavski's theatrical universe is the expression of his self-critical nature and restless mind, and Strasberg's 'Method' reflects his need to see and explain acting the only way he can.

To the central question, What are these actors doing? They are taking fragments from very many sources, and piecing them together into what we might call 'personal belief systems', or matrices. It seems to me much more useful to think of an actor's work as a matrix—or mandala—rather than a method or a process. As I said at the beginning, I'm prejudiced against the word 'method' as applied to acting. The idea of a method, or a methodical approach, seems every bit as crude to me at the end of this project as it did at the beginning. Art is not about ticking boxes, nor living inside a theoretical—or even practical—cage. One needs a method to make an omelette, not to make a Hamlet. These actors use discipline. Disciplined intuition, disciplined *patterns* and 'weaves'. Their impulses and fancies, their talent, is guided and forged by discipline, and by methodical fragments, not by methods. Does that mean they are making it up as they go along? Well, yes and no. I liked Joel Edgerton's take on this particularly: that we are making it up in the same way that the electrician or the hairdresser is doing so in their daily work. We are improvising, but our improvising is based on skill and experience. Among the ways in which we might think of actors as special, this is perhaps a reminder of one of the ways in which our practice is not particularly special at all, but common as muck.

I am struck by how much talk there is about growing up, shifting, changing in one's life, and of how the growth of the person cannot be disentwined from the growth of the actor. That finding one's self as an actor is in fact the same journey as finding one's self as a person, and that this quest is one of reconciliation with one's past, one's childhood and family. The journey back to the source that is universally treasured by artists of other hues—painters, novelists, playwrights—is just as necessary for us. Show me the child at seven and I'll show you the actor? No, that's too simplistic, but there is a link, a connection, and these good actors seem to be searching for or travelling down that organic path. It is about literally finding one's 'self' in the work. I think of John Clark's regular and astute advice to NIDA auditionees: Don't think about wrong and right ways to do the piece, just show us how you want to do it.

The other searing impression that I take from the interviews is that it is not only about finding one's self, but finding everyone else too. This is something no acting book covers. Acting is—as my teacher Nick Enright was wont to say—an act of moving toward others. Nick's talk—the year before his death—at the Rex Cramphorn Memorial Lecture was a noble and necessary reminder that this 'moving toward' is the central reality off stage as well as on: industrially, if you like, as well as artistically. There is no theory outside of that rehearsal room. There is no approach outside of the collective. We will collaborate, or do nothing.

I'd hate to be understood as arguing against theory and theorising, or against actor-training itself. In fact I believe that the Australian theatre has been too shy of a rigorous engagement with the world of theatrical and performance thinking, and the words of the actors in this book don't incline me, generally, to change my mind. Mainstream theatre and academia seem suspicious of each other, and hostile to each other, with each side commonly characterising the other as irrelevant. Our National Institute of Dramatic Art—for legitimate reasons—has been historically disinterested in making the two camps friends. This two-way snobbery is unhelpful and unnecessary. Actors should read more, and academics should engage with the mainstream. The mutual disrespect is self-fulfilling. It is striking that our theatrical history has had very few people who have conducted serious performance research within the mainstream. Rex Cramphorn comes to mind, and the marvellous Jenny Kemp. But largely, our contributors to the written word on the art of the theatre, and our leading practitioners, are mutually exclusive mobs. If it is true that the actors in this book are less than thoroughly supported by acting theory in their views, it is also true that our theatre academics often don't know much about the reality of being on stage (though this is not a peculiarly Australian phenomenon).

Pamela Rabe makes the point that learning is taking 'what sticks'. So to the young actors reading this I say, What sticks? What is your way? You may have found a school, a teacher of repute, but is she or he your teacher? You may have found a process, a series of exercises or an enveloping philosophy of acting that fascinates you or intrigues you or turns you on, intellectually, but is it yours? Does it work in your body, in your psyche? How can you appropriate it to help you find your way?

Why train to be an actor? Because there is much to learn, and training provides the beginnings of that learning. Training provides a series of acting simulations. None of them may make total sense, but they all contain good things to be extracted by the talented and enthusiastic student. When I was packing bags to go to acting school, an old actor said to me, It's good that you're going to NIDA. It will prepare you to start learning about acting. I expect I considered it a facetious comment at the time, but it seems more true to me with every passing year, every role, each acting failure I accumulate, and every few seconds of success.

But where is this lifelong learning to take place in today's theatre, with most of the regional companies long dead, and the remaining larger companies offering work opportunities at perhaps a third of the rate that they were offered 20 years ago? We're back to the industrial problems, back to the challenges of this watershed era between Australia's flirtation with theatre subsidy, and whatever rescue is to be found. We are back to the mammoth challenges that are facing our Artistic Directors, the challenges they are clearly wrestling with, and sometimes obviously ducking. In a way we're back to the 1950s, the time when any serious young stage actor had to go abroad for experience.

What a revolting and depressing thought!

How to avoid ending on it?

I think of the youth, beauty, integrity and guts of my students, of the mirror they are holding up to us with their work, allowing us to see whatever remains of our own youth, beauty, integrity and guts.

We're back to the reason this book exists.

Break a leg.

ACKNOWLEDGMENTS

My principle debt of thanks is pretty obvious. It is to the actors, my 'co-authors', who contributed their time, talent, wisdom, memories and bared souls to the project with the professional generosity that sustains our cottage industry.

Thanks are also due to the actors' agents. Particular credit must go to Wendy Millyard at Shanahan Management, who represents no fewer than seven of the fourteen actors in this book. Wendy has a theatre-based degree, and I was very lucky to strike her sensitivity to the project. She quickly accepted the responsibilities of a firm colleague, put in hours of work, and smiled through my constant hassling. I don't know how I could have done it without her.

Dr Ian Maxwell of Sydney Uni provided welcome encouragement.

I'm grateful to Victoria Chance and all at Currency for their faith and support, and to Dean Nottle for his careful criticism of the text.

Thanks to Vicki Dymond at the Victorian Arts Centre, for organising a meeting room at short notice, and to my sister-in-law, Andrea Haren, for sustenance and transport in Melbourne.

I am privileged to have enjoyed the collegiality of many fine teachers, actors, designers and directors over the years, all of whom have contributed to the theatrical thinking that guides these pages.

Huge thanks are due to all the students with whom I've quested, fumbled and flown. I am humbled by the fact that they now number in their several hundreds. I sincerely hope for many hundreds more.

Final thanks are due to Louise MacMahon, for all happy adventures.

Terence Crawford began his career as an actor in 1980 with the Hunter Valley Theatre Company in his home city of Newcastle. He is particularly proud to have carried many spears for that company in the premiere production of John O'Donoghue's acclaimed *Essington Lewis: I Am Work*. After graduating from the National Institute of Dramatic Art (NIDA) in 1984, he spent four years with the State Theatre Company of South Australia where he created roles in the premiere productions of plays by Australian writers as diverse as Stephen Sewell, Barry Dickins, Patrick White and Nigel Krauth. In a career that has increasingly focussed on writing and teaching, his acting highlights of the last decade have continued to be Australian premieres, including Debra Oswald's *Gary's House*.

This passion for Australian plays led him to serve on the board of the Griffin Theatre Company, teach playwriting at the University of Western Sydney and engage with various small 'cells' of play-development activities. His own plays have been produced by Griffin, New England Theatre Company, Theatre of Image and Sydney Theatre Company. They include *Pushin' Up Daisies*, *Autumn* and the verse comedy, *Love's Triumph*, which enjoyed a hugely successful season at Darlinghurst Theatre in 2003. He has also had work produced on radio and television, and short fiction published.

Terence began teaching acting in 1986 at the Centre for Performing Arts (now Adelaide Centre for the Arts). In 1989 he began a long association with Theatre Nepean, becoming Head of Acting in 1997, and leaving at the end of 2002. He has also taught for NIDA, Australian Theatre for Young People (ATYP) and at the Theatre Training and Research Programme in Singapore, where his 2004 multi-lingual production of Chekhov's Seagull led to his current position of Head of Acting.

Terence achieved his Masters (Hons) from James Cook University in 2000 with a dissertation on Chekhov in an Australian context.